LIBRARY OF HEBREW BIBLE/
OLD TESTAMENT STUDIES

688

Formerly Journal for the Study of the Old Testament Supplement Series

Editors
Claudia V. Camp, Texas Christian University, USA
Andrew Mein, University of Durham, UK

Founding Editors
David J. A. Clines, Philip R. Davies and David M. Gunn

Editorial Board
Alan Cooper, Susan Gillingham
John Goldingay, Norman K. Gottwald, James E. Harding,
John Jarick, Carol Meyers,
Daniel L. Smith-Christopher, Francesca Stavrakopoulou, James W. Watts

JONAH AND THE HUMAN CONDITION

Life and Death in Yahweh's World

Stuart Lasine

LONDON • NEW YORK • OXFORD • NEW DELHI • SYDNEY

T&T CLARK
Bloomsbury Publishing Plc
50 Bedford Square, London, WC1B 3DP, UK
1385 Broadway, New York, NY 10018, USA
29 Earlsfort Terrace, Dublin 2, Ireland

BLOOMSBURY, T&T CLARK and the T&T Clark logo are trademarks of
Bloomsbury Publishing Plc

First published in Great Britain 2020
This paperback edition published in 2021

Copyright © Stuart Lasine, 2020

Stuart Lasine has asserted his right under the Copyright,
Designs and Patents Act, 1988, to be identified as Author of this work.

All rights reserved. No part of this publication may be reproduced or
transmitted in any form or by any means, electronic or mechanical,
including photocopying, recording, or any information storage or retrieval
system, without prior permission in writing from the publishers.

Bloomsbury Publishing Plc does not have any control over, or responsibility for, any
third-party websites referred to or in this book. All internet addresses given in this
book were correct at the time of going to press. The author and publisher regret any
inconvenience caused if addresses have changed or sites have ceased to exist, but
can accept no responsibility for any such changes.

A catalogue record for this book is available from the British Library.

Library of Congress Cataloging-in-Publication Data
Names: Lasine, Stuart, author.
Title: Jonah and the human condition: life and death in Yahweh's world / Stuart Lasine.
Description: 1 [edition]. | New York: T&T Clark, 2019. |
Series: Library of Hebrew Bible/Old Testament studies, 2513-8758; volume 688 |
Includes bibliographical references and indexes.
Identifiers: LCCN 2019016127 | ISBN 9780567683236 (hardback) |
ISBN 9780567683243 (epdf)
Subjects: LCSH: Death in the Bible. | Death–Biblical teaching. |
Life–Biblical teaching. | Spirituality. | Bible. Jonah–Criticism,
interpretation, etc.. | Jonah (Biblical prophet)
Classification: LCC BS1199.D34 L37 2019 | DDC 221.6–dc23
LC record available at https://lccn.loc.gov/2019016127

ISBN: HB: 978-0-5676-8323-6
PB: 978-0-5677-0060-5
ePDF: 978-0-5676-8324-3
eBook: 978-0-5676-9112-5

Series: Library of Hebrew Bible/Old Testament Studies, 2513-8758, volume 688

Typeset by Deanta Global Publishing Services, Chennai, India

To find out more about our authors and books visit
www.bloomsbury.com and sign up for our newsletters.

To my parents,
Jack Lasine and Fay Braude Lasine
and my sisters,
Arlene Kaplan and Dorothy Troy

CONTENTS

List of Figures	ix
Preface	x
List of Abbreviations	xiii

Part One
PERSPECTIVES ON THE HUMAN CONDITION IN THE HEBREW BIBLE

Chapter 1
INTRODUCTION: CHARACTERIZING THE HUMAN CONDITION — 3
1. Biblical answers to "What is the human being?" — 4
2. Are humans born for trouble and toil? — 7
3. Comparing biblical and Greek answers to "What is the human being?" — 10
4. Biblical and modern conceptions of the human condition: Part One of this study — 16
5. Jonah's human condition: Part Two of this study — 18

Chapter 2
PESSIMISM AND THE HUMAN CONDITION IN THE HEBREW BIBLE — 21
1. What exactly is "pessimism"? — 22
2. Are Qoheleth's pronouncements on death and injustice pessimistic? — 25
3. Pessimistic divine and human leaders in Deuteronomy 31 — 32
4. Pessimism among the prophets: When is death better than life? — 35
5. Conclusion — 45

Chapter 3
AT SEA IN YAHWEH'S WORLD: NAVIGATING THE HUMAN CONDITION IN THE HEBREW BIBLE — 46
1. The "Life is a sea voyage" metaphor — 46
2. Images of enclosure and exposure in Jonah 1–2 — 47
3. Images of enclosure and exposure in the Psalms — 49
4. Storms at sea in Psalm 107 and the issue of theodicy — 52
5. Death—and birth—as shipwreck — 53
6. Coping with the storms of life in Yahweh's world — 57
7. Conclusion — 60

Chapter 4
READING ABOUT DEATH IN BIBLICAL NARRATIVE — 62
1. The psychology of reading about death — 63
2. Reading about death and resuscitation in 2 Kings 13 — 64
3. Power and immortality: Exalting Elisha's bones — 69
4. Readers' fear of death and the prospect of an afterlife — 71

Part Two
JONAH AND THE HUMAN CONDITION IN YAHWEH'S WORLD

Chapter 5
JONAH AS A LITERARY CHARACTER — 79
1. Psychological judgments on Jonah's character — 80
2. What we are, and are not, told about Jonah's situation and character — 81
3. "Jonah complexes" and our own — 88

Chapter 6
THE PLOT OF JONAH, CHILDHOOD CRISES, AND THE PERILS OF ADULTHOOD — 98
1. Fears of being swallowed and eaten — 99
2. Fantasies of being swallowed and killing the monster from within — 102
3. Jonah and other mature ancient heroes — 105
4. Yahweh's character and his relationship with Jonah — 110

Chapter 7
CONCLUSION: LIVING AND DYING IN THE HEBREW BIBLE — 114
1. Orwell's "essential Jonah act" — 114
2. Life and death "keeping house together": The end of the book of Jonah — 118
3. Vulnerability and the human condition — 121
4. *Weltende?* Visions of death, exposure, and enclosure in Jeremiah and Qoheleth — 126
5. My death in Yahweh's world — 132

Bibliography — 135
Index of Ancient Sources — 155
Index of Authors — 161

FIGURES

1   The device of Philips van Marnix van St. Aldegonde, detail from *Portrait of Philips van Marnix Heer van Sint Aldegonde (1540–1598)* by Jacques de Gheyn, II, 1599. Image courtesy: Rijksmuseum, Amsterdam x

2   Maarten van Heemskerck, *Jonah Fleeing from the Presence of the Lord to Joppa*, 1566 (detail). Photograph © 2018, Museum of Fine Arts, Boston xi

PREFACE

The drawings below present a key component of the "human condition" in compact fashion. Both include the biblical God as part of that condition. Figure 1 is a device designed by the sixteenth-century Calvinist politician and writer Philips van Marnix. Figure 2 is a contemporary depiction of the popular "Jonah cast over the side" motif by van Maarten van Heemskerck. Both drawings feature a three-masted ship on a turbulent sea, accompanied by a curly-tailed sea monster and a rocky shore nearby. In both pictures, Yahweh is shown in the skies above. One way in which Marnix signals God's guiding presence is by writing the Tetragrammaton in Hebrew letters above the scene. Around the border of his drawing is his French motto *repos ailleurs*—rest elsewhere. In Heemskerck's rendering of the Jonah story, God's body is depicted larger than the ship below. While Jonah is being cast overboard during the storm in Heemskerck's drawing, Marnix's device does not

Figure 1 The device of Philips van Marnix van St. Aldegonde, detail from *Portrait of Philips van Marnix Heer van Sint Aldegonde (1540–1598)* by Jacques de Gheyn, II, 1599. Image courtesy: Rijksmuseum, Amsterdam.

include a corresponding figure. Here it is all humans who are potentially under threat of being shipwrecked and cast away.

In effect, Marnix's drawing presents human life as a perilous voyage through space and time. Heemskerck's image suggests that the story of Jonah may do so as well. As I will discuss in Chapter 3, Marnix's point is that we can successfully navigate through the choppy waters of our storm-filled world only if we take scripture—and especially the "reliable Pole Star of the Gospel"—as our guide. Then, we will be rewarded with rest elsewhere, that is, in the afterlife.

But what if our only guide is the Hebrew Bible? For me and other Jewish readers, this is the entire Bible, the Tanakh. Can these readers of Hebrew scripture ensure their safety from metaphorical shipwreck if they rely on Yahweh as their navigational guide, in the sense illustrated by Marnix? Can they at least count

Figure 2 Maarten van Heemskerck, *Jonah Fleeing from the Presence of the Lord to Joppa*, 1566 (detail). Photograph © 2018, Museum of Fine Arts, Boston.

on Yahweh to provide a lifeboat or "big fish" to save those who are cast over the side during our life voyage? Does the Hebrew Bible allow its readers to remain optimistic about their existence in God's world or do some of its narrators cast a pessimistic shadow over the canon? And while Jewish scripture offers little or no prospect of a positive afterlife, does it at least offer its readers other ways of coming to terms with their mortality and death fear? I will address these fundamental theological, ethical, and existential questions as well as others in the course of this investigation.

Part One of the book examines different ways in which the human condition has been characterized over the centuries, as well as the various attitudes toward that condition expressed or implied by specific texts within the Pentateuch, the Prophets, and the Writings. Part Two engages in a detailed case study of one biblical character's "human condition." This is the prophet Jonah. I will then conclude by drawing more general conclusions about life and death in Yahweh's world, as well as in the world of the Hebrew Bible's present-day readers, including myself.

This enquiry is necessarily personal in another sense as well. I could have focused on other biblical texts and given more emphasis to other aspects of the human condition. I could have compared biblical concepts of human life and death with those expressed by ancient and modern texts different from the ones I have chosen. Other scholars could have made use of insights from the relevant disciplines about which I am ignorant. Finally, I suspect that authors with different personalities, genders, values, and life experiences would have come up with somewhat different understandings of the human condition in the Hebrew Bible, if they accepted that there is such a thing as "the human condition" at all. In short, I have not attempted to produce a definitive study of this difficult topic. I will be happy if this book leads at least a few readers to ask themselves what they think the Hebrew Bible is telling us about human reality and how that vision of the human condition might relate to their own life-worlds.

I would like to thank the LHBOTS series editors Claudia Camp and Andrew Mein for their support throughout this project. Thanks also to Catherine Menefee for her careful proofing of the submitted manuscript. As always, I am most grateful to my wife, Rannfrid Thelle, for her companionship and encouragement as I wandered through the house muttering "Is this really a book?"

Portions of Chapter 5 and 6 incorporate, in revised form, parts of the following article: "Jonah's Complexes and Our Own: Psychology and the Interpretation of the Book of Jonah," *Journal for the Study of the Old Testament* 41.2, pp. 237–60. Copyright © Stuart Lasine, 2016. DOI: 10.1177/0309089215641397. http://JSOT.sagepub.com. Reprinted by permission of SAGE publications. Portions of Chapter 4 incorporate, in revised and expanded form, material from the following book chapter: "The Character of Elisha and his Bones." Forthcoming in *Characters and Characterization in Samuel-Kings, Volume 2*. Edited by Keith Bodner and Benjamin Johnson. LHBOTS. London: Bloomsbury. Used with permission.

ABBREVIATIONS

2H4	Shakespeare, *Henry IV, Part 2*
AB	Anchor Bible
ABD	*Anchor Bible Dictionary*. Edited by D. N. Freedman. 6 vols. New York, 1992
ÄgAbh	Ägyptologische Abhandlungen
ANE	Ancient Near East[ern]
Ant.	Josephus, *Jewish Antiquities*
Antig.	Sophocles, *Antigone*
ATD	Das Alte Testament Deutsch
b.	Babylonian Talmud
B. Meṣiʿa	*Baba Meṣiʿa*
BBET	Beiträge zur biblischen Exegese und Theologie
Bib	*Biblica*
BibInt	*Biblical Interpretation*
BTB	*Biblical Theology Bulletin*
BZAW	Beihefte zur Zeitschrift für die alttestamentliche Wissenschaft
CBQ	*Catholic Biblical Quarterly*
CJ	*Classical Journal*
CP	*Classical Philology*
DRN	Lucretius, *De Rerum Natura*
Ep.	Horace, *Epistulae*
Ep. mor.	Seneca, *Epistulae morales*
ESV	English Standard Version
Eth. nic.	Aristotle, *Ethica nichomachea*
ExpTim	*The Expository Times*
FAT	Forschungen zum Alten Testament
FOTL	Forms of the Old Testament Literature
Fr.	Fragment
GE	*The Gilgamesh Epic*
Gen. Rab.	*Genesis Rabbah*
GR	*Greece & Rome*
GW	Sigmund Freud, *Gesammelte Werke*. Edited by Anna Freud. London, 1940–
Heb.	Hebrew
HeyJ	*Heythrop Journal*
Hipp.	Euripides, *Hippolytus*
Hist.	Herodotus, *Histories*
HS	*Hebrew Studies*
HTR	*Harvard Theological Review*
HUCA	*Hebrew Union College Annual*
IBC	Interpretation: A Bible Commentary for Teaching and Preaching

ICC	International Critical Commentary
IDB	*The Interpreter's Dictionary of the Bible*. Edited by G. A. Buttrick. 4 vols. Nashville, 1962
Il.	Homer, *Iliad*
Inf.	Dante, *The Inferno*
JAAR	*Journal of the American Academy of Religion*
JANES	*Journal of the Ancient Near Eastern Society*
JBL	*Journal of Biblical Literature*
JBQ	*Jewish Bible Quarterly*
JBTh	*Jahrbuch für Biblische Theologie*
JEA	*Journal of Egyptian Archaeology*
JHS	*Journal of Hellenic Studies*
JNES	*Journal of Near Eastern Studies*
JPS	Jewish Publication Society of America
JSOT	*Journal for the Study of the Old Testament*
JSOTSup	*Journal for the Study of the Old Testament: Supplement Series*
KBL	Koehler, L., and W. Baumgartner, *Lexicon in Veteris Testamenti libros*. 2nd ed. Leiden, 1958
LCL	Loeb Classical Library
Leg.	Plato, *Laws*
LHBOTS	Library of Hebrew Bible/Old Testament Studies
ll.	lines
LXX	Septuagint (the Greek Old Testament)
Mek.	Mekilta
Mem.	Xenophon, *Memorabilia*
Metam.	Ovid, *Metamorphoses*
Midr.	Tehillim Midrash Tehillim
MT	Masoretic Text (of the Hebrew Bible)
NABRE	The New American Bible, Revised Edition
NASB	New American Standard Bible
NCBC	New Century Bible Commentary
Nem.	Pindar, *Nemean Odes*
NETS	New English Translation of the Septuagint
NIB	*The New Interpreter's Bible*. Edited by Leander E. Keck, et al. Nashville: Abingdon, 1994–
NIBCOT	New International Biblical Commentary on the Old Testament
NICOT	New International Commentary on the Old Testament
NIV	New International Version
NRSV	New Revised Standard Version
NovT	*Novum Testamentum*
NT	New Testament
OB	Old Babylonian
Od.	Homer, *Odyssey*
OED	*Oxford English Dictionary*
Oed. col.	Sophocles, *Oedipus coloneus*
Ol.	Pindar, *Olympian Odes*
OT	Old Testament

OTE	*Old Testament Essays*
OTL	Old Testament Library
OtSt	*Oudtestamentische Studiën*
Phaed.	Plato, *Phaedo*
Phil.	Sophocles, *Philoctetes*
Pirqe R. El.	*Pirqe Rabbi Eliezer*
Pol.	Plato, *Politicus* (*Statesman*)
Proof	*Prooftexts: A Journal of Jewish Literary History*
Pyth.	Pindar, *Pythian Odes*
Qoh. Rabb.	Qoheleth Rabbah
RB	*Revue biblique*
RelEd	Religious Education
Resp.	Plato, *Republic*
RSV	Revised Standard Version
Sanh.	Sanhedrin
SemeiaSt	Semeia Studies
SJOT	*Scandinavian Journal of the Old Testament*
TDOT	*Theological Dictionary of the Old Testament.* Edited by G. Johannes Botterweck, Helmer Ringgren, and Heinz-Josef Fabry. Translated by J. T. Willis, G. W. Bromiley, and D. E. Green. 8 vols. Grand Rapids, 1974–
Theog.	Hesiod, *Theogonia*
TMT	Terror Management Theory
Vg.	Vulgate
VT	*Vetus Testamentum*
WBC	Word Biblical Commentary
WBCom	Westminster Bible Companion
WW	*Word and World*
ZAW	*Zeitschrift für die alttestamentliche Wissenschaft*

Part One

PERSPECTIVES ON THE HUMAN CONDITION IN
THE HEBREW BIBLE

Chapter 1

INTRODUCTION: CHARACTERIZING THE HUMAN CONDITION

Ever since Pope Innocent III introduced the phrase "human condition" (*conditio humana*) in the twelfth century,[1] many writers have attempted to express their understanding of the problematic features of existence with which every person must cope. These understandings of course vary according to culture, one's situation within that culture, and one's personality (i.e., their specific "human natures"). Among the negative factors which have been most consistently cited as basic to the human situation are ephemerality, mutability, frailty, contingency, vulnerability, lack of control, the need to labor, and, at the most fundamental level, mortality. It would be difficult to deny the role played by these sobering realities in human life; in fact, our awareness of our evanescence and vulnerability is itself a key aspect of our condition, although we may work hard to obscure that knowledge.[2]

In this study I will investigate the human condition in the biblical world, both in general and as it is experienced by the prophet Jonah. The book of Jonah—and the differing ways in which it has been interpreted—will be examined

---

1. The *OED* defines "human condition" as "the state or condition of being human, especially regarded as being inherently problematic or flawed." It locates the first appearance in English of *humaine condition* in Alday's 1566 translation of Boaistuau's *Le théâtre du monde*, which refers to "*la grande fragilité & misere de notre condition humaine*" (1570, 121). Howard notes that Montaigne has often been viewed as the author who introduced this term in the sixteenth century (Howard 1969, xiii). Innocent's 1196 work, *On the Misery of the Human Condition* (Segni 1969), was written before the author, Lothario dei Segni, became pope; see Howard (1969, xxi). The author cites many biblical verses to support his arguments; see n. 30 in this chapter. A number of other eleventh- to sixteenth-century European works also focus on the most wretched and most contemptible aspects of human existence; see, for example, Howard (1974, 53–63).

2. The concept of a "human condition" should not be equated with the idea of "human nature." Theorists disagree about whether there is such a thing as "human nature." For example, Sartre believes that "it is impossible to find in each human being a universal essence that would be human nature," although "there nevertheless exists a human universality of *condition*" (1946, 67). Also see the well-known debate between Noam Chomsky and Michel Foucault (Chomsky and Foucault 2006, 1–67). On this debate, see Wilkin (1999).

from literary, psychological, philosophical, and theological perspectives. This investigation will include a crucial element of the human condition which I did not list above: the need to live in relation to the personal god Yahweh. Throughout the book, I will be asking what biblical texts reveal about human existence, not only for characters who dwell within the textual world but also for readers of the Hebrew Bible.

1 Biblical answers to "What is the human being?"

The human (האדם) became a living being (נפש חיה).

(Gen. 2:7)

What is the human being?

(Ps. 8:5; Job 7:17; 15:14; Ps. 144:3)

Every human is entirely vapor.

(Ps. 39:6)

The first step in this investigation is to inquire about the nature of the being whose condition we will be studying. Within the Hebrew Bible the question "What is humanity?" is asked four times and answered in four different ways.[3] The speaker in Psalm 8 wonders what we must be, considering that God remembers and visits us. He answers by declaring that God has made the human being "a little less than god," crowned him with glory and honor, given him "dominion over the works of your hands," and "put all things under his feet" (Ps. 8:5-7). This passage recalls Gen. 1:26-27, which reports that humans are made in the image and likeness of God. And in both Psalm 8 and Gen. 1:28, humans have power and control analogous to that of a king over his subjects,[4] complete with a regal aura of glory.

Job answers the question of human identity and worth in a very different manner. Like the psalmist, he acknowledges human smallness, but he complains about the significance granted to us by our Creator: "What is the human being that you magnify him and that you set your heart on him, visit him every morning and scrutinize him every moment?" (Job 7:17-18). Here God's constant attention and testing is experienced as onerous, oppressive, and inappropriate, given our basic insignificance and lack of power. Job is no sea or sea monster, yet God keeps

---

3. A number of different terms are used to denote human beings in the verses discussed in this chapter (אנוש, בן-אנוש, גבר, איש, אדם and בן-אדם). The only terms I render as "man," as opposed to "human," "human being," or "humanity," are איש and גבר. While אנוש is often assumed to denote humans as frail, Clines (1989, 216) denies that this is the case.

4. The verbs רדה (Gen. 1:26, 28), כבש (Gen. 1:28), and משל (Ps. 8:7) are all employed elsewhere to denote the exercise of royal power (see, for example, 1 Kgs 5:1, 4; Ps. 72:8; 2 Sam. 8:11).

him under such constant surveillance that he cannot even swallow his spit (7:12, 17-19). Job's belief that he is ignorant and insignificant (קלל) remains until the end of the book (40:4; 42:5-6).

Job's friends go further, interpreting our insignificance in terms of our basic lack of purity and moral worth. Eliphaz asks, "What is the human being, that he can be pure? Or he who is born of a woman, that he can be righteous? Behold, he puts no trust in his holy ones, and the heavens are not pure in his eyes; how much less one who is abhorrent and corrupt, man (איש) who drinks injustice like water" (15:14-16; cf. 4:17).[5] Both Eliphaz and Bildad focus on our being born of a woman rather than on being created by the God who made us in his likeness (15:14; 25:4).

At the same time, both Eliphaz and Bildad speak as though they themselves are exceptions to their rule, being so close to God that they know exactly how God views his creations. While Job recognizes that "God does not see as humans see" (10:4), the friends talk as though they know how God views both humans and the rest of his creations. They are certain that in God's eyes humans are contemptible, impure, and iniquitous, especially in light of the fact that God allegedly does not even trust in his "holy ones" and views the heavens and the luminaries as impure (cf. Job 4:17-20; 25:4-6). And for Bildad, our affinity with maggots and worms is not merely a reminder of our mortality; our entire being is as vile and filthy as these fellow creatures (25:4-6). In effect, Bildad is asserting that God made us in the image and likeness of a maggot.[6]

The final occurrence of the question "What is humanity?" is found in Psalm 144. The royal speaker begins by giving thanks to "his rock," Yahweh, for having trained him for battle. Yahweh has not only been "my fortress, my high refuge, my deliverer and my shield" but also "my covenantal loyalty (חסד)" (v. 2); that is, the psalmist feels sheltered by Yahweh's loyalty to the covenant he has made with the speaker and, presumably, with the speaker's people. God's aid has granted him the power to defeat aliens and (according to the MT) the power to "subdue my people under me" (144:2). It is at this point that the psalmist poses his question to Yahweh: "What is the human being (אדם) that you know him, the son of a human (אנוש) that you think of him? The human being is like vapor (הבל); his days are like a passing shadow" (Ps. 144:3-4). The speaker stresses human ephemerality and insubstantiality, not lack of purity. He then asks for Yahweh to descend in his power, making mountains smoke and sending forth his arrows of lightning. He wants to be rescued and delivered from "many waters,"[7] which, in this instance, means rescue from the hand of "the sons of aliens" who speak

---

5. In his study of "being human in God's world" McConville omits Job 15:14 when he discusses the "What is humanity?" verses (2016, 9, 174). For a brief survey of the ways in which the Hebrew Bible presents human life, see Marlow (2016, 295-308).

6. On the friends' perspective and its implications, see the detailed discussion in Lasine (1988, 32-38).

7. On this and similar metaphors, see Chapter 3 §1-4.

falsely (vv. 5-7, 11). The poem concludes with a depiction of a fertile, prosperous, and secure society. Looked at as a whole, this Psalm acknowledges both extremes of the human condition as the speaker understands it: the power which God has granted his king as well as the king's vulnerability and total dependence upon his God for survival.

The emphasis on human insubstantiality and evanescence expressed in Psalm 144 is not unique to this poem. For example, the afflicted speaker in Psalm 39 twice asserts that all humanity is vapor (הבל) and that "a man walks about as a transient image"[8] (39:6-7, 12). Similarly, Qoheleth, who is anything but "afflicted" in the ordinary sense, laments the human inability to know "what is good for a human being in life, during the days of his vain life (חיי הבלו), which he spends like a shadow" (Qoh. 6:12). In addition to highlighting our insubstantiality, Qoheleth laments our epistemological vulnerability. Lack of knowledge exacerbates our lack of control over our "vain lives."[9]

Like Qoheleth, the sufferer Job views human life as short and full of hardship: "Has not the human being a warlike service (צבא) on earth, and are not his days like the days of a hireling?" Later he answers his question by declaring that "a human who is born of a woman is few of days and full of turmoil" (Job 14:1; cf. 7:1-3). In these verses neither God nor humans themselves are explicitly blamed for our troubled days on earth; it's simply the way it is. In other words, this is the human condition.[10]

The epigraphs from the book of Job also focus on other aspects of the human condition with which we will become very familiar in the course of this study.[11] These include our vulnerability and the futility of sheltering ourselves from forces which threaten to overwhelm us. As Eliphaz puts it, we dwell in houses of "clay" founded on "dust" (4:19).[12] We ourselves are as short-lived and fragile as an easily

---

8. See KBL (804) on the nuance of צלם here.

9. It is hardly surprising that so many writers cite Qoheleth when they want to illustrate the Old Testament view of the human condition, considering the number of explicit statements made in the book about human life and its meaning—or lack of meaning. Qoheleth has been cited as a precursor of modern worldviews as diverse as psychoanalysis, existentialism, and philosophical pessimism. See, for example, P. Marcus (2003, 119–37), Christianson (1997, 40–45, 49–50) and Chapter 2 §2. On the enigmatic poem in Qoh. 12:1-7, see Chapter 7 §4.

10. Commentators disagree dramatically about the thrust of Eliphaz's statement in Job 5:6-7; see §2 in this chapter.

11. For a discussion of these texts in terms of the fundamental polarity between destiny and inheritance, see Habel (1981). He contends that "this opposition has its existential manifestation where the specific fate of individuals is juxtaposed to their actual human condition" (1981, 373).

12. I am taking "dwell in houses of clay" literally (with, for example, Clines 1989, 134–35) rather than in the sense that our bodies are themselves the clay dwellings (as does, for example, Habel 1985, 128–29).

crushed moth. As Clines points out, in these verses Eliphaz is calling Job's attention to "the *danger* [humans'] precarious existence lays them open to" (1989, 135). Our mortality reveals our kinship to the insects which devour our dead bodies, such as the worm and maggot mentioned by Bildad. Job himself stresses our ephemeral and painful existence; we are like temporary day laborers whose pay is the grave when their work is done.

We will find that these aspects of human reality are evoked in the book of Jonah as well—albeit indirectly—when God prepares a worm to destroy the *qiqayon* plant after it has existed for only a day (4:7). As noted by Sasson (1990, 301, 318), the fate of the plant recalls "the fragility of human existence" in a manner similar to Ps. 90:5-6 and Ps. 144:3-4, while the worm (תולע) is elsewhere shown to be a "voracious consumer of human remains" (e.g., Isa. 14:11). The scene with the plant also alludes to the role of toil in human life, as I will discuss in the next section.

2 Are humans born for trouble and toil?

Yahweh Elohim took the human and put him in the garden of Eden, to work it and guard it.

(Gen. 2:15)

And to Adam (ולאדם) he said, ... cursed is the ground because of you; in painful toil (עצבון) you shall eat of it all the days of your life. ... By the sweat of your face you shall eat bread.

(Gen. 3:17, 19)

The human being (אדם) is born for trouble (עמל).

(Job 5:7a)

God reminds Jonah that the prophet had not "toiled" (עמל) to cultivate the *qiqayon* plant. According to Yahweh, Jonah "pities" the plant's demise, while not feeling mercy toward the humans and animals in Nineveh (Jon. 4:10-11).[13] The verb עמל can denote exhaustive labor, misery, suffering, trouble, and/or mischief, although not all scholars agree about which nuance is at work in a specific passage.[14] Crenshaw (2014, 120) believes that "the basic sense of עמל suggests the onset of tiredness." Together with various "companion words," עמל indicates "activity that brings on exhaustion and the psychological state of distress." For "the author of the book of Job," however, עמל "always describes the human condition" (2014, 121). Otzen (2001, 199) would certainly agree, since he holds that the nuance of עמל which predominates in the entire wisdom tradition is "the affliction, or rather the misery, that is part of the fundamental human condition."

---

13. On this scene, see Chapter 5 §2.
14. See, for example, Fox (2010, 97–102) and Seow (1997, 104).

Similarly, Crenshaw contends that "the human condition" in Genesis 3 "was characterized by a single word, עָמָל"; for the author of this story "life was full of hardship" (2014, 119–20). Few readers would dispute that the garden of Eden narrative shows the necessity of painful toil for humans, whether it take the form of labor pains or painful working of the cursed ground. The fact that the term עמל is not employed by the narrator is irrelevant. The element of painful toil is one consequence of the first couple having eaten from the tree of knowledge. Labor itself was part of human existence from the start; Yahweh puts the first earthling in the garden in order to work it (עבד; Gen. 2:15). As Westermann puts it, far from being pessimistic, Gen. 3:17-19 is "sober realism"; work and toil are "part of human existence" (1994, 265–66). In short, saying that the entire "human condition" is characterized by trouble and toil overlooks far too many other aspects of human life which also have their origins in this narrative.[15]

My third epigraph, in which Eliphaz asserts that "the human being (אדם) is born for trouble (עמל)," has been understood in a variety of ways. Fox (2010, 98) argues that Eliphaz is saying that "misery, and not only labor, is the human condition." Driver (1921, 52) interprets the statement less broadly: "It is as natural for man to experience misfortune as it is for sparks to fly upwards."

How one interprets vv. 6-7 depends in part on whether or not one accepts the MT,[16] as well as how one understands Eliphaz's character. Eliphaz's dim view of humanity elsewhere in his speeches leads commentators such as Zuckermann to take vv. 6-7a as a "pessimistic assessment of the human condition" (2010, 6.6). Taking עמל as denoting "mischief" here and און as "evil," Zuckermann concludes that Eliphaz is accusing "mankind" of "inherent wickedness"; we were "born to do mischief." Clines (1989, 141–42; cf. 116) agrees that v. 7 expresses the principle that "the suffering (און, עמל) that humans undergo is 'begotten' by themselves." But in contrast to Zuckermann, Clines believes that "this is no pessimistic view of humankind," because it does not make them "inherently incapable of good." Whybray (1998, 46) offers yet another perspective. He takes Eliphaz to be saying that while humans are made from the earth, "that is not the root cause of their troubles." Trouble "falls on each individual from his birth." If we re-vocalize the passive "is born" to active "begets," then "human beings create their own misery

---

15. To mention just a few examples, humans acquire knowledge of good and evil in this chapter, as well as shame and other manifestations of a new consciousness of self, as well as the *ersatz* immortality provided by having children. None of these features of our condition can be completely characterized by the term עמל.

16. If one emends MT *pual* יוּלָד to *hiphil* יוֹלִד, then humans "beget" trouble instead of being "born for" (or "to") it, a change which functions as anthropodicy. Another suggested emendation is to replace לֹא in v. 6a ("affliction does not come out from the dust") with לְא ("affliction assuredly springs from the dust"). While Clines (1989, 141) rejects this emendation, Habel accepts it, rendering "evil also springs from the ground and trouble sprouts." He concludes that the earth is a continuing source of mortals' suffering on earth (1985, 117, 132).

by the way in which they live their lives." Whybray concludes that these verses present "a realistic if pessimistic view of human nature," whichever grammatical option we prefer.

The core issue is whether the עמל we experience is caused by our own behavior, our flawed nature as humans, our relation to the ground from which we were formed, and/or our difficulty coping in the world in which Yahweh has placed his fallible and frail human creatures. Together these factors ensure that we will inevitably suffer pain and failure and remain vulnerable to uncontrollable external (if not internal) forces.

Many commentators would object that Eliphaz is not referring to all these variables in 5:6-7; his focus is on humans' impure and corrupt nature as the cause of suffering, as his statements in 4:7-8, 17-21, and 15:14-16 make clear.[17] Driver offers a more nuanced reading on this issue. He argues that v. 7 expresses the nonjudgmental view that it is as natural for humans to experience misfortune as it is for sparks to fly upward. He then adds that, "if pressed, Eliphaz *would have* said that humans 'did not merely fall into misfortune, but brought misfortune upon himself by following the impulses of his evil nature'" (1921, 52; emphasis mine). In other words, Eliphaz is making his point in a non-accusatory fashion (for the moment), instead of stating his own view bluntly. Readers of the book of Job can therefore interpret v. 7 as stating a general truth that (in American slang) "stuff happens" while simultaneously being aware that Eliphaz himself blames humans for causing their own עמל.

Other passages also challenge readers to decide whether a character's statement about the human condition has general validity or merely represents that character's perspective at a particular point in time. Earlier I cited Job asking whether humans have warlike service on earth, so that his days are like those of a hireling (שכיר) or slave laborer (עבד), who await their wages but only receive "months of emptiness and nights of suffering (עמל)," until death puts them out of their misery (7:1-10 cf. 14:1-2). Clines (1989, 183) believes that Job is "project[ing] upon the human condition his own experience," rather than depicting some form of Hebrew pessimism. Rowley (1980, 65) sees both a universal and a particular aspect to Job's statement in 7:1-3. Job "realizes that the common lot of man is a hard one"; his own "experience, while exceptional in the intensity of his sufferings is typical in the fact of suffering." Whybray (1998, 54) finds that in vv. 1-2 Job is reflecting "about the state of human existence in general," while in vv. 3-5 he applies "these reflections to his own case." Clearly, generalizations about the human condition such as those examined in this section invite readers to think about their own general understanding of human existence and ask whether that understanding is harmonious with their own life experience.

---

17. When Eliphaz parallels עמל and און in Job 4:8, he is definitely using און in the sense of "iniquity." When he parallels these terms in 5:6, however, און may signify only "sorrow" or "affliction." For the pairing of עמל and און, see also Pss. 10:7, 55:11, and 90:10.

3 Comparing biblical and Greek answers to "What is the human being?"

Creature of a day. What is someone? What is no one?
—Pindar, *Pythian Ode* 8.95 (Gildersleeve 1885, 106)

Fearful wonders are many, and none is more fearfully wonderful (δεινότερον) than the human being.
—Sophocles, *Antigone* 334 (D'Ooge 1900, 52)

Nothing human is worth taking very seriously.
—Plato, *Resp.* 604b-c (Adam 1897, 309; cf. *Leg.* 803b)

It is hardly surprising that the same wide spectrum of opinion on human worth and experience can be found in other ancient and modern cultures. A brief survey of some ancient Greek statements on the human condition can alert us to similar key issues in biblical texts. When Pindar asks "What is someone?" his answer is that a human being is a "dream of a shadow" (σκιᾶς ὄναρ). However, when he takes into account our relationship with the god Zeus we hear a more positive message: "But when the Zeus-given splendor comes, a bright light is on men (ἀνδρῶν), and a gentle lifetime" (*Pyth.* 8.96-97). Yet taken as a whole, the ode is reflecting "on the inevitability of defeat for all victors, and for all human beings" (Lefkowitz 1977, 210).[18]

Perhaps the most famous praise of human power and potential in Greek literature is the second choral ode from Sophocles's *Antigone*. The ode begins by invoking human mastery over the sea: "This one [the human being] advances across the sea surging white in the wintry south wind, passing beneath swelling waters that engulf all around" (ll. 335–37). The song goes on to laud human mastery over earth goddess Gaia, the oldest of the gods, thanks to human ingenuity in fabricating plows. Hunting nets, yokes, and horse bridles force other animals to submit to our use and benefit. Our quick thinking and resourcefulness also allow us to escape inclement weather and to cure all diseases—with the notable exception of death. By teaching ourselves speech and controlling our emotions, we have also created the shelter of life in human societies, as long as we honor our country's laws and honor justice by swearing on the gods.

The very first line of this ode should alert us to the possibility that human mastery over our condition is not the whole story. We are praised for being "the most wonderful" of phenomena (*Antig.* 334). Sophocles uses the term δεινός, which can also mean "terrible" or "fearful," as when Homer's Odysseus and his shipmates face mortal danger from the "terrible" whirlpool Charybdis

---

18. At the same time, Lefkowitz does not agree with the many scholars who find a "sense of despair" in the poem. She believes that the poet is inviting his listeners and readers to ponder the "manifold connotations" of victory in general, not simply the wrestling victory being celebrated in the ode (1977, 218–19).

(*Od.* 12.260). Does the *Antigone* ode include a less sanguine view of human reality than it may initially appear? Knox (1971, 109) points us toward an answer when he notes that the ode expresses "a fully 'secular' view of human progress." Gods are mentioned only when Gaia is scoured by the plow and in the concluding proviso to swear by the gods in order to honor justice (*Antig.* 337–40, 369). Most strikingly, this glorious self-portrait of human success is subverted by the death and disorder which occur in the drama following the Chorus's song. Destructive actions by Creon and Antigone which qualify as δεινός hardly constitute an example of human ingenuity, laws, and success at survival in a civilized and orderly society.[19]

Elsewhere in Greek literature of the sixth to fourth century one can find many expressions of the brevity and shadowy unreality of human existence, as well as numerous examples of human moral failings and depravity (see, for example, Dodds 1968, 29, 214–17). In his late and most pessimistic work, *The Laws*, Plato's spokesperson ("the Stranger") goes so far as to claim that humans have very little true reality about them (*Leg.* 804b). In addition, we humans imagine that we know everything when we know almost nothing, and we are jerked around by our emotions like marionettes pulled by their strings (*Leg.* 732a, 644e). The fact that we are the god's "plaything" is the best thing about us. We are not worth being taken seriously apart from the role assigned us by the gods (*Leg.* 803c; 804b). After expressing these views, one of his dialogue partners concludes that the Stranger considers the human race to be of very little value.

The complex myth in Plato's earlier dialogue, the *Statesman* (also known as the *Politicus*), describes *two* alternating "human conditions." The crucial factor differentiating these sets of circumstances is the gods' role (or lack of direct role) in the two continuously alternating periods of human history.[20] During the original age of Cronus, the creator God is directly involved in governing his creation, assigning lesser deities their appropriate functions as shepherds for the various animals. Many features of this era are familiar from stories of the "Golden Age."[21]

---

19. Aeschylus's Prometheus includes the fabrication of sea-going ships among the gifts he bestowed upon humankind: "It was I and no one else who discovered the sailor's sail-winged wagons that wander over the sea" (line 467). The frailty of ships in the unbounded sea will be discussed in Chapter 3 §5–7. When Sophocles wrote and presented the later two plays of his Theban trilogy, *Oedipus the King* and *Oedipus at Colonus*, he offered his audiences a much more sobering portrait of humanity. The great knower Oedipus turns out to be abysmally ignorant (see Lasine 2001, 68–71). Creon's exercise of political power threatens disaster for his city. These more somber depictions of the human condition parallel historical events in Athens from the year in which *Antigone* was first presented (around 441 BCE) to the production of the *Colonus* (presented posthumously in 401 BCE).

20. On the myth as a presentation of the "human condition," see White (2007, 51–52) and Ambuel (2013, 215–16, 222–23, 225).

21. For example, foods grew in abundance without humans having to plant seeds. Humans were naked and had no need for houses or other shelter. There was no violence

Because humans have a body and the world itself has a material element, this state of affairs cannot go on eternally in this fashion; only the divine is unchanging. Changes, including total reversals, characterize human existence.[22] At a certain point, "the pilot of the universe let go of the rudder's handle and withdrew to his place commanding a wide view" (*Pol.* 272e), as do the lesser shepherding deities. Thus, the God becomes a spectator of what follows. The earth's motion then reverses itself. The sudden change causes earthquake and tumult, killing most animals and humans. At this point, survivors stop growing older; instead they grow younger until all earth-born humans finally disappear.

During the next period, the "age of Zeus," the world must control and care for itself insofar as humans recall the instructions which their divine creator and father had given them in the past. Over time, these are increasingly forgotten or ignored. The human condition is now one of vulnerability and exposure. Many animals become fiercely wild, while humans are now "feeble and unguarded" (*Pol.* 274b). At first, humans are also without a means of coping and without skill. Food no longer grows spontaneously. Various deities therefore have to intervene on their behalf.[23] Governments and civic institutions now begin to be installed. Nevertheless, the material element in the humans and their world leads to increasing disorder, including the entry of evil and unrighteousness. Eventually disorder becomes so great that the world is threatened with ruin, leading the God to intervene in order to prevent the world's destruction.

Given the Greek view of cyclical time shared by Plato, these two "human conditions" will continue to alternate forever (see Guthrie 1965, 63–79). Yet, one can argue that these two "eras" and two human conditions, both take place within any individual's life span.[24] From this perspective, the myth illustrates human development from a condition of total dependence similar to that of an infant to a stage of adult resourcefulness and self-protection. These stages of life, and their characteristic challenges, will be discussed extensively in relation to the book of Jonah in Part Two of this study.

In Genesis, it is the primal couple's transgression which leads to the necessity of toil and pain as well as the acquisition of survival skills (Gen. 3:16-17). As discussed earlier, Crenshaw seems to regard this as the main point of the story, in terms of defining the human condition. The ancient Greeks had varying views of toil and pain as elements of the human condition. The Greek word πόνος comes

---

or war, and animals did not devour one another. There were no governments and no possession of property by males, including possession of women and children. Humans sprung directly from the earth with no memory of the past.

22. In fact, one root denoting "change" (μεταβολή; μεταβάλλω) appears seven times in the myth.

23. These are Prometheus, Hephaestus, Athena, and Demeter. At this point, children begin to be born from mothers and grow older.

24. The idea of the eras coexisting is also noted by Vidal-Naquet (1978, 137), although he does not explain what he means by saying that both are "aspects of the same world."

closest to being an equivalent for Hebrew עמל; πόνος can denote distress, misery, and suffering, as well as toil (Loraux 1982, 171–72). Unlike עמל, however, πόνος does not have "mischief" as one of its possible meanings. Nor is it paired with a Greek term equivalent to Hebrew און.[25]

Burckhardt (1998, 101) makes the blanket statement that "to the Greek way of thinking, the obligation to work, life as toil, was itself a form of suffering."[26] This is an overgeneralization. Greek "ways of thinking" varied over time and among different groups at any given time. Heroic toil can result in glory, as the much-toiling[27] Heracles tells the isolated sufferer Philoctetes in Sophocles: "Having toiled at and persisted to the end in how many toils (πονήσας . . . πόνους) I achieved immortal excellence . . . and to you . . . it is owed to suffer this—to make your life glorious after and through these toils (πόνων)" (*Philoc.* 1419–22; Schein 2013, 336–37, modified). In Euripides's *Heracles*, the Chorus declares that excellent actions accomplished through "noble toil" (ἀρεταὶ πόνων) are glory for the dead (356–57). And in fifth-century Athens, athletic πόνος and rigorous training help to define an aristocrat's identity, virtue, and his status as a privileged member of the elite—as long as the painful efforts are made voluntarily and have no relation to servile labor (Johnstone 1994, 235–40; Csapo, 2005, 306–09).[28]

Like Hebrew עמל, πόνος is also used in statements which take toil and suffering to be an unavoidable part of the human condition. For example, in the *Iliad* Agamemnon tells Menelaus that they should toil in battle themselves, since Zeus sent "heavy misery" on us when we were born (*Il.* X.70–71). Pindar declares that all humans are much-toiling (πολύπονος; *Nem.* 1.33). "No one is without a share of toils or will be" (*Pyth.* 5.54; cf. Euripides, *Hipp.* 189–90). Xenophon's Socrates quotes Epicharmus's saying that "the gods sell us all good

---

25. On און, see n. 17 in this chapter.

26. Burckhardt adds that toil "is probably the age-old cause of pessimism." On the various causes for pessimism, in ancient Greece and Israel (as well as today), see Chapter 2 §1.

27. Euripides uses the epithet ὁ πολύπονος (the "much-toiling" or "much-suffering") to describe the hero in his *Heracles* (1192).

28. Arendt's well-known study on the human condition stresses the "*Vita Activa*," the three categories of which are labor, work, and action. The distinction between the first two elements is influenced by the Greek distinction between work and labor; see Arendt (1989, 79–84). She mentions the biblical presentation of work and toil only in passing, focusing on Gen. 3:17-19. Arendt claims that the "curse by which man was expelled from paradise" made "birth full of sorrow" (1989, 107, n. 53). However, the human couple are not said to be expelled as a curse. The term "curse" (ארור) is used only in reference to the serpent and the ground (3:14, 17). As von Rad (1973, 97) puts it, the expulsion has a merciful aspect, "namely, the withholding of a good [eating from the tree of life] which for man would have been unbearable in his present state" (Gen. 3:22). Finally, in Gen. 3:16 birth is said to involve pain and toil (עצב; עצבון), not the emotion of "sorrow."

things for the price of toil" (*Mem.* 2.1.20; see Johnstone 1994, 239). Socrates then recites Prodicus's essay "On Heracles," in which young Heracles encounters two women, Excellence and Evil, who give him opposite advice. Excellence tells him that for everything good and beautiful, the gods "give nothing to humans without toil (ἄνευ πόνου) and diligence" (*Mem.* 2.1.28).

That suffering and toil as an inescapable part of human life is also implied in Euripides's *Bacchae*, when Teiresias calls wine the only "medicine for misery (φάρμακον πόνων)" capable of stopping mortal's suffering and pain (ll. 280–83). This prescription recalls Prov. 31:6-7, in which it is recommended that one gives intoxicating drink to those who are perishing and wine to those whose lives are bitter, for drinking allows them to forget their poverty and עמל. Finally, the πόνος associated with human life may be contrasted with that of other beings who live without toil, such as the Hyperboreans (Pindar, *Pyth.* 10.41–43) or the good who have an afterlife without toil, as opposed to the wrongdoers who have to endure "toil that is unbearable to look at" (Pindar, *Ol.* 2.62–72).

The myth in Plato's *Statesman* remains the most provocative parallel with the situation of humans in the Hebrew Bible. The myth, like the Bible, shows what can occur when humans are given direct divine care and shepherding, and when the deity withdraws and becomes an observer of human successes and failures. Biblical texts offer many examples of Yahweh caring for and shepherding humans who find themselves in an otherwise hostile environment. Most dramatically, Yahweh guides the Israelites through the wilderness, feeding the people with manna and quail. In this scenario, the people's role is to gratefully accept their God's parental nurturing and obey all his rules. Later I will ask whether Yahweh wants the "children of Israel" to remain in this state of childlike dependence upon him, rather than have them become autonomous adults. One thing is immediately clear: Yahweh's many-faceted personality and emotions make his relations with his human children more complicated and perilous than is the case with the faceless deity of Plato's myth.

When God Yahweh first creates humans in Genesis 1–2, he forbids them from acquiring survival skills for which "knowledge of good and evil" is necessary. After they nevertheless disobey and digest "knowledge of good and evil," their initial actions do not exactly show mastery of their environment. The clothing they fabricate is made from fig leaves, and their ignorance of their new situation is so great that they attempt to hide themselves from an all-seeing God. This may be appropriate behavior for little children playing "hide-and-seek" with their parents, but it is not an indication that they are now equipped to cope with the world outside this Edenic kindergarten.

Ten generations later, after God destroys almost all life on earth with the Flood, the threat of future destruction remains, even after the war bow in the sky has been transformed into a rainbow "peace symbol." In Plato's myth the helmsman god periodically withdraws from direct control of the world, but he remains on watch and intervenes when humans are about to destroy themselves. While this is sometimes the case with Yahweh as well, on other occasions Yahweh abandons his people in order to punish them, leaving them to cry out for his aid when they are in danger and near death.

Perhaps the only examples of human mastery over external threats comparable to that found in the *Antigone* ode are those which directly follow from our being given the power to rule and dominate by God, as in Genesis 1 and Psalm 8. Yet the Bible often reports cases in which royal and parental power have been misused. In his speeches to Job from the whirlwind, God lets us all know—in no uncertain terms—that humans have no mastery over animals and weather unless he allows it. And whoever the speaker may be in Job 28, that chapter makes it clear that humans have no access to wisdom, so that fear of Yahweh and obedience to his wishes is our only "wise" option. Even this may not ensure our security. As Ps. 107:23-32 dramatically illustrates, God can make even the greatest human ingenuity (in this case, seafaring) seem stupid when he chooses to do so.[29]

The praise of human origins and potential found in Genesis 1 and Psalm 8—as well as in *Antigone*—contrasts violently with the denigration of humanity expressed by Eliphaz and Bildad in the book of Job and the many evocations of human folly and evanescence found throughout ancient Greek literature. The copresence of such opposing views is also found in later times, perhaps most dramatically in medieval and Renaissance Europe, when Bildad-like condemnations of human nature generated passionate defenses of unique human dignity, potential, and freedom.[30] Because the Hebrew Bible includes both opposing positions within one canonical body of texts, each of its readers is called upon to decide where they stand on the issue of human worth and the appropriate role God should play in their lives.

---

29. On this passage, see Chapter 3 §4.

30. See Howard (1974, 55-57), Cassirer (1963, 83-86), and Bayertz (1996, 73-76). For example, Pope Innocent III's influential essay on human misery illustrates the negative pole of this opposition: Humans are "formed of dust, slime, and ashes . . . of the filthiest seed and . . . conceived from the . . . stench of lust." Once born, we defile ourselves by committing "depraved and . . . shameful acts." And in the end, we become "food for the worm . . . [and] a mass of rottenness which will forever stink and reek" (1969, 6). Writers such as Pico della Mirandola rebut this view, by stressing the uniquely high status given to humans by their Creator. Pico gives a number of reasons—including "David's" affirmation (in Ps. 8:6, Vg.) that we are "little lower than angels"—to justify his view that the human being "is the most fortunate and therefore worthy of all admiration"; in fact, our "condition . . . [is] to be envied not only by beasts but even by the stars and the intelligences dwelling beyond this world" (*Oration* §6; 2010, 113). To explain the copresence of such radically contrasting opinions, historians often point to the influence of the Protestant Reformation and Counter-Reformation as well as the "New Science"; see, in addition to the works cited above, Stark (2012, 173-74).

4 Biblical and modern conceptions of the human condition: Part One of this study

Many modern characterizations of human life highlight two basic aspects of human experience mentioned earlier: danger and death.[31] For example, Ortega y Gasset argues that "the progressivist idea anesthetized the European and the American to [the] basic feeling of risk," obscuring the fact that "the very substance of our life is danger" (1963, 26, 27, n. 4). He contends that "the condition of man [sic] . . . is essential uncertainty"; we can "only be sure of insecurity" (1963, 25). Others highlight our lack of control over our situation.[32] As one Malraux character puts it, we have not chosen to be born, we did not choose our parents, and we "can do nothing against time." Every person feels the "independence of the world with regard to himself," at least at certain moments (Malraux 1997, 111). It is hardly surprising that the vulnerability highlighted in these statements may lead a person to fear taking risks, including the risk of exposing oneself to danger when seeking to become an autonomous adult. The feeling of lack of control may also lead us to deny or gloss over anxiety-producing facts such as the inevitability of our own death.[33] In Ricoeur's blunt formulation, "immortality is what we attempt to confer upon ourselves in order to endure our mortal condition" (1983, 62).

While these modern writers and ancient characters such as Job's friends make disconcerting blanket statements about the human condition as a whole, this is not the norm with the Hebrew Bible. When narrators report the words and actions of most biblical characters, they do not ordinarily include parenthetical asides telling readers what the characters' behavior implies about human nature as a whole. Admittedly, after the Flood, Yahweh says to himself that "the inclination (יצר) of the human heart is evil from his youth" (Gen. 8:21; cf. Jer. 17:9). Readers must continually reconsider this sweeping judgment about the human inclination toward evil as they read along and encounter characters who exhibit no such

---

31. The statements by Freud and A. Huxley discussed in Chapter 7 §2 also illustrate this emphasis on danger and death.

32. Social psychology has shown that individuals also have a hand in creating their own situation. See Chapter 6 §3.

33. In Malraux's novel *La Condition Humaine*, the philosopher Gisors states that it is very rare for a human being to endure "*his* human condition" (emphasis added). Each of us therefore resorts to some form of "intoxication"—that is, some kind of coping device, escape, or defense—in order to free ourselves from "our human condition" (1946, 185). In Thomas Mann's *Joseph and his Brothers*, which was written about the same time as Malraux's novel, the narrator asks what "'unbearable' (*unerträglich*) means when it must be borne and absolutely nothing remains but to take it, as long as the person is in his right mind?" (1964, 427). As we shall discover in Chapter 2 §3-4 and Chapter 5 §1, the point at which something difficult to bear becomes something unbearable varies for different biblical characters, including prophets from Moses to Jonah.

propensity toward evil as adults. The same is true concerning Yahweh's earlier statement to the first woman, which ends with the still influential proclamation that her husband will rule over her (Gen. 3:16). Even within Genesis, readers will discover women who dominate or control males (including their husbands) rather than being lorded over by them. In general, biblical narratives show humans as they act—and interact with others (including their God)—rather than telling readers how to understand the human condition by making general pronouncements.

In Chapter 2, I will examine the optimistic and pessimistic attitudes toward the human condition exhibited by characters within the textual world of the Hebrew Bible and by readers of biblical texts. I begin by outlining the various senses in which the concepts of pessimism and optimism have been understood and employed. Next, I consider Qoheleth's seemingly pessimistic statements on death and the vanity of human life, in part by comparing these passages with similar statements in ancient Greek texts. I will then turn from pessimism in the Writings to examples of pessimism in the first two divisions of the canon. In the Pentateuch, I will focus on Deuteronomy 31, asking whether the characters Moses and Yahweh display pessimistic attitudes toward God's people, if not toward humans in general. The next section asks whether Jeremiah and the other biblical prophets who desire death are exhibiting pessimism. The chapter then concludes after discussing the theological implications of human and divine pessimism: What does "pessimism" mean when we are referring to the biblical world governed by God Yahweh?

In Chapter 3, I will trace the implications of a core metaphor, namely, human life as a sea voyage. The Hebrew Bible says relatively little about ships and sea voyages. While some scholars associate water and fear of drowning imagery in the Psalms with the "mythical drama" of the *Chaoskampf*, I will argue that this is not the appropriate lens through which to view the variations of sea, storm, and shipwreck imagery in Psalms and Jonah 1–2. Further implications of this metaphor will be discussed through an analysis of works by Philips van Marnix, John Donne, and several other authors. In the biblical context, the life as sea voyage metaphor points to unsettling aspects of the human condition in Yahweh's cosmos. While the biblical God can rescue those who are drowning and provide a safe haven for those whose life-ships are in peril, even the most loyal of his human children cannot take for granted that their divine father will play these roles whenever storms threaten their existence. Taken together, this cluster of nautical metaphors indicates that the difficulties of navigating through life in Yahweh's world are not merely the result of Yahweh's complex personality but of the complex and forbidding cosmos in which he has chosen to place us.

Chapter 4 concludes the first part of this investigation by asking whether reading about human mortality can lead modern readers to become more aware of their own inescapable demise and, if so, do biblical texts offer a way of coping with this uncomfortable awareness? After briefly surveying research on the psychology of death, I will turn to the Elijah-Elisha narratives, which include an unusually large number of stories involving illness, human vulnerability, death, and the resuscitation of the dead. How do biblical characters—and readers of Kings—react to stories which challenge our ordinary understanding of the boundaries separating life and death? And how should we understand the fact that the Hebrew Bible does not offer its readers the prospect of a positive afterlife?

5 Jonah's human condition: Part Two of this study

Part Two of the book examines one biblical character in detail. Jonah might seem to be a surprising choice for a case study on the human condition, since the book of Jonah does not include the kind of generalizations on human existence found in texts such as Qoheleth or Job. Nevertheless, the book manages to touch upon some of the most fundamental aspects of human experience, highlighting the most paradoxical aspects of our relationship to the biblical God and God's complex character. The methods I will employ to analyze the book of Jonah are various. The value—and ultimate inadequacy—of psychological approaches to Jonah's character will receive extended treatment. The philosophical and theological implications of the book's plot, dialogues, and root metaphors will also receive considerable attention.

The first section of Chapter 5 is a detailed examination of what readers are, and are not, told about Jonah's situation and character. Many biblical scholars have analyzed Jonah's personality and made definite judgments about his character and his relationship with God. A number of commentators view the prophet Jonah as an "Everyman/Everyone," a human being very much like ourselves—although they disagree about Jonah's character and therefore about his similarity to themselves. I will argue that the text of Jonah does not furnish us with sufficient data to support *any* definitive psychological profile of the prophet, whether complex *or* simple, unique *or* universal. The book's informational gaps, quoted speeches, and network of intertextual allusions are examined closely in this section. I conclude that the book's subtle narrative rhetoric often leads readers to interpret Jonah's personality in ways which express more about their own personalities, expectations, values, academic paradigm, and group identity than they say about this elusive biblical figure.

The second section of Chapter 5 examines the many attempts made by commentators to judge Jonah's character, including the evaluations made by psychologists who posit different versions of a "Jonah complex." I ask whether these "complexes" actually illuminate the character of the biblical Jonah and/or reflect aspects of human behavior and the human condition experienced by modern readers of the book. Commentators often point to the book's many metaphors of enclosure and conclude that Jonah consistently chooses to be "embedded," as a psychological defense against risk. In support, they usually cite Maslow's version of the "Jonah complex." After analyzing Maslow's approach, I consider the Jonah complexes conceived by Jung and the related theories by Fromm, Bettelheim, and others. All these versions of the Jonah complex focus on the topological dimension of human existence, especially the opposition between enclosure and exposure. After considering the evidence adduced by each of these theorists, I conclude that Jonah's actions do not suggest that he is attempting to avoid risk through embeddedness, let alone that he displays a "fear of engulfment." In fact, Jonah consistently displays a readiness to *expose himself* to danger, rather than striving to avoid it.

In Chapter 6, I concentrate on the plot of the book of Jonah, from both literary and psychological perspectives. The first section examines how the book's action evokes many of the childhood crises all of us must endure. In fact, the book's plot and mode of narration make this text uniquely capable of evoking readers' fundamental fantasies and fears. What George Orwell calls the "hold that the Jonah myth has upon our imaginations" has more to do with the book's plot and root metaphors than it does the perceived personality of the character Jonah. In light of all the versions of the story transmitted over many centuries in words and images, and the continuing popularity of the Jonah story in children's literature and videos, it is difficult to deny that the narrative has indeed had a powerful effect on a wide variety of readers. To investigate the reasons for this effect, I compare Jonah's stay in the belly of the big fish with the experiences of mythical and fairy-tale heroes who either experience being swallowed up, engulfed, and devoured or are in mortal fear of such a fate. The crucial challenges faced by children discussed in this chapter may continue to play a role in one's adult life as well, especially when they have not been resolved successfully during one's early years.

In the second section of Chapter 6, I attempt to show that the plot of Jonah also prompts its readers to ponder the perils of adulthood, suggesting that this is another reason for the book's continuing appeal to audiences over time. Jonah 3–4 are viewed here in terms of the threats to autonomy and integration faced by all adults as they navigate their way through their lives. Jonah's actions are contrasted with those of others who face danger at sea and on dry land, such as the Egyptian shipwrecked sailor and the quintessential mature male hero in Greek literature, Homer's Odysseus. These comparisons lead to the conclusion that Jonah's flight may express a refusal to let God's command control his behavior, even if his refusal results in his annihilation or being entombed alive in a fish. On the ship, Jonah controls what the sailors do with him, once he has told them that he had fled from Yahweh. Jonah 4 shows that the prophet's resistance to God's authority remains even after he has completed his mission. His words imply that his resistance stems from moral objections to the task, while his twice-repeated request to die expresses both the futility of resistance and a desire to—at least—control when and how he will escape his untenable situation. From this perspective, the death wish stems from a refusal to live on Yahweh's terms, rather than being an expression of wounded narcissism, a longing for embeddedness, or a desire to protect himself from being viewed as a false prophet.

This book's final chapter surveys the results of our investigation, making it possible to draw some wider conclusions about living and dying in Yahweh's world—and in our own world. The preceding chapters demonstrated that the fundamental opposition between enclosure and exposure plays an important role not only within the book of Jonah but also in the individual and collective life-worlds of the book's readers. The final chapter begins with an analysis of George Orwell's understanding of the contemporary "human condition" as life "inside the whale." I consider the appropriateness and desirability of a life of embeddedness, maintaining the stance of a detached observer who does not risk involvement in the events outside his or her womblike shelter. The second section takes its lead from William James's description of "life and death keeping house together" in our world and asks how this perspective might shed light on the abrupt ending of the book of Job. This discussion is followed by an examination of the way vulnerability has been viewed as an element of the human condition in both ancient and modern texts, with and without religion being taken as a factor in determining our fragility. I then return to biblical speakers, focusing on Jeremiah 4 and Qoheleth 12 in relation to the issues of mortality and annihilation. The study concludes by asking how the Hebrew Bible's silence on the topic of an afterlife might affect our understanding and experience of our own death in Yahweh's world.

Chapter 2

PESSIMISM AND THE HUMAN CONDITION IN THE HEBREW BIBLE

In this chapter, I ask whether specific biblical texts express an optimistic or pessimistic view of the human condition. I begin by examining the various senses in which the concepts of pessimism and optimism have been understood and employed. I then consider how we should evaluate wide-sweeping pessimistic statements in the Hebrew Bible and ancient Greek texts, especially the claim that it is best never to have been born and, once alive, to die as soon as possible. Are such pronouncements merely clichés which should not be taken very seriously?

In the remainder of the chapter, I look for the presence of pessimism in each of the three sections of the Hebrew Bible. I begin with Qoheleth as my example from the Writings,[1] paying close attention to the sage's statements on death and its relation to divine justice. Next I turn to the Pentateuch, asking whether the leaders Moses and Yahweh display pessimism in Deuteronomy 31. Then I will focus on the prophets, specifically, whether the prophets who desire death are exhibiting pessimism. The chapter concludes by tracing the theological implications of human and divine pessimism: What does "pessimism" mean when we are referring to the biblical world governed by God Yahweh?

---

1. If readers were asked which book in the canon has the most pessimistic view of the human condition, there is little doubt that the most frequent answer would be Qoheleth. However, Crenshaw (2013, 127–28, n. 14) notes that "in recent commentaries there seems to be a trend toward a positive interpretation of Qoheleth's thought, as opposed to earlier pessimistic treatments." This raises the question whether the earlier interpretations were affected by the interpreters' own pessimism, instead of (or, as well as) highlighting pessimism expressed by the dramatized narrator in the received text. More recently, Crenshaw has stressed that Qoheleth's hatred of life is not a temporary phenomenon and that optimistic readings of the book are consequently unpersuasive (2014, 119, 127–28).

1 What exactly is "pessimism"?

> Nor is any mortal (βροτός) blessed, but wretched are all mortals (θνητοὺς) upon whom the sun looks down.
>
> —Solon (Fr. 14; Stobaeus 1856, 227)

The view expressed in this epigraph can be found in a number of extant Greek texts. This should not be surprising, considering the Greek observations on the brevity, fragility, and toilsomeness of human existence that I discussed in Chapter 1. Burckhardt claims that "Greek consciousness . . . , probably exceeds anything in other literatures in its total pessimism and despair" (1998, 94).[2]

While some of Burckhardt's examples echo biblical speakers such as Qoheleth and Job, the Hebrew Bible is rarely taken as evidence of Israelite pessimism.[3] In fact, the opposite has been asserted. In 1903, Adolph Guttmacher published a dissertation in which he argued that "the optimistic view of life came naturally to the ancient Hebrews" (1903, 57). In support he cites Schopenhauer's view that "the Old Testament was a religion of Optimism," and agrees with the philosopher's assertion that Gen. 1:31 "holds the entire philosophy of Optimism."

---

2. For examples of "archaic pessimism" in Greek texts of the eighth to fifth century BCE, see Versnel (2011, 152–55, 210). Murray (1998, xxxix) lauds Burckhardt's insight that "the real problem and the real achievement of the Greeks lay in their inability to accept the existence of an afterlife of any significance." There are exceptions, however, such as the more positive views found in Greek mystery religions and the rise of ideas such as reincarnation, as well as in the fate of those (such as Homer's Menelaus) lucky enough to be transported to Elysium (*Od.* 4.563). See the compact survey in N. Richardson (1985; cf. Sourvinou-Inwood 1996, 298–300).

3. Some scholars have also characterized ancient Mesopotamian and Egyptian culture as pessimistic, quite apart from the fact that each produced examples of what has been called pessimistic wisdom literature. Lambert (2016, 19) notes that Irkalla, the Mesopotamian underworld, is depicted as a "dreaded, gloomy place"; this gave "a certain pessimistic tinge to Mesopotamian thought." Among non-Assyriologists, N. K. Sandars refers to the "pervasive pessimism of Mesopotamian thought" (1972, 22–23). As evidence, she points to precarious life in the city-states, the threats of flood, drought, and "turbulent neighbors," as well as dependence upon the gods. Eliade (1969, 74) also speaks of the "pessimism characteristic of Mesopotamian culture," citing the creation of humans in *Enuma Elish* and the impossibility of gaining immortality demonstrated in *The Gilgamesh Epic*. Interestingly, in spite of a positive afterlife belief in ancient Egypt, Egyptologist R. B. Parkinson claims that the Egyptian worldview was also "fundamentally pessimistic" (1998, 22). He cites the constant presence of chaos "waiting to overwhelm the ordered cosmos" and the generally negative Egyptian view of human nature, which is viewed as "tending to the wild" (1998, 204).

(1903, 58; cf. Schopenhauer 1965, 449).[4] Guttmacher detects a "predominant note of cheerfulness running through the Old Testament," thanks to the characters' complete dependence on "a God who had ordered all things for a beneficent purpose." He concedes that Job, Ecclesiastes, and a few Psalms are exceptions, but "the pessimistic tendency was successfully overcome by faith in a Creator and the goodness and wisdom of his work." In short, the Old Testament portrays life as "full of victory over troubles" (1903, 58).

Guttmacher's appeal to Schopenhauer is ironic; Schopenhauer actually condemns optimism as "not only a false, but also a corruptive doctrine, because it depicts life as a desirable condition for us" which has "as its purpose the happiness of humankind" (1960, 748-49). According to Schopenhauer, Jews "cannot be humbly thankful enough, and sufficiently laud Jehovah, for an ephemeral existence full of wailing, anxiety, and privation" (1965, 450).[5] The only thing which "reconciles" Schopenhauer to the Old Testament is the myth of the Fall, which supplies the required "pessimistic element" (1960, 743, 1965, 447). Schopenhauer laments that in the Old Testament this story "stands there isolated and is put to no further use" (1960, 795). He himself believes that it is "far more correct to regard work, deprivation, hardship, and suffering—crowned by death—as the purpose of our life"—as does "genuine Christianity"—because "it is these which lead to the negation of the will to live" (1960, 749).

Clearly, whether one views the entire Hebrew Bible as optimistic or pessimistic will depend upon how one understands these terms and how one evaluates Yahweh's role in the life of his human creatures. Crenshaw (1987, 47) astutely observes that the book of Qoheleth reflects the interpreter's worldview, which is why opinions vary so widely on Qoheleth's optimism or pessimism and other issues. Specific texts within the Hebrew Bible have been repeatedly called "pessimistic." Sneed (2012, 9) cites Job 3, Lamentations,[6] and psalms of lament in addition to Qoheleth. Chin (1994, 101) speaks of "the drastic mood shift from extreme pessimism to almost equally extreme optimism" in Job 13-14, and Weitzman (1997, 53) finds "intellectual pessimism" in Deuteronomy 31-32.[7] Jeremiah has been dubbed the "prophet of pessimism," as I will discuss later. Less frequently Naomi is described as

---

4. In Gen. 1:31, God sees everything he has made as being "very good." Schopenhauer quotes the Greek version.

5. The love of life in spite of all the negative aspects of the human condition is captured nicely by Woody Allen's character Alvey Singer in the 1977 film, *Annie Hall*: "That's essentially how I feel about life. Full of loneliness and misery and suffering and unhappiness, and it's all over much too quickly" (Allen 1982, 4).

6. Krašovec (1992, 231) cites Lam. 3:18 as an "utterly pessimistic statement," but notes that it "gives way to a sense of tranquility" by 3:24.

7. Weitzman (1997, 53) believes that this runs counter to the "pedagogical optimism implicit in much of the rest of Deuteronomy."

pessimistic in the opening chapter of Ruth.[8] Passages in the LXX such as Sir. 40:1-17 have also been described as pessimistic (e.g., Skehan and DiLella, 1987, 469). The salient aspects of the human condition in the wisdom passages are suffering and the inevitability of personal death. In the case of Qoheleth, Job, and Sirach, innocent suffering is also stressed, thereby conceding that injustice is present in a world which is said to be governed by a just God.

Before proceeding, we must clarify the various senses in which the term "pessimism" has been used by scholars in various fields. Among biblical commentators, Sneed states that pessimism is "a negative emotion" characterized by a "sense of futility," as well as a mood and a psychological strategy (2012, 7, 231, 233). According to Crenshaw, pessimists believe that "chaos has the upper hand"; once pessimism "sets in . . . [it] spawns sheer indifference to cherished convictions" (1981, 191).

Among psychologists, pessimism is usually regarded as an attitude, outlook, or the result of a negative mood or depression.[9] In the past twenty-five years, personality theorists and social psychologists have made experimental studies of the optimism-pessimism continuum. Here pessimism is understood to "reflect an expectation that bad things will happen" (Chang 2000, 5). Some researchers distinguish between rational and defensive pessimism on the one hand and neurotic or unrealistic pessimism on the other. Others contrast pessimism as a disposition or attributional style with pessimism as the temporary result of a negative mood.[10] In all cases, the focus is on "the benefits and costs of . . . pessimism" for people with specific personalities, goals, and life experiences (see Norem and Chang 2000, 362).[11] The implied goal is clearly eudaemonic.

Philosophers are more concerned with pessimism as a general worldview. In fact, many philosophers in late-nineteenth-century Germany held that "modern pessimism" was exclusively philosophical (Beiser 2016, 4). More atypical is William James's claim that "pessimism is essentially a religious disease"

---

8. For example, Hall asserts that Ruth carefully refutes Naomi's "realistically pessimistic vision" (2012, 563). Zakovitch sees Naomi infecting Ruth with Naomi's pessimism (Brettler 1993, 179–80).

9. See, for example, Keltner (1993, 740). Nesse views pessimism as a functional manifestation of depression which allows one to cope with "unpropitious situations" (2000, 17). Sim (2015, 13) contrasts the medical condition of depression with pessimism, which he views as "more in the nature of a personality trait." One common feature of these descriptions is that "negativity" can result in a pessimistic attitude, although in some cases the negativity is not viewed negatively if it corresponds to the perceived reality.

10. The terms employed are "dispositional pessimism," "pessimistic attributional style," "neurotic and rational pessimism," "unrealistic pessimism," and "defensive pessimism" (Norem and Chang 2000, 348–49).

11. Norem (2000, 96) notes that "one might reasonably predict that defensive pessimists would be relatively averse to risk," but adds that their "extensive preparation might also make them more willing to take some kinds of risks."

(1962, 8–9).[12] Recent philosophical studies of pessimism dispute the assumption that pessimism must lead to a sense of futility or spawn indifference, even in the face of the inescapability of death. In Dienstag's formulation, "to say that our lives are always on the way to death is not at all to say that they are pointless, but simply to set out the parameters of possibility for our existence." Pessimism may "warn us to acknowledge our limitations—but it does not urge us to collapse in the face of them" (2006, 22). In fact, pessimism "relieves us from the unhappiness that optimism, quite unwittingly, generates and guarantees" (2006, 110; cf. Sim 2015, 10, 21–22, 172). In other words, admitting our human vulnerabilities does not necessarily lead one to become indifferent, depressed, or resigned to being powerless.[13] In fact, the pessimist philosopher Bahnsen considers those who withdraw into an attitude of resignation to be "grouches" or "whiners" (*Murrköpfe*; qtd. in Beiser 2016, 282).

Clearly, we must distinguish between cases in which a person views his or her situation or capabilities in a negative way and those in which negative judgments are made about an entire culture, environment, or humanity as a whole. In the former case, if others perceive someone to be acknowledging only the difficult or painful aspects of their situation while ignoring more positive indicators, they might as well view this person as a pessimist. In the latter case, others may label someone a pessimist if that person calls their attention to unsettling aspects of human condition which they themselves would rather ignore or obscure. This person's attentiveness to life's negative features could then be written off as a function of despair, rather than being viewed as a serious attempt to acknowledge unpleasant realities in order to cope with them more effectively. This is not to deny that perceivers can project their own negativity onto the world at large. We must therefore consider the possibility that people's perceptions may sometimes say more about their own state of mind or personality than they do about external realities.

2 Are Qoheleth's pronouncements on death and injustice pessimistic?

And I commended the dead who have already died more than the living who are still living. And better than both of them is he who has still not existed and who has not seen the evildoing which is done under the sun.

—Qoh. 4:2-3

---

12. For more on James's view, see Chapter 7 §2 of this book.

13. In contrast, Crenshaw claims that once pessimism "sets in . . . [it] spawns sheer indifference to cherished convictions" (1981, 191). Crenshaw draws a distinction between skepticism and pessimism in biblical wisdom literature and concludes that only the teachings of Agur and Qoheleth are pessimistic in his sense (1981, 259, n. 5). Intellectual historians who trace the history of pessimism tend to cite only Qoheleth as a biblical example (if they mention the Bible at all), just as they typically cite Schopenhauer as the quintessential example of philosophical pessimism (e.g., Dollimore 2001, 36–42; Dienstag 2006, 100).

> It is best of all for earthlings not to be born and not to look upon the rays of the piercing sun, but once born it is best to pass through the gates of Hades as swiftly as possible and to lie under a great heap of earth.
>
> —Theognis, 425–27 (Clement 1869, 252)

As I mentioned earlier, statements within the book of Sirach are among the biblical texts which have been called "pessimistic." Sirach outlines the "heavy yoke" which God (*'el*) has allotted to us over the course of our lives, whether we are awake or asleep (40:1, 5–7; cf. Qoh. 2:23). This "yoke" includes anger, jealousy, anxiety, dread, fear of death, strife, contention, bloodshed, fever, drought, and famine (vv. 5, 9). The fear of death is described with great precision: "Perplexities and fear of heart [are everyone's] and anxious thought of the day of their death, . . . fear of death (φόβος θανάτου) and fury and strife. . . . O death, how bitter is the reminder of you to one who lives at peace among his possessions" (Sir. 40:2, 5; 41:1; NRSV, slightly modified). To say with Collins (1978, 182–83) that "Sirach is not insensitive to the common fear of death" is putting it too mildly.[14]

Are Qoheleth's alleged pessimism and focus on human mortality also linked to fear of death? Bickerman (1967, 151) has no doubt about the answer: "Kohelet echoed the primeval and eternal voice of the frightened man trying to fool Death. . . . The Sage of Jerusalem feared Death and repeatedly denied a survival after death." Williamson implies the same, when he argues that for Qoheleth "the anxiety-buffering worldview of Proverbs 10–29" has become impaired, so that the sage is "forced to grapple—unbuffered—with 'the worm at the core' of human existence" (2014, 382).[15]

Commentators also differ on the degree to which Qoheleth focuses on death. Fox points to Qoheleth's unparalleled obsession with death (1989, 294; cf. 2010, 343), while Sneed believes that Qoheleth's "brooding over death" is a "major component of [his] pessimism" (2012, 8). For Burkes (1999, 1) the problem of death is "the driving theme and main concern of Qoheleth." In contrast, Walsh insists that Qoheleth does *not* "give the impression of being obsessed with [death]" (1982, 46).

---

14. Collins (1978, 182) balances this statement by pointing out that for Sirach "death is not necessarily terrible" for the wise who do not "succumb to fears or bitterness," even though death remains "the limiting end of life." It remains to be seen whether canonical Hebrew scripture also includes evidence of a fundamental fear of death, *even among* those who "live at peace among their possessions"—and whether a similar fear might influence how modern readers understand the biblical narratives in terms of their own life situations and impending demise.

15. The "buffer" metaphor is employed by most exponents of TMT; see Chapter 4 §1. Among some psychologists who study optimism and pessimism, a key question for future research is "whether optimism could buffer individuals from the disruptions in everyday activities that typically stem from major life changes" (Affleck et al. in Chang 2000, 149–50).

There is little doubt that the pessimism readers perceive in Qoheleth has much to do with the fact of mortality. Priest asserts that "the real crux of his pessimism [is] the immutable fact of death which brings an end to all human aspiration, striving, and realization" (1968, 324). Williamson (2014, 364) argues that "Qohelet faces the reality of his own inevitable demise, judging life lived in death's shadow to be nothing more than a vain shepherding of the wind." Here mortality renders life meaningless. Crenshaw goes further, noting that Qoheleth views death, meaninglessness, and justice in relation to one another. He believes that for Qoheleth, "life devoid of equity, both human and divine, is hollow mockery" (1978, 207). Similarly, Murphy argues that Qoheleth "forms an exception" to the biblical rule that mortality "was never deplored as unjust fate." For this sage, "human death seems to be blamed on an arbitrary God, who makes no distinctions between people." Finally, Sneed argues that Qoheleth's pessimism is a strategy for coping with an irrational and unfair world: "His mood lowered his expectations about the world" (2012, 233).[16]

If Bickerman and Williamson are correct about Qoheleth's fear of death, it should be easy to point to verses in which the narrator Qoheleth expresses death anxiety. Qoheleth realistically describes human vulnerabilities on both the individual and social levels, but does that necessarily imply that this dramatized narrator is responding to those realities by experiencing anxiety?[17] If there is no textual basis for this view, how can we explain Bickerman's certainty that Qoheleth fits his template of the "frightened man trying to fool death"? Should we entertain the possibility that a commentator's own psychology may affect his or her readings of the biblical texts, or should we retain our pose of objectivity and detachment at any cost?

Qoheleth's seemingly pessimistic utterances about mortality can be more fully understood if we view them in their literary context and ask what functions they may serve. For example, Qoheleth claims that the dead are more fortunate than those who are still living, but best of all is not to have existed, thereby avoiding the

---

16. Sneed finds this to be a healthy attitude, as long as it does not "lead to a largely inactive, passive kind of life style."

17. Similarly, does contemplating one's mortality necessarily imply that one is "obsessed" with death? Are, for example, Seneca and Montaigne obsessed with mortality because they write so much about it? Montaigne, for one, admits that "from the outset there was no topic I ever concerned myself with more than with thoughts about death," but he takes this as evidence that he is "not so much melancholic as an idle dreamer" (2003, 97). The literary character Gilgamesh, on the other hand, offers a perfect example of obsession with death after his friend Enkidu dies, although in the end he is reconciled to his mortality, thanks, in part, to the symbolic immortality imparted by fame, potential progeny, and the erection of monumental structures in which tablet boxes are deposited. In the case of Qoheleth, the narrator seems more obsessed with control than he is about personal annihilation. Specifically, he is concerned with his inability to control the wealth he has acquired once he has died.

need to witness the evil actions and oppressions which characterize the human life-world (4:1-3). Krüger (2004, 95) notes that this passage "is often claimed as a testimony to the 'pessimism of Qoheleth.'" As the second epigraph to this section makes clear, the same idea is expressed in a Greek text attributed to Theognis. In fact, these lines are echoed in the writings of a number of other Greek and Roman authors, as well as in modern literary works.[18] One classical scholar calls them "the classic formulation of Greek pessimism" (Knox 1989, 103). Another notes that the "pessimistic outlook [in these lines] appears in many authors and became proverbial" (Gerber 1999, 235, n. 1). Burckhardt also acknowledges the prevalence of pessimistic statements in Theognis and other Greek texts, adding that pessimism is "a fact of ordinary life, and . . . not at all . . . the outcome of reflection" in this culture (1998, 99, 106). Finally, Steiner contends that tragedy itself expresses a "world-view summarized in the adage, 'It is best not to be born, next best to die young'" (qtd. in Goldhill 2012, 153).

We should not be so quick to label an entire culture as pessimistic on the basis of gloomy proclamations such as these, whether we are talking about ancient Greece or biblical Israel. We must first view each example in its own context and then consider the functions of such generalizations for those who invoke them. Each of the "best not to be born" passages turns out to be less wide-sweeping when viewed in its wider context than it does when read in isolation. For example, when the Chorus in Sophocles's *Oedipus at Colonus* (*OC* 1225–31) offers this adage, they are speaking to the old blind Oedipus and therefore stress the many sources of suffering which accompany adulthood—and especially old age. They also concede that youth is a time of thoughtless levity. In Baccylides's *Ode* 5, the adage is uttered by Heracles, in reference to the *psyche* of deceased Meleager, with whom Heracles is conversing in Hades. Heracles uses the saying as a way of putting an end to Meleager's laments, as well as halting his own pity for the fallen warrior. Heracles observes that bewailing our condition produces no good result (ll. 155–64). In so doing, he shifts the conversation to what can be still be done in order for Meleager to gain some form of *ersatz* immortality.[19] Throughout, Heracles gives no indication that death is better than life for *himself*.

---

18. The most well-known example is Sophocles's echo of Theognis in *Oed. col.* 1225. Other examples include Bacchylides, *Ode* 5, l. 160, Plutarch, *Consolation to Apollonius*, section 27, and *The Contest between Homer and Hesiod* 315 (Evelyn-White 1914, 572–73). The thought reappears in a poem by Heine written when he was confined to his "mattress-grave" during his agonizing fatal illness: "Good is sleep, death is better—certainly best is never to have been born" ("Morphine," ll. 15–16). Nietzsche, focusing on the story in Plutarch's *Consolation*, calls this attitude the "wisdom of Silenus" (1964a, 58, 64, 82, 185).

19. Heracles has in mind marrying Meleager's sister, Deianeira. Heracles is not aware of a fact well known to ancient readers of Bacchylides's ode: Deianeira will later be the cause of Heracles's own horrible death (Hesiod, *Catalogue of Women*, Fr. 98; Evelyn-White 1914, 216–17; cf. Ovid, *Metam.* 9.99-272).

Even Theognis's seemingly universal version of the adage is qualified, when one views it in the context of the theogonic corpus as a whole. In other statements, Theognis asserts that death is better than a life of oppressive poverty and that raising hateful and ungrateful children is worse than death; he does not assert that *all* human lives are worse than death (*Theog.* 181-82, 271-78).[20] When we examine Qoh. 4:1-3 in its total context, we will find that this passage is also less wide-sweeping than it may seem at first glance. And later in this chapter, we will discover that the same is true for the biblical prophets who state that they want to die or wish that they had never been born.

In terms of psychological and social function, Goldhill points out that in the Greek context the "it is best not to be born" adage is "a cliché, exposed as such in tragedy" (2012, 163). According to Zijderveld, proverbial statements and clichés are incorporated into the cultural repertoire of intellectually accepted "facts" in a way which "avoids reflection upon meanings" rather than promoting reflection (1987, 28). Lifton even characterizes one type of cliché as "thought-terminating" (1961, 429).[21] If this is the case, in the biblical context, we do not need the buffers of "symbolic immortality" (Williamson 2014, 371-73) offered by Proverbs in order to manage our death anxiety; intellectual acknowledgment of the dreaded facts in easily quotable form can do the same. Unfortunately, however, intellectual lip service to inconvenient truths—without an emotional component—blocks true "death acceptance" rather than promoting it.[22] Thus, the narrator Qoheleth cannot be assumed to have experienced anxiety because he utters pessimistic adages about death being superior to life.

Before drawing any conclusions about Qoheleth as a pessimist, we must first recognize that we are reading the words of a dramatized first-person narrator, who often employs the emphatic אני for "I." When I refer to "Qoheleth" I am referring to this narrator, not to the book's author.[23] This narrator tells his own life story and

---

20. Lines 1013-16 call the person "blessed, happy and fortunate" who goes down to the black house of Hades without experiencing struggles, such as submitting to enemies, sinning of necessity, and learning that his friends may not be loyal. Left open is how long one can live without experiencing one or more of these causes of suffering.

21. According to Lifton (1961, 429), this type of cliché characterizes "the language of the totalist environment.... The most far-reaching and complex of human problems are compressed into brief, highly reductive, definitive-sounding phrases."

22. See Kübler-Ross (1970, 112-37) and Klug and Sinha (1987-88, 229-30).

23. I cannot agree with Sneed's view that Qoheleth "refers to the rich and powerful as if he were neither" because he refers to rich who lose money "as if this were impossible for himself" (2012, 139-40). The narrator is explicitly said to have amassed wealth, and there is no hint that he has somehow lost his money. When Sneed says that Qoheleth speaks of the poor and oppressed "*as though* he were neither" (2012, 138; emphasis added), we must reply that this is because Qoheleth *is* neither.

reflects upon what he has concluded from his experiences.²⁴ To determine whether Qoheleth's reflections on mortality imply an obsession with death, we must ask whether his comments imply a failure in the normal defenses which allow us to keep death anxiety at a distance.²⁵ Could his statements on mortality be a sign of his mental strength? If so, Qoheleth would be in agreement with Freud's view that it is "better to give death the place in reality and in our thoughts that is its due" (1990, 38).²⁶

When analyzing Qoheleth's reflections, we must distinguish between his descriptions of the human condition and his opinions about those aspects of human existence. The former includes his references to the perceived brevity of human life and its consequent insubstantiality, such as "the few days of [a person's] futile life, which he passes like a shadow" (6:22; cf. 2:3). Many other verses stress that there is "one fate or event for all"; we all must die, whether we are wise or foolish, just as all beasts die.²⁷ Qoheleth also stresses the poor quality of our existence; life is filled with misery, vexation, and madness, in part because human hearts are filled with evil (2:23; 9:3). His social world also includes innocent suffering, oppression, and a delay in enforcing justice (4:1; 5:8; 7:15; 8:11). If a reader finds that these perceptions accurately reflect unfortunate aspects of actual human existence, they will view Qoheleth as being realistic, rather than pessimistic.

What does this view of life say about the *personality* of this first-person narrator? That question can be answered by focusing on Qoheleth's attitude toward the human condition he has sketched. He summarizes that attitude with the multivalent word הבל. Among the aspects of human existence which can qualify as הבל (futile, insubstantial, vain, or absurd) for Qoheleth are life's brevity, its "shadowiness," and the fact that the fool and wise both die. The oppression arising from misuse of power makes death preferable to life. While being stillborn is best even for those who have amassed wealth but do not enjoy it, Qoheleth also prefers life to death. While the living know that they will die, they can also remember the past, gain reward, and have trust and confidence (בטחון; 9:4), while

---

24. Greenwood (2012, 479–80) claims that there are three distinct voices in the book: one optimistic and two pessimistic. The optimistic voice is that of "Qoheleth, the Preacher"; this "is the true voice of wisdom." One of the two pessimistic voices is "Qoheleth speaking as Solomon"; this voice serves as Qoheleth's "foil." The final voice is the frame narrator of chs 1 and 12. Dividing Qoheleth's statements among multiple personae is not a new strategy; several seventeenth- to eighteenth-century writers argued that the book must be read as a dialogue between Solomon and an atheist; see R. Watson (1994, 34, 336, n. 108).

25. This perspective stems from Ernest Becker and continues with his followers, several of whom developed TMT; see Chapter 4 §1 and §3. This attitude is illustrated by La Rochefoucauld's maxim that we can no more look directly at death than we can look at the sun; see Lasine (2004, 117–19).

26. On whether Freud actually "practiced what he preaches" in this comment, see Chapter 7 §5.

27. Qoh. 2:14, 16; 3:19; 7:2; 8:8; 9:2-3, 5.

the dead have and know nothing at all. And while Qoheleth asserts that the hearts of humans are filled with evil, he also acknowledges that there are righteous men (8:14) and innocent victims (4:1; 5:8). He repeatedly responds to his evocations of our mortality by recommending pleasures such as eating and drinking (see Rindge 2011). Yet at the same time, he counsels that it is better to go to a house of mourning than to one of feasting and merrymaking.

In general, Qoheleth's judgments on the human condition are made from the perspective of a member of the privileged elite. As Dollimore points out, "It is in the nature of privilege that it takes itself for granted, even when under attack from itself" (2001, 41). The most striking examples of this attitude are Qoheleth's statements on social injustice. He speaks as someone who *observes* the oppressed and their tears, but *does* nothing to comfort those who have no comforter or to chastise the high officials who abuse them—even though he himself has been the highest political official (Qoh. 1:1, 12). Sneed (2012, 139–40) believes that Qoheleth is "touched by" and "demonstrates sympathy" for the poor and oppressed. In contrast, Francis Watson notes that Qoheleth analyzes oppression in 4:1-3 as "part of the tragedy of the human condition" and adds that the sage's approach "subtly evades and distorts the experience of oppression . . . the oppressed desire not their own non-existence but the non-existence of oppression" (1994, 283–84). Watson captures Qoheleth's detached stance toward others' suffering: "For all his gentle compassion, he will not lift a finger to help . . . even if his own eyes are filled with tears as he passes by on the other side."

Qoheleth's attitude contrasts sharply with the passion expressed by Job when he rails against God's indifference to the exploitation of the poor and helpless who cling to the rock for lack of shelter in the storm (Job 24:1-12). Qoheleth asserts that it is from the hand of God that a man should eat and drink (2:24), but he does not point out that the poor people he has mentioned may lack food and drink, as well as the opportunity for leisure. As a member of the elite, he is in an ideal position to take his own advice about indulging in pleasure. Most others are not so fortunate. Qoheleth rationalizes the status quo—and excuses his failure to aid sufferers—by saying that God is in control and we cannot change, let alone straighten, anything that God has twisted (7:13), including the injustice God allows.

So, is Ostriker correct when she calls Qoheleth "the most brilliantly pessimistic tract of all time" (2007, 76)? To answer, we must consider two factors. First, has Qoheleth omitted important aspects of the human condition which might lead to a less gloomy picture of human life? And second, is the narrator Qoheleth's attitude toward the human condition the *only* possible way for one to respond to the aspects of human existence he mentions?

On the first issue, we might ask whether he gives enough weight to experiences of self-transcendence. He says nothing about devotion to a good cause or wanting to experience a direct revelation from a personal God. He *does* counsel males to enjoy our futile life "with the woman whom you love" (9:9). However, unlike Siduri in an Old Babylonian fragment of *Gilgamesh*, Qoheleth says nothing about the joys of parenting, such as looking at "the child (*ṣeḫru*) who takes hold of your hand" (George 2003, 278–79, modified). Each reader must decide if Qoheleth's reference to a woman one loves and his repeated advice to enjoy the pleasures of eating and drinking are meant to represent all the fulfillment which life has to offer.

On the second issue, we must ask whether all people would—or should—share Qoheleth's attitude toward the inescapability of our own death, our lack of knowledge and control over our future, and our other vulnerabilities. *Must* we conclude that these realities render life futile and meaningless? Readers who deny that this is the case, including pessimistic philosophers such as Hartmann and Bahnsen, may view Qoheleth as unreasonably pessimistic, if not a "whiner."

3 Pessimistic divine and human leaders in Deuteronomy 31

A number of commentators have included Deuteronomy 31–32 among the Bible's "pessimistic" texts.[28] However, it is not often mentioned that the characters Yahweh and Moses are *themselves* presented as pessimistic in ch. 31.[29] Yahweh claims to know exactly what will happen to Israel in the future and it isn't pretty. He then tells Moses to repeat this dire forecast to the people and even teach it to them in poetic form. By so doing, Yahweh is actually *slanting the future* in a negative direction. Hearing this message, delivered by their God and his reliable spokesperson, had to be demoralizing for Moses's immediate audience in the land of Moab, if not lead the new generation to resign themselves to future failure.

One might object that this situation is not unique, since at the end of his life Joshua also gives a speech which implies that it is impossible for the people to keep the covenant (Josh. 24:1-27). Yet Joshua—who is speaking on his own authority—may be challenging his listeners to recommit themselves to the covenant, which they do immediately (Josh. 24:21, 24). Moses, on the other hand, uses Yahweh's authority to impugn the people's basic character, their "rebelliousness and stiff neck" (Deut. 31:27); in his view, they are constitutionally incapable of succeeding—whether "they" are his present listeners in Moab or later readers and hearers who have experienced the exile. Neither generation of rebels is offered an opportunity for recommitment by Moses.[30]

Viewing Deuteronomy 31 in its larger context only increases the impression of pessimism. In ch. 28, the recitation of possible future blessings and curses had at least implied that the people were *capable* of choosing the good life. And while ch. 29 begins with Moses's statement that Yahweh did not give people the psychological means of choosing good, he may be saying this ironically, as though he were saying "up to now you've behaved so foolishly and disastrously that it is *as*

---

28. For example, Weitzman (1997, 53), Lundbom (2013a, 838), Kissling (1996, 41–42), and Boda (2009, 111–12).

29. Tigay points out that Moses "is not entirely pessimistic" at the start of ch. 30; later he notes an "unexpected note of pessimism" in parts of ch. 31 (1996, 284, 289).

30. As Sanders (1996, 344) puts it, Yahweh "is determined to strike his people and nothing can stop him."

though you didn't have eyes in your heads or the intelligence to process what you saw and heard." Moses goes on to assure the people that Yahweh will single out perpetrators from the community (29:17-20); this implies that at least some in the community will be obedient and not have to suffer innocently. However, Moses goes on to speak of foreigners coming and seeing the whole country in a state of Sodom-like devastation because "they" abandoned Yahweh (29:21-27).

Deuteronomy 30 begins by addressing what occurs after all this devastation has taken place. Here the forecast seems quite optimistic for a much later generation. After having been scattered in exile, the people will "turn to their heart" and then return to Yahweh, who will bring them home and circumcise their hearts. Here Moses predicts that the exiles will repent and consequently be restored. Yahweh will enable them to remain receptive to his word through his surgical procedure on their hearts. Enemies will then be the ones to bear the brunt of Yahweh's wrath. Verses 11-19 then express in emphatic terms that Moses's listeners have the means and opportunity to choose life—a possibility which Moses seemed to rule out in 29:1-3.

Whether their hearts will remain open and receptive to Yahweh's demands remains to be seen. Moses had already suggested the possibility of exile in Deuteronomy 4 and then predicted that if they return to Yahweh with all their heart and soul and obey him, their compassionate God will not forget the ancestral covenant (4:26-31). Yet just a chapter later, when Yahweh is impressed by the people's display of fear after they hear his divine voice, he can only express the wish that "this their heart" was such that it would continue to fear and obey him, so they would do well forever (5:26 Heb.). In other words, even after their hearts return to him during the exile, Yahweh does not take it for granted that this will remain the case.

After the preceding mixed messages, it seems likely that the majority of those addressed by Moses will choose evil and be annihilated, while the remnant of their descendants can rebuild the future which their forbears threw away. In one sense, Deuteronomy 31 clarifies and dramatizes this impression, but with troubling new elements. The chapter begins with Moses giving his present audience a "be strong and courageous" pep talk, in reference to conquering the indigenous peoples under Joshua. Yahweh then prepares Moses and Joshua to appear before these people.

In vv. 15-21, however, Yahweh tells Moses—as a fact—that a nightmare scenario will follow Moses's death. In v. 19 Yahweh tells Moses to write and teach a song so that it can serve as a witness against the people after prosperity in the promised land has led them to serve other gods.

As evidence that the people will backslide after they occupy the land, Yahweh cites the people's tendency in its behavior[31] "today" (31:20-21). He speaks of the people as a whole here ("*its* יצר"), with no mention of the possibility that at least

---

31. Literally, "its inclination (יצרו) that it is doing." For people's יצר leading them to sin and prompting divine punishment, see Gen. 6:5. For God being merciful because (כי) the inclination of the human heart is evil from youth, see Gen. 8:21.

some of them might resist the inclination to rebel and heed the warnings contained in Moses's song. Yahweh is concerned about having proof that he had "warned" the people ahead of time, so that he will not be blamed for their failure. Because he tells Moses to announce all this to his present audience and make them internalize it, the people have to face the future *knowing* that they will fail and, therefore, that they will choose death over life. This, in turn, necessitates the exile, which will then lead to the chance for the still stiff-necked remnant to choose life in the future. How could these speeches not confuse and dishearten those who hear them?

In Deuteronomy 31, Moses himself reinforces Yahweh's bleak message, telling the people—yet again—what fools they have been in the past, even though he is now talking to the new generation. Moses claims that he has repeatedly witnessed their recalcitrant and rebellious nature. He assumes that their character will be their destiny, even though he had earlier implored the people to circumcise the foreskins of their hearts and no longer be stiff-necked (Deut. 10:16). Echoing Yahweh in vv. 20-21, Moses expresses certainty that the people will act even worse after he has gone.[32] Moses is being very personal here; in v. 29 he says "I know" that you will act corruptly, not "God told me that you would" do so. All this makes Moses's earlier exhortations to do right in the future seem hollow, if not cynical.[33]

Moses's song in ch. 32 ends with the prospect of ultimate reconciliation and happiness for God's people, along with the destruction of their enemies. This certainly seems to be a reason for optimism. However, the fact that both God and Moses had attributed the people's repeated failures to robust traits such as stiff-necked rebelliousness implies that such optimism may be premature. The same is true of Jeremiah's prediction of a time when God will write his *torah* directly upon his people's hearts, eliminating the need for teaching (Jer. 31:32-33). This "utopian"[34] idea is based on the failure of all previous attempts at educating the people, so that God's words might go from the people's uncircumcised ears into

---

32. Moses apparently has little confidence in Joshua's ability to keep the people loyal to Yahweh. Could that be the reason why Moses did not suggest Joshua as his replacement in Num. 27:16-17?

33. Tigay (1996, 432) suggests that Moses mentioning future restoration and forgiveness in Deut. 4:29-31 and 30:1-10 might weaken the effectiveness of his warnings to his audience concerning exile. He could also cite Moses's exhortation for the people to no longer be stiff-necked in Deut. 10:16 (cf. Hezekiah in 2 Chron. 30:8). Moses's emphasis on the people's chronically rebellious and stiff-necked temperament in ch. 31 goes far beyond mere warnings of exile. Even in Deut. 9:7, Moses had accused his people of being consistently rebellious since they left Egypt. And Deut. 9:24 goes all the way back to Moses's first acquaintance with the people; readers of the Torah know that this was the day when Moses intervened between two fighting Hebrews, only to be betrayed by one of them and have to flee Egypt (Exod. 2:11-15).

34. Carroll (1986, 612; cf. McKane 1996, 827).

their hearts.³⁵ In spite of Jeremiah's prediction that in the future Yahweh will write his *torah* on his people's hearts—and Ezekiel's claim that Yahweh will give them "hearts of flesh" (Ezek. 11:19)—the later books of the Hebrew Bible give no sign that the people have changed in any fundamental way.

4 Pessimism among the prophets: When is death better than life?

Cursed be the day that I was born; the day that my mother gave birth to me, let it not be blessed. . . . Because he did not kill me from the womb and my mother be my tomb,³⁶ and her womb enlarged forever.

—Jer. 20:14, 17

My death is better than my life.

—Jon. 4:3, 8

The epigraphs from Jeremiah and Jonah echo the preference for death over life expressed in Qoh. 4:1-3 and the Greek texts discussed earlier. If Qoheleth is the quintessential pessimist in biblical wisdom literature, Jeremiah has been dubbed "the prophet of pessimism and despair" (Macdonald 1937, 326), and his experiences have been called "a complete study of Hebrew pessimism" (Kaufmann 1904, 188). According to McKane (1980, 53), the prophet's opponents also regarded him as "a pathological pessimist whose utterances reflected his own fits of depression and were not 'word of God.'"³⁷

The attitude expressed in Sophocles's version of the "best not to be born" adage has often been cited with approval by pessimistic philosophers (see Beiser 2016, 4; Schopenhauer 1960, 752). Readers of the Hebrew Bible might find it difficult to fathom how not being born is best; after all, God himself created humans, called his creative acts "very good," and intended that humans be fruitful and multiply. A full, normal human life includes building a house, marrying, having children, and enjoying the harvest from the ground over which one has labored, as Jeremiah himself suggests in his letter to the exiles in Babylon (Jer. 29:5-6; cf. Deut. 20:5-7; 28:30).³⁸ In addition, Psalms 1, 33, and 112 hold out the prospect of happiness

---

35. Jeremiah repeatedly talks about the people's failure to "incline their ear" to hear and follow God's words (e.g., Jer. 7:24, 26; 11:8; 17:23; 25:4; 34:14; 35:15; 44:5). During Jeremiah's lifetime, however, not even Josiah's obedience and "tender" heart could prolong that king's life, let alone avert the destruction of Jerusalem (2 Kgs 22:19).

36. The Hebrew has "grave" (קבר), but pairing "tomb" with "womb" reflects the rhyming of Hebrew אמי and קברי.

37. As evidence, McKane points to Jer. 23:33-40, especially the "satirical use of משׂא" ("burdensome word") in v. 33.

38. Jeremiah himself is denied the possibility of such fulfillment when Yahweh orders him not to take a wife (16:2).

and blessedness to those whose delight is in Yahweh's *torah*. McConville (2016, 196) believes that "this foregrounding of happiness as the true human condition is wholly realistic," because "happiness has to do with the fundamental orientation of the self to God." McConville takes this to mean that "in general, a person's happiness is not contingent on their circumstances."[39]

Several of Yahweh's best known prophets (as well as his servant Job) might balk at the notion that happiness is not dependent upon one's situation. Their death wishes are motivated by their perception of their circumstances, including their position vis-à-vis their God. Here I will focus on Jeremiah's wish that he had never been born, viewing it together with the death wishes expressed by three other prophets: Moses, Elijah, and Jonah.[40] While the requests by these three appear to be quite similar, there are vast differences in their situations, their attitudes toward their role, and their reasons for wanting God to participate in an assisted suicide. Once again, the key question is whether an individual's negative view of his or her situation—and that of her community—actually reflects the "facts" as we readers know them, without ignoring counterevidence. If this is true, then the individual in question is being realistic, but not necessarily pessimistic. In the present case, does the available biblical evidence allow us to determine whether any of these prophets is presented as having a pessimistic disposition, especially when their circumstances might be interpreted in a more positive and hopeful manner by another observer?

---

39. McConville points to Hellenistic philosophy for a similar idea. Perhaps the most compact description of this view is Schopenhauer's rather optimistic account of will-less aesthetic contemplation, in which it is all the same whether we see the sun set "from the dungeon or from the palace" (1819, 284).

40. Many commentators believe that Elijah's, Jonah's, and Jeremiah's desperate wishes echo Moses's request to die in Numbers 11, if not his earlier call to be blotted out of God's book (Exod. 32:32). A number of scholars believe that the biblical order of events "reverses the true relationship" between Moses and Elijah, because the Moses story is a later tradition based on the experience of Elijah (e.g., Geller 1996, 193; Auld 1983, 20). In contrast, Allison (1994, 44) concludes that "certain stories about the Tishbite were composed or recast so as to make the prophet like the lawgiver [Moses]." Some believe that the link between these two prophets is designed to show Elijah's similarity to Moses, if not his superiority to Moses (e.g. Masson 2001, 122-23, 130). Others contend that the echoing is contrastive, showing Elijah to be inferior to his incomparable predecessor (e.g., Robinson 1991, 528-30; Gregory 1990, 145-46). The vast majority of interpreters also take the link between the Moses and Jonah stories to be contrastive; Jonah is often grouped together with Elijah in terms of self-concern and is contrasted to Moses (e.g., Robinson 1991, 529; Gregory 1990, 145-46). Echoes of Moses's story in Jeremiah have been taken to show that Jeremiah is the last Mosaic prophet (Seitz 1989, 11-12; contrast Petersen 2006, 321-22). When one examines studies of Moses, Elijah, and Jonah, it is striking how many of the same negative traits are attributed to two or more of them. For example, all three have been criticized for their self-pity, self-centeredness, and petulance. Moses, Elijah, and Jonah have all been accused of hubris. Elijah and Jonah have both been called arrogant and narcissistic and so on (for Moses and Elijah, see Lasine 2012, 64-67, 115-19; for Jonah, see Chapter 5 §1).

Scholarly evaluations of these prophetic rejections of life tend to be surprisingly harsh. Given the negative attitude toward pessimism which is characteristic of today's Western cultures (see Dienstag 2006, ix–x), we might ask whether some commentators are taking the prophets' feelings of hopelessness and resignation as equivalent to lack of faith and/or courage. Some of the negative assessments made about the prophets' motivations and intentions involve quasi-medical diagnoses. Thus, Moses is said to experience a "collapse" or "breakdown" in Numbers 11,[41] and Elijah has been diagnosed as suffering from an impressively wide array of mental disorders in 1 Kings 18–19.[42] In a similar vein, McKane (1986, 351) concludes from Jer. 15:15 that Jeremiah has reached the point at which he "will crack under the pressures . . . he has to endure." According to Becking (2007, 61–62), Jeremiah's depression and "periods of bitter alienation" stem from the distortion of his internal balance. And, as I will discuss in Chapter 5 §1, Jonah has been said to suffer from narcissism, an inferiority complex, and other maladies.

Other exegetes also view these prophets' intentions and motives with great suspicion. While Good accepts that Elijah's despair is "genuine," he believes that Jonah's despair and "sullen" death wish rise out of mere "vexation" at God's acceptance of Nineveh.[43] Lockwood (2004, 54) dismisses Elijah's "prayer to die" as a familiar attention-seeking "ploy of those who threaten to commit suicide." Walsh (1996, 267) reasons that if Elijah *truly* wished to die, then he would have no reason to flee from Jezebel. Others, like Sommer, simply condemn the desire to die out of hand; he calls Moses's death wish "damnable" (1999, 619). Moses and Jonah have both been dubbed "anti-prophets" in the scenes in which they ask to die and Jonah is often called an "anti-hero."[44] Sometimes one of these prophets is characterized by contrasting him with one of the others. Thus, Jeremiah has been called an "anti-Moses" (Schökel 2000, 27), while Jonah has been viewed as the opposite of Moses, Elijah, *and* Jeremiah.[45]

If we are to evaluate the prophets' longing for nonexistence, we must ask why each one finds his present life intolerable. One thing is clear: they all share the perception that others want to harm or kill them. Bishop Hall once observed that "our cradle stands in the grave" (1837, 183). This is literally true for Moses, who is

---

41. For example, Milgrom (1990, 85, 378, 1992, 1153) and Sasson (1990, 285).

42. As I describe elsewhere (Lasine 2012, 117–18), the suggested disorders include generalized depression, manic depression, paranoia, prophetic or ministerial burnout, a midlife crisis, a messianic complex, and the hopelessness and selective abstraction of a depressed introvert who is engaging in distorted, maladaptive thinking. For these commentators, Elijah presents symptoms such as excessive sleeping, loss of appetite, suicidal urges, distorted perceptions, feelings of loneliness, inability to cope, and even "psychomotoric retardation."

43. Good (1981, 51; cf. Driver 1920, 325) and Simon (1999, 38).

44. For example, D. Marcus (1995, 96), Sherwood (2000, 27, 110, 243), and T. Thompson (1999, 395).

45. Ben Zvi (2003, 121–22), LaCocque and LaCocque (1990, 150), and Wolff (1986, 120). See further in Chapter 5 §1.

placed in his little ark (תבה) in order to evade the death ordered by the Egyptian king (Exod. 1:22–2:10). Later Moses kills an Egyptian, and the Pharaoh seeks to kill him (2:15). Then, soon after God tells Moses that all the men who sought his life are dead, God himself seeks to kill "him" (Exod. 4:19-24), that is, Moses or one of his sons.[46] In Exod. 17:4 Moses himself claims that the people are nearly ready to stone him.[47] Later Moses asks Yahweh to kill him so that he will not have to look upon his evil situation, sandwiched as he is between a murmuring people and their wrathful divine parent (Num. 11:10-15).

Readers are also aware of Ahab's attempts to extradite Elijah and Jezebel's warning to Elijah of her intent to end his life (1 Kgs 18:10; 19:1-3), as well as Elijah's unsupported claim that the Israelites themselves seek to kill him (1 Kgs 19:10, 14). Elijah's relations with death and mortality are particularly complex; he evades death, defeats it, inflicts it, flees it, desires it, forecasts it, and ultimately escapes it forever (see Lasine 2012, 122–35). Jonah's death-related words and experiences will be discussed in Part Two of this study.

Is Jeremiah's fear of assassination justified by his situation? If Moses's "ark-cradle" threatened to become his grave, Jeremiah wishes that his mother's womb had become his grave (Jer. 20:17). For good reason, both Yahweh and the narrator make it clear that Jeremiah's enemies seek his life, and the narrator reports several instances in which Jeremiah is physically abused or left for dead (Jer. 11:18-21; 20:2; 26:11; 37:15; 38:6).

With all these prophets except Jonah, a form of the phrase בקש נפש is used to describe others' intention to kill the prophet. In fact, in Exod. 4:19 and Jer. 11:21, the phrasing is nearly identical.[48] In contrast, the only seeming attempt on Jonah's life is made by God, in the sense of requiring Jonah's immersion in the deep. On the other hand, the verbal similarities between the requests of Elijah and Jonah

---

46. The verb בקש ("to seek") is used only three times in the Pentateuch in the sense of "seeking to kill" someone, and in all three cases that "someone" is Moses (Exod. 2:15; 4:19, 24), if "him" at the end of 4:24 refers to Moses. In Exod. 4:19-24, there are three references to attempts at killing, one in the past (4:19), one in the present (4:24), and one in the future (4:23). On this baffling episode, see Lasine (2010, 42–48).

47. The desire to stone one's leaders is mentioned again in the story of the spies' expedition into Canaan (Numbers 13–14), although in the later instance the mob's primary desire is to stone the younger generation of leaders, Joshua and Caleb (Num. 14:10). Milgrom is inconsistent on this point. First he claims that it is Joshua and Caleb whom the people want to stone, but then asserts with equal certainty that it is Moses and Aaron (1990, 108). Similarly, Widmer initially states that "the text is not absolutely clear whether Moses and Aaron were also physically threatened" but goes on to conclude that "there is no evidence that . . . not all four leaders were threatened to be stoned" (274, 274 n. 71).

48. "All the men/the men of . . . seeking your life." In Exod. 4:19, Yahweh is directly addressing Moses. In Jer. 11:21 MT, Yahweh is directly addressing Jeremiah (see McKane 1986, 258). In 1 Kgs 19:10, after Elijah exclaims "they seek my life," he adds "to take it" (לקחתה; cf. Elijah's request for God to "take" his life in v. 4).

are striking. Both implore their God to take their lives saying, "Now, Yahweh, take my life" (עתה יהוה קח נפשי; 1 Kgs 19:4; Jon. 4:3).[49] In both cases, the narrator says, literally, "and he asked[50] for his life to die" (וישאל את נפשו למות; 1 Kgs 19:4; Jon. 4:8). There is no such verbal similarity between Elijah's words and those used by Moses, either at Sinai/Horeb in Exod. 32:32 or in the wilderness in Num. 11:15.

Elijah seems to have endured much less hostility from his people than did Moses, so that he would have less reason to be pessimistic. Unlike Elijah, Moses did not wish to die immediately following a great victory for the Lord. In fact, Moses put up with the hostile ambivalence of the Israelites for quite a while before he asked God to kill him if things were not going to change (Num. 11:14-15). And while Elijah attempts to cast himself in the role of victim, Moses is the one who is totally isolated and betrayed by his closest relatives (Num. 12; 16). And while there is no textual evidence to support Elijah's claim that his own people want to kill him,[51] Moses's complaint that the people are nearly ready to stone him *is* supported by the narrator's reports of the people "murmuring against" Moses (Exod. 15:24; 16:2; 17:4; Num. 14:2; 17:6). Moreover, Elijah does not have to worry about leading the people himself, as does Moses. And unlike Elijah, Moses does not *want* to be the unique, lone prophet of Yahweh, if we take at face value his statement to Joshua that he wishes "all Yahweh's people were prophets" (Num. 11:29).[52] Finally, the biblical Moses does not have Elijah's ability to disappear without trace whenever the going gets tough.[53]

---

49. The only difference is that Jonah is more polite, adding "please" to his request (קח-נא).

50. For the use of the verb שאל in asking God for a death, see Job 31:30 and Thelle (2002, 218).

51. On this, and the lack of textual evidence supporting Elijah's other charges against his people, see Lasine (2012, 127–29).

52. Apparently Moses is less gratified by Joshua's jealousy for his sake than Yahweh was when Phineas exhibited jealousy on Yahweh's behalf (Num. 25:11-13).

53. When Moses's complaint in Numbers 11 is compared to Elijah's in 1 Kings 19, it is clear that Moses's perceptions are more in alignment with what we are told about his situation by the narrator and shown by other characters. Is this why Yahweh responds to Moses's complaint by bringing a sort of relief to him, but does not grant the wishes of Elijah, whose perception of his situation does not jibe with the reported facts? Another potential similarity between Moses and Elijah is that both are replaced by a successor after they have failed in some way, if one accepts that Yahweh dismisses Elijah in 1 Kgs 19:18 (see, for example, Cogan 2000, 457, n. 3); for a rabbinic example, see *Mek. Pisḥa*, I, 99–100. In the cases of Elijah and Jonah, it is partly through converse with Yahweh that the prophet's personality is revealed to readers. Is this equally true of Moses? Moses complains to God, is said to be intimate with him, and argues with him on principle as did Abraham, but it is unclear whether that reveals his *personality*, as opposed to revealing his ethical standards and his assumptions concerning *God's* ethical standards.

Even Jonah's complaints seem better-founded than those of Elijah. Jonah's mission is directed at a notoriously sinful pagan city, rather than at his own people. Elijah's people actually *affirm* his authority and *help* him to corral the Baal prophets that he proceeds to slaughter single-handedly. This is just before Elijah asks to die, charging that his people seek to kill him (1 Kgs 18:39-40). Moreover, Elijah has not had to endure the harsh treatment which Yahweh metes out to Jonah.[54] Defenders of Jonah ask whether Yahweh has given the prophet too difficult and "unbearable" a task, implying that any blame which Jonah's request might deserve should rest on Yahweh himself (see Frolov 1999, 89–90, 92; see Chapter 5 §1).

Jeremiah has also been viewed as a Moses- or Elijah-figure. Holladay (1964, 153, 1986, 2, 5) claims that "it was in the light of the figure of Moses that Jeremiah lived out his own ministry." Schmidt (2001, 3, 16) cites Elijah as a key precursor of Jeremiah, partly because he believes that Jeremiah, like Elijah, expresses his despair and failure by wishing to die. Commenting on Elijah's complaints and accusations in 1 Kgs 19:4, 10, and 14, Long (1984, 201) notes that Elijah's "lamenting words" here are reminiscent of the "complaint song of the individual," such as those that we find in Jer. 11:18-20; 15:15-18; and 20:7-12, 14-18, although he adds that "formally speaking," the parallels are "fairly imprecise." If one focuses on content rather than form, there are some striking differences as well as some similarities. In all three of these chapters Jeremiah asks God for vengeance (נקמה) against those who have been pursuing him (20:11-12; cf. 15:15), insulting and threatening him (15:5; 20:8), or plotting to kill him (11:19-20). In Jeremiah 11 and 20, the prophet explicitly "opens up his case (ריב)" to Yahweh (11:20; 20:12); in chs 15 and 20, he explicitly blames Yahweh for his suffering (15:15, 17-18; 20:7-8) and his aloneness (15:17).

Like Jeremiah, Elijah claims that he is being pursued: the Israelites are supposedly seeking to take his life. He too emphasizes his aloneness. However, while Elijah claims to have been very jealous for Yahweh, he does not claim that Yahweh caused him to be this way, so that Yahweh is to blame for his plight. Nor does Elijah claim that he was drafted into the prophetic corps, let alone that he objected, as did Moses, Jeremiah, and Jonah. Elijah lays no ריב before Yahweh in the sense that Jeremiah did.

---

54. See Provan (1995, 144), Frolov (1999, 92–98), and Simon (1999, xxiv). In 1 Kgs 21:28-29, Ahab "repents" after hearing Elijah's words of doom, prompting Yahweh to tell Elijah that he will defer Ahab's punishment to his son. However, Yahweh does not command the prophet to inform Ahab of this reprieve and the narrator gives no sign that Ahab is so informed. This raises the question whether Yahweh is making a point of directing Elijah's attention to Ahab's apparently humble submission to him (1 Kgs 21:28-29), implying that this is an attitude which the self-willed prophet should himself adopt. If so, Yahweh's words to Elijah about Ahab's repentance resemble Yahweh's words to Jonah after Nineveh repents. Of course, in both cases the prophet could answer by saying "big deal; he/they could go back to their wicked ways tomorrow."

One thing which all four prophets have in common is that they blame God for something. Jonah explains his own actions in terms of his perception of *Yahweh's* character. Both Jonah and Jeremiah use the fact that Yahweh is "long to anger" (ארך אפים) against him, in the larger context of either wanting to die or wishing that he had never been born, although they differ in how and why they appeal to this divine character trait (Jon. 4:2; Jer. 15:15). Another feature shared by Jeremiah and Jonah is their association with images of enclosure and interiority. Gunn and Fewell suggest that Jonah's flight from God "could be read as a retreat into the womb" (1993, 130). If Jonah may seek womblike security,[55] Jeremiah wishes that his mother's womb had been his grave. More generally, Jonah finds shelter inside enclosures, while Jeremiah's focus is on *his own* "interior." One other key difference was mentioned in passing earlier: Moses's requests for God to kill him or blot him out of his book are conditional, while Elijah's and Jonah's requests for God to take their life are *not*. The latter two seem to have decided that there is no remedy for a situation which has wounded their self-image.

Of the four prophets, it is Jeremiah whose grievance is most directly aimed at Yahweh, for it is God who is most directly responsible for the situation in which the prophet finds himself. That situation is the prophet's entire existence. God knew and consecrated Jeremiah to his service from the womb (רחם, בטן; 1:5). Yahweh warns Jeremiah that he will be under attack from all groups in Judah, and others do, in fact, beat, imprison, and plot to kill the prophet. Yahweh also warns Jeremiah that if he allows these adversaries to make him panic, God will make him panic (חתת) before them (Jer. 1:17; cf. 17:17-18). Violence from the community and from God threatens to "overcome" Jeremiah.[56]

Yahweh says that he will armor the prophet for his mission by making Jeremiah into a fortified enclosure—a city with an iron pillar and bronze walls. He assures Jeremiah that while he will be attacked, he will not be overcome, since Yahweh will save him (Jer. 1:17-18). Yahweh later repeats these promises[57] after the prophet bemoans the fact that his mother bore him (15:10) and asks Yahweh to avenge him by punishing those who pursue him. He begs God *not* to "take him," by allowing his divine "longness to anger" to enable Jeremiah's enemies to cause his

---

55. In Chapter 5 §3 I will argue that this interpretation of Jonah's actions is not supported by the text.

56. Holladay (1986, 465) notes that the adjective "violent" (עריץ) occurs in Jeremiah only in 15:21 and 20:11. In ch. 20 it is an attribute of Yahweh, "dread (warrior)," while in ch. 15 it is an attribute of Jeremiah's enemies.

57. In Jer. 15:20 Yahweh repeats that he will make Jeremiah a fortified bronze wall. In 15:20 Jeremiah is a wall against "this people"; in 1:18 he is "against the whole land, to the kings of Judah, to its princes, to its priests, and to the people of the land." Jeremiah's fellow-sufferer Job describes himself as a city (Job 16:14), but he was stressing how easily God and his troops breached his walls.

death (15:15; cf. Exod. 34:6).[58] Daube cites Jeremiah as an example of someone who never embraces suicide as a "second-best" solution; in fact, "it is as if he never heard of it" (1983, 192–93).[59] This misses the point. The reason that Jeremiah does not mention suicide is because he wants Yahweh to help him remain *alive*.[60]

Being armored as a fortified city affords Jeremiah little protection. As Shakespeare's *Henry IV* puts it, this kind of armor "scalds with safety" (*2H4* 4. 5. 30). Looking at the book as a whole, it is difficult to agree that Yahweh protects and delivers Jeremiah. Jeremiah himself certainly doesn't feel saved. Considering that he has to announce the fall of his listeners' fortified city, he, like Moses, could easily be viewed by his own people as threatening them with death. The prophet whom God makes into a fortified wall describes the uselessness of city walls against death, which will come up through their windows and into their palaces, cutting down children in the streets and town squares (Jer. 9:20).

In ch. 20, Jeremiah wishes that his mother's womb had been "forever pregnant" with the corpse of her unborn son (v. 17). This formulation is particularly unsettling,[61] for it also constitutes a terrible curse against the mother who eternally

---

58. Admittedly, Jeremiah also expresses the desire never to have been born, but if his ultimate desire is to be unconscious, that is equally available before and after the short span of human life. Cf. Schopenhauer: "If what makes death seem so frightful to us were the thought of *not-being*, we would have to think with equal shuddering of the time when we did not yet exist" (1960, 595).

59. McKane (1986, 486) dismisses the absence of any reference to suicide in Jeremiah 20 and Job 3, concluding that it "is probably sufficiently explained by the circumstance that it was not part of the literary pattern of cursing birthday." Daube (1983, 192) cites Euripides's Andromache, Job, and Ecclesiastes as other examples of characters who behave as if they had never heard of suicide.

60. Sasson proposes a typology of "individuals [who] ask God to shorten their lives" (1990, 283), which includes all four of the prophets under discussion here. His classification is also problematic. As just mentioned, Jeremiah does not ask God to shorten his life. Also, Sasson (1990, 284–85) claims that Elijah asks God to die when he suffers from the "fierce," "merciless" heat which is "haunting" him even though this is nowhere said or implied in 1 Kings 19. Apparently Sasson is assimilating the Elijah story to the Jonah narrative (see Jon. 4:8). He also seems unclear where to place Jonah in his schema. At one point he claims that in Jonah's case the theme of wanting God to shorten his life "is not to be confused with . . . suicide," but later he describes Jonah as becoming "suicidal" in ch. 4 of the book (1990, 283, n. 1, 349). The LaCocques also view Jonah's request for the sailors to dispose of him as a gesture of suicide (1990, 88). Wohlgelernter (1981, 140) believes that the death wishes of the prophets Jonah, Elijah, and Jeremiah are similar in that the reasons each gives for desiring death "are not to be taken at face value." In fact, "they are for the most part cover-ups" for feelings such as fear, shame, and disappointment. Because they are prophets fulfilling a public function, the "unsympathetic, almost harsh reaction of God to each of them is certainly understandable" (1981, 139).

61. McKane (1986, 485) stresses the "terror of [Jeremiah's] pessimism" in this passage.

carries her child's dead fetus within her, a condition which could lead to her death by infection or internal bleeding. The pain which Jeremiah expresses in ch. 20 is partly physical: a fire burns in his heart, restrained in his bones. But it is the mental pain which dominates. He feels himself to be a man of strife; he feels himself being subjected to jeering, disgrace, curses, and contempt, whispered about and informed upon, surrounded by terror, and experiencing shame.

The contrast with Jonah's lack of expressed feeling is stark and telling. According to the *Qur'an*, if Jonah had not glorified God inside the fish, he would have remained inside it until the Day of Resurrection (*Sura* 37.142-45). If so, this prolonged stay in an enclosure bears no resemblance to what Jeremiah sought in wishing that he had remained forever unborn in his mother's womb. Jonah is obviously conscious when praying inside the fish, while Jeremiah wants to become insensate in order to escape the pain of his life situation. Some readers ask why Jeremiah does not beseech God to kill him. After all, if Jeremiah's wish is for unconsciousness, that is equally available to all of us before and after the short span of human life. While we are alive that avenue to oblivion is closed and the infinity before our birth is rarely lamented (see n. 57 in this chapter). If Jeremiah seeks unconsciousness in order to escape the pain of his life situation, the pain-ridden Job begs God to put him into Sheol until God's fit of fatherly rage passes (Job 14:13-15). Job is not yearning for analgesia or unconsciousness; he merely seeks a "safe house" in which to take shelter until the divine father's storm of rage abates (see Lasine 2001, 224–25, n. 21).

We are now in a position to repeat the earlier question: Why *do* so many commentators judge Moses, Elijah, and Jonah—but not Jeremiah—so harshly when their complex situations (and perhaps their characters) could be interpreted much more generously? A negative attitude toward suicide could be one reason. Even pessimistic philosophers such as Schopenhauer and Hartmann view suicide negatively (Schopenhauer 1819, 572–77; Hartmann 1904, 569). In fact, Dienstag asserts that no pessimistic philosopher recommends suicide (2006, 37, 103). While Daube (1983, 191) contends that "biblical theology" certainly approves of Samson's and Saul's suicides, others read biblical theology very differently. Gregory (1990, 146) points to the fact that both Elijah and Jonah "entertain suicidal sentiments" and calls this a "dubious distinction." Calvin is less subtle, calling Moses's offer to be blotted out of God's book "culpable arrogance" (*superbia*; qtd. in Hahn 1981, 94). Lockwood even assumes that the *character* Elijah "knows that suicide is taboo" when he asks Yahweh to take his life, making the request "inherently shocking" (2004, 53–54). His Elijah takes for granted that Yahweh is willing to dishonor the sanctity of life and contravene his own holy will. Lockwood does not point to the absence of laws prohibiting suicide in the Hebrew Bible or note that characters who do commit suicide are not explicitly condemned for it.[62]

---

62. Young lists Saul and his armor-bearer, Ahithophel, and Zimri as suicides, but not Samson (1962, 453–54). Wohlgelernter (1981, 131) also finds four suicides, but she includes Samson rather than Zimri. Droge (1992, 227–28) includes Gideon's son Abimelech, adding

However, there could be a more basic reason why some scholars explain prophetic pleas for death in terms of negative traits such as self-concern,[63] self-pity, and petulance. By asserting themselves and wanting to choose the time of their death are these prophets breaking the rules of submissive obedient conduct which these scholars see the Bible as setting? Comedian Bill Maher once defined suicide as "our way of saying to God, 'You can't fire me. I quit.'" Are critics easier on Jeremiah because he does not ask God to help him "quit" living? This seems to be what J. Thompson (1980, 458–59) admires about Jeremiah's way of complaining: "Only one who walked intimately with God would dare to speak as Jeremiah did. But despite such strong words, he continued his calling steadfastly to the end."[64] In American political parlance, he "stayed the course."[65] At the same time, the Bible shows Yahweh choosing assertive, independently minded people such as Moses, Elijah, and Jonah to be his spokespersons.[66] Ironically, while Jeremiah is the only one of the four prophets who does not ask God to kill him, he is also the one who, as far as we know, ends his time on earth most unhappily.[67]

"to these one might add Samson"; cf. Shemesh (2009, 157). Both Young and Droge note that there are no specific biblical prohibitions of suicide and the act as such is not condemned. Droge believes that the lack of censure leads one "to conclude that in ancient Israel that act of suicide was regarded as something natural and perhaps heroic" (1992, 228). In contrast, Young (1962, 454) interprets this narratorial silence in the opposite way, as implying a negative attitude toward the act.

63. On the role of culture in determining social attitudes toward self-concern and "healthy" narcissism, see Kohut (1972, 364–65). On our tendency to attribute negative traits to others when judging their character (what social psychologists call the "negativity bias"), see Lasine (2012, 218–20).

64. Stulman (2005, 203) is less sanguine about Jeremiah's continued steadfastness: "Now we encounter a prophet who is unable to exert himself against Yahweh." Yahweh's "behemoth control" on Jeremiah's life "deprives him of freedom, leaving him weak and wounded."

65. Whether he is fully resigned to his fate by the end of his life is of course another matter. Moses apparently resigns himself to dying outside Canaan, but not before repeatedly appealing Yahweh's death sentence. In Elijah's case, Yahweh ends up giving the prophet the exact opposite of his request to die. As for Jonah, the book ends before we can discover his final attitude toward his situation.

66. Compare Yahweh's treatment of Job, who, although not a prophet, has been compared to the first prophet Abraham for his actions in Job 42; see, for example, Habel (1985, 580, 584–86). In the end, Yahweh rewards the self-assertion of Job, if not the others. Of course, the book of Job also conveys the terrible price one must pay if one is either totally submissive like the Job of chs 1–2 or assertive like the Job of chs 3–31.

67. The abrupt ending of the book of Jonah precludes our being able to gain information about Jonah's last years (including the resolution of his dispute with his God, if any) or the manner of his death.

5 Conclusion

It is often noted that Qoheleth's God is very unlike the deity described in most of the Hebrew Bible.[68] Qoheleth does not directly address his impersonal God, and divine revelation is absent.[69] Could Qoheleth's pessimism be attributed to the fact that his deity is not the personal God Yahweh, to whom he might appeal for justice and understanding and with whom he could enter into dialogue, as does Job?

I would argue the opposite, that Yahweh's complex personality could provide readers (and characters such as Moses, Jonah, and Jeremiah) with the most profound reasons for adopting a pessimistic outlook. Yahweh describes himself as just and compassionate, leading his followers to expect fair and merciful treatment when they obey his dictates. Yet, as I will show throughout this study, the Hebrew Bible reports glaring examples of these expectations being disappointed. Yahweh also lists jealousy, wrath, holiness, and unaccountability among his defining traits. At times he is indeed the Rock who shelters us (Deut. 32:4, 15, 18), but on other occasions he is more like the inanimate rock mentioned by Job, to which naked victims cling in the storm (Job 24:8). And, as we have also noted, Yahweh can be quite pessimistic about his people's ability to obey him and flourish.

An optimist might reply that we are better able to navigate through Yahweh's universe because the Hebrew Bible acknowledges God's complexity and unpredictability, that is, if we follow the Bible's lead and acknowledge the dark side of reality, including the "dark side" of our divine guide, as does Jeremiah.[70] Our loyalty must surely pay off in the long run. The optimist might add that Isaiah was correct to predict that the wolf will reside with the lamb and the leopard will lie down with the young goat (11:6). However, as Jewish pessimist Woody Allen reminds us, "the lion and the calf shall lie down together, but the calf won't get much sleep" (1983, 28).

Should we who are descendants of the Israelites sleep with one eye open, because we know that God—in both the distant and the recent past—has allowed us to become innocent "sheep led to the slaughter" (Ps. 44:23; cf. v. 12)? Given the nature of the Bible's divine lion Yahweh,[71] is remaining wakeful a realistic—but not necessarily pessimistic—attitude for Jewish sheep to adopt? Such questions will be easier to address once we come to terms with Yahweh's relationship with his risk-taking prophet Jonah in the next several chapters of this study.

---

68. See, for example, Sneed (2012, 2–3) and Ostriker (2007, 92–97).

69. At times Qoheleth's God even resembles Zeus, who mixes evils and good gifts for individuals from his two jars without any regard to merit (Homer, *Il.* XXIV.527–33; cf. Qoh. 6:1-2). This famous image is put into the mouth of Achilles, who is consoling Priam for his many losses. Plato (*Resp.* 379de) faults this passage not for failing to consider merit but for assuming that gods cause evil.

70. On Yahweh's so-called "dark side," see Lasine (2016a, 465, 472–75).

71. For example, Job 10:16; Lam. 3:10; Hos. 5:14.

Chapter 3

AT SEA IN YAHWEH'S WORLD: NAVIGATING THE HUMAN CONDITION IN THE HEBREW BIBLE

In this chapter, I will focus on the time-honored notion that a human life span resembles a perilous sea voyage, as illustrated by the device of Marnix described in my Preface. After viewing this core metaphor in relation to Jonah's sea journey, I will explore the fate of the mariners in Psalm 107 and the enclosure imagery in other psalmic texts. The life as a sea voyage metaphor can be a vehicle for expressing either optimism or pessimism, depending upon the extent to which we can rely on a divine guide in navigating our way through life. This will be illustrated by examining a variety of non-biblical texts which employ this root metaphor.

1 The "Life is a sea voyage" metaphor

As noted by Blumenberg, "humans . . . seek to grasp the movement of their existence above all through [the] metaphorics of a perilous sea voyage" (1997, 7). Over the centuries, many works of literature, philosophy, theology,[1] and the fine arts[2] have appealed to this metaphor in order to get to the fundamental nature of

---

1. In fact, the sea voyage may be "the commonest metaphor in literature" (Edwards 1997, 1). Examples are also found in religious works. The *Zohar* employs this metaphor when alluding to Jon. 1:4; the human soul is in the body as are people in a ship which is in danger of breaking up. On this passage, see Wineman (1990, 58). Wineman also cites the thirteenth-century poet Berdisi who "likened the world to a raging sea and the human body to a hotel for the soul, one which, employing the same biblical phrase, is 'in danger of breaking up'" (1990, 58). Tucker (2006, 19) takes the verb חשב in Jon. 1:4 literally, translating "the ship thought that it would break up." Among philosophers, Plato speaks of our "passing through this sea-voyage of life" (*Laws* 803b). However, it is Ortega y Gasset whose formulation is most radical: "Life is, in itself and forever, shipwreck" (1968, 136). What "we call 'civilization'" is merely a system of "insecure securities" which allows us to cope with our situation, "like a raft in the initial shipwreck" (1963, 26).

2. Pictorial representations of this metaphor usually emphasize human "suffering, turmoils, and disasters" caused by the forces of nature (Goedde 1989, 36; cf. Bonner 1941, 50, 55, 59; Judson 1964, 145). This is also true of some prose accounts of human life.

human existence. The related theme of a lone castaway struggling to survive on land is also familiar from many works of literature and philosophy.[3]

In contrast, the Hebrew Bible says relatively little about ships and sea voyages, apart from the book of Jonah.[4] Brown (2002, 107) associates water and fear of drowning imagery in the Psalms with the "mythical drama" of the *Chaoskampf*. Through this optic, even God himself can become "the embodiment of chaos." I will argue that this is not the appropriate lens through which to view the variations of sea, storm, and shipwreck imagery in Jonah 2 and Psalms such as 88 and 107. These metaphors actually point to unsettling aspects of the human condition in the controlled cosmos which Yahweh created *from* chaos. Taken together, these nautical metaphors suggest that the difficulties of navigating through life in Yahweh's world are not merely the result of God's often uneasy relations with his human creations but also the forbidding cosmos in which he has chosen to place us. While the realities to which these biblical metaphors point may not always be pleasant to contemplate, I will argue that they do not illustrate Crenshaw's view of pessimism, according to which "chaos has the upper hand" (1981, 191).

2 Images of enclosure and exposure in Jonah 1–2

After Jonah has been ingested by the big fish, he prays to God. The prophet describes himself as speaking from the "belly" or "womb" (בטן) of Sheol after God has exposed him by "casting" him into the depths in the heart of the seas and "driving" him from God's sight (2:3-5).[5] Jonah refers to himself as "surrounded,"[6] constricted in all directions, and engulfed by the flood and the deep. With seaweed around his head and the earth's bars closing upon him, he

---

For example, in his description of the "fragility and misery of our human condition," Boaistuau evokes the "great abyss of miseries in which the human being is submerged from birth to the sepulcher" (1570, 151). He adds that "this sea of misery" is not caused by the hatred of God but by human malice and corruption (1570, 171; see Chapter 1, n. 1).

3. Literary examples include Homer's Odysseus, the protagonist of the Egyptian *Tale of the Shipwrecked Sailor*, Sophocles's *Philoctetes*, and Defoe's *Robinson Crusoe*; see §2 and §5 in this chapter and Chapter 6 §2. Examples of this metaphor in the works of the philosophers Lucretius and Schopenhauer are discussed in §5 of this chapter.

4. See 1 Kgs 22:49; 2 Chron. 20:37; Jon. 1:4; 48:7; Pss. 48:8; 107:23-28; Ezek. 27:25-29.

5. The verbs שׁלח and גרשׁ are also used in Genesis to describe God's eviction of Adam and Eve from the garden (Gen. 3:23-24). God also employs both of these verbs when he predicts that the Pharaoh will send and drive away the Israelite slaves after the tenth plague (Exod. 6:1; 11:1).

6. In vv. 4 and 6, the verb denoting enclosure is סבב. In v. 6, אפף is also used, as is also the case in Ps. 116:3: "The cords of death surrounded (אפפוני) me." See Chapter 5 §3 for more on the enclosures in which Jonah finds himself.

descends before being brought up from the "pit." The prayer gives no indication that Jonah welcomes his impending annihilation or views death as peaceful, as do the afflicted individuals described so vividly by the sufferer Job (Job 3:20-23). Nor does Jonah mention having resisted his descent, having struggled against the waves, or having attempted to remove the seaweed from around his head. His only reported action is praying.

Jonah attributes his plight directly to God, even though in ch. 1 we were told that he had fled on his own volition and then told the sailors to throw him into the sea. Jonah experiences God's waves and billows passing over him (Jon. 2:4-5).[7] Yet God is also the one who brought up his life from the pit (v. 7). In other words, God is responsible for enclosing Jonah in life-threatening danger and also for rescuing him by extricating him from these enclosures.[8]

When Jonah is ejected from the fish's belly, we are given no clue about his feelings and no information about his actions when he is again on dry land. The castaway Robinson Crusoe, who is likened to Jonah by the captain of Crusoe's former ship,[9] initially responds to his plight by fending for himself with no thought of God, most notably by erecting a massive wall and cave dwelling against danger from outside.[10] In contrast, "the word of Yahweh" comes to Jonah at this point, but nothing is said about Yahweh offering the prophet shelter, a means of cleansing himself, or providing him with food after his ordeal.[11] Instead, God merely repeats the earlier command to arise and go to Nineveh.

Later Jonah exposes himself to the wind and the heat of the sun and then protects himself in a Crusoe-like manner by erecting a *sukkah*. God immediately thwarts these attempts at self-help; the *sukkah* suddenly vanishes from the story in favor of the shelter of the *qiqqayon* plant provided by—and then destroyed by—Yahweh (Jon. 4:5-7). When we examine the book of Jonah in detail later on, I will ask whether the deity is attempting to convince Jonah that he cannot escape the need to depend upon Yahweh for shelter, whether that be a fish's belly or a fickle plant's shade.

---

7. By naming God as the cause of his predicament, is Jonah implying that Yahweh had left him no choice but to jump—or be thrown—overboard, if the ship were not to go down in the storm?

8. Jonah is not the only prophet whose song dramatically depicts God as the one who both endangers and rescues his creatures. In Deuteronomy 32, Moses, who was himself exposed on water as an infant, likens Israel to an infant exposed on dry land in a howling desert wasteland (vv. 10-11). When Yahweh discovers this abandoned baby, he encompasses and cares for him as "the little man in his eye." See further in Lasine (2016a, 469–70).

9. "Perhaps this has all befallen us on your account, like Jonah in the ship of Tarshish" (Defoe 1994, 12).

10. Fisch (1986, 218) suggests that Jonah's many trials "may be used as a kind of midrash on *Robinson Crusoe*." On Crusoe's alleged fear of being swallowed up, see Heims (1983).

11. For more examples of information withheld by the narrator, see Chapter 5 §2.

In the Hebrew Bible (as in ancient Greek writings), rough waters and quaking earth are among the ultimate dangers with which humans can be confronted.[12] While the dry ground does not shake beneath Jonah after he is vomited out onto *terra firma*, being on land does not protect Jonah from the ills to which the sun and wind expose him. Elsewhere in the Bible, the very ground beneath one's feet *can* become just as unstable and turbulent as stormy waters.[13] As I will discuss further in Chapter 6 §3, earthquake, like the sea, can "swallow one up" and send one downward toward Sheol while still alive.[14] The message is clear: those who act in a manner which rouses God's jealousy or his wrath cannot expect that God will continue to act as their safe haven or refuge. In fact, if one incurs Yahweh's displeasure there is no safe place to stand on earth any more than there is in a ship at sea. In a sense, Jonah is an exception to this rule. When God issues his initial command to Jonah and the prophet flagrantly disobeys, God expresses no anger, and Jonah is not destroyed by God's "waves."

3 Images of enclosure and exposure in the Psalms

In the book of Psalms, being surrounded can be either a positive or negative experience. Speakers are sometimes protectively encompassed by God,[15] but they may also be surrounded by negative forces.[16] This is of course true in other genres of biblical literature as well. For example, Job is first "hedged in" protectively by

---

12. The same double danger is experienced by Robinson Crusoe. After enduring shipwreck, this castaway has to contend with an earthquake on his island. The shelter he had meticulously constructed, including a cave surrounded by a wall, offered no protection. The ground became as unstable as a stormy sea: "I had no sooner stepp'd down upon the firm Ground, than I plainly saw it was a terrible Earthquake. . . . The Motion of the Earth made my Stomach sick, like one that was toss'd at sea; . . . I thought of nothing then but the Hill . . . burying all at once . . . . The fear of being swallow'd up alive made me that I never slept in quiet; and yet the Apprehensions of lying abroad without any Fence was almost equal to it" (1994, 59–61). In these conditions, neither enclosure nor exposure guarantees safety.

13. One key difference between these situations is that those who dwell on dry land typically expect the ground to remain *firma*, while those who venture out on the waters should have no such expectation, no matter how invulnerable their *Titanic*-like vessel may seem to them.

14. This is most dramatically illustrated by the "new" fate of the rebels Dathan and Abiram (Num. 16:30). Sheol "swallowing" people "alive" or people going down "alive" to Sheol is also mentioned in Prov. 1:12 and Ps. 55:16. In Exod. 15:10-12, the earth is said to swallow Pharaoh's army after they had sunk into the waters of the sea.

15. For example, Pss. 32:7, 10; 125:2.

16. For example, Pss. 17:9, 11; 22:13; 88:18; 140:10.

Yahweh, and then "hedged in" with suffering, when that same deity allows him to be tortured (Job 1:10; 3:23). In fact, Yahweh tells the satan (השטן) that he "swallowed" (בלע) Job for no reason (Job 2:3).

In terms of imagery and vocabulary, the Psalms most often cited in relation to Jonah's prayer are Psalms 18, 22, 69, and 88. The speaker in Psalm 69 asks that he not be overwhelmed (שטף) by the flood, swallowed up by the deep, or have the pit close its mouth over him (v. 16). When he urges Yahweh to rescue him, he does so by appealing to Yahweh's self-declared traits of covenantal loyalty, fidelity, and womblike compassion (vv. 14, 17; cf. Exod. 34:6-7). While the psalmist fears being swallowed up, Jonah, who *was* swallowed up, does not express fear in his prayer. As I will discuss later, Jonah does not even acknowledge that he had been residing in a fish's belly.

The speaker in Psalm 22 is also encompassed. In v. 13, he mentions being surrounded by bulls, while in v. 17, he reports that dogs have surrounded him and an assembly of evildoers have enclosed him.[17] In Ps. 18:5-6, the speaker includes his emotional reaction to having been constricted by the "cords" and "snares" of death and Sheol: "The torrents of Belial terrified (בעת) me." The speaker in Psalm 55 expresses his emotions even more vehemently when he is beset by an enemy: "My heart writhes within me, the terrors of death have fallen upon me. Fear and trembling come upon me, and horror overwhelms me."[18] He longs to rush to a place of escape in the wilderness, away from the storming wind and tempest (55:5-9).[19]

When speakers in Psalms 22 and 71 mention the "belly" (בטן), they are referring to the maternal womb, rather than the metaphorical belly of Sheol evoked by Jonah. The speaker in Psalm 22 expects no nurturing protection once he emerges from the womb unless it comes from God, whom he believes to be far from him (vv. 2-3, 10-12). He makes no mention of his human birth mother or father or other possible sources of human support. These verses stress how protection comes from Yahweh as soon as one is separated from the womb. God takes us from the womb; it is on him that we are cast from the womb; it is he with whom basic trust is established when we are nursing at the mother's breasts, not the mother

---

17. In these verses the verbs used to describe the act of enclosure are סבב, כתר, and נקף.

18. The LXX has "the fear of death (δειλία θανάτου) fell upon me" (LXX Ps. 54:4). The Hebrew word for "terror" in the MT of Ps. 55:5 is אימה, which also describes the terror reported in Exod. 15:16. The verb which denotes "trembling" in the following verse (רעד; Ps. 55:6) is also employed in Exod. 15:15. The term for "horror" in 55:6 is פלצות, which appears elsewhere only in Job 21:6, Ezek. 7:18, and Isa. 21:4.

19. The fact that Jonah makes no reference to this kind of emotion in his prayer reinforces the "pastness" of his words, as though these events are being viewed from a position of comfort, looking back on a crisis that has already ended.

herself (22:10).²⁰ The speaker in Ps. 71:6 expresses a similar assumption. He says that he has "leaned upon Yahweh from the womb," adding, "from the innards (ממעי) of my mother you excised me."²¹

Finally, in Psalm 88 the speaker describes his life as "full of evils." His life "draws near to Sheol." He is likened to "those who go down to the pit (בור),"²² forsaken among the dead "like the slain that lie in the grave," who are "cut off from your hand" (vv. 4-6). The speaker knows the cause of his near-enclosure in death: God himself has "put [him] in the lowest pit, in dark places, in depths."²³ Once again God is said to place an individual into a situation from which only God can rescue him.²⁴ In contrast to Jonah (and Job), in Psalm 88, it is wrath which leads God to afflict this speaker "with all [his] waves" (vv. 7-8). In my next section, I will show that in Psalm 107, the most extensive example of nautical imagery in the Hebrew Bible, God sends "his waves"—in a literal sense—against seafaring believers who have *not* aroused his wrath.

20. Although Job initially declares that he came naked out of his mother's womb and will be naked when he returns there (1:21), by ch. 3 he feels sufficiently abandoned and exposed to ask why "*the* knees" received him and "*the* breasts" were there for him to suckle (3:12). The mother herself, as a protective nurturing *person*, has vanished. And while God has not disappeared, by chs 6-7 Job feels the deity's presence to be oppressive and terrifying.

21. In his poem "Paradise," George Herbert expresses his trust in divine enclosure when he asks "what open force, or hidden charm can . . . bring me harm while the inclosure is thine arm?" (2007, 464). As R. Watson points out (1994, 264), this "is consoling as theology . . . [but it] proves equivocal as psychology," since "agoraphobia of an infinite universe can quickly give way to the no less terrifying claustrophobia of a grave."

22. On the nuances of the word בור see Chapter 7, n. 28.

23. The psalmist continues in a manner reminiscent of Job whom God has hedged in with disaster: "You have distanced my acquaintances from me; you have set me up as an object of repugnance to them; I am shut up, and I cannot go out" (Ps. 88:9; cf. Job 3:23).

24. Elements within the books of Job and Jonah also suggest that utter and total dependence on God is necessary—but not sufficient—in order for one to fare well. After Job loses his children, the rest of the family steers clear of the sufferer (Job 19:13-19), except for the mother of the dead children who is scorned by Job (Job 2:9-10) and then ignored by the narrator. It is as though God and the satan are stripping away the illusion that safety and success are guaranteed if one is totally loyal to God. And once Jonah is "vomited out" by the fish he too is made to understand that safety can only be found (if at all) by acknowledging his total dependence upon God. However, Yahweh does not put Jonah into a situation which is as obviously unbearable as that of Job, whose life has been wrecked by Yahweh as thoroughly as the "ship" Tyre was wrecked in "the heart of the seas" (Ezek. 27:26).

4 Storms at sea in Psalm 107 and the issue of theodicy

While ships and shipwreck are mentioned in 1 Kings and Ezekiel,[25] we must wait until Jonah 1–2 and the Psalms if we are to experience the full force of our fundamental vulnerability at sea. Psalm 107 includes the most powerful and fully developed example:

> Those who went down to the sea in ships, . . . saw [Yahweh's] . . . wonders in the deep. For he spoke and raised the storm wind and it lifted up its waves. They went up to heaven; they went down to the depths; their life (נפש) melted away in their evil plight; they reeled and staggered like drunkards and all their wisdom was swallowed up. And they cried to Yahweh in their anguish, and he delivered them from their distress (vv. 23-28).

These verses give no hint that the storm represents a divine punishment for some misdeed. God simply commands the winds and waves to violently threaten the sailors, who have already witnessed his "wonders." The mariners' response to the danger is pious; they cry out to Yahweh in their distress. Their evil situation may "swallow up all their wisdom,"[26] but there is no indication that they had thought that their wisdom was equal to Yahweh's or that God's favor was not needed in order for them to conduct their "business in great waters" (v. 23).[27] All we are told is that Yahweh causes their plight and then delivers them from it: "They were glad that the waters were quiet,[28] and he guides them to their desired haven (מחוז)" (v. 30).

Psychologist John Bowlby points to infants who yearn for "a haven of safety" when they are frightened (1982, 303). For theologians such as Gordon Kaufman, the biblical God represents such a haven. Yahweh is "a protective and caring parent who is always reliable and always available" when needed (1981, 67). At first glance, the conclusion in Ps. 107:30 seems to support Kaufman's assertion. However, a key

---

25. On Solomon's fleet, see 1 Kgs 9:26; 10:22. Jehoshaphat's "Tarshish ships" are wrecked at Ezion-Geber (1 Kgs 22:49). According to 2 Chron. 20:37, the wreck is punishment for Jehoshaphat having worked together with Ahaziah. The wreck of Tyre's Tarshish ships in Ezek. 27:25-34 is also presented as divine punishment.

26. Cf. the many fine, brave sailors in the Egyptian *Tale of the Shipwrecked Sailor* (ll. 28–39) who have the ability to predict storms before they happen, but could not prevent their ship from "dying"—or themselves from drowning—in a gale. On this tale, see Chapter 6 §2.

27. The absence of any reference to culpability or punishment is acknowledged by both Mejía (1975, 64) and Kartje (2014, 154). However, Mejía hedges his bet by adding that there "seems to be a certain connotation of imprudence in the fashion the seafarers commit themselves for the sake of trade, to the dangers of the 'great waters.'"

28. The rare verb שתק is also used to describe the quieting of the sea in Jon. 1:11-12.

question remains, one which I will address in the remainder of this study: Can God's loyal followers *always* count on him to provide safety for them?

Psalm 107 itself points to this problem by underscoring the absence of any divine motivation for the storm. It does so in several ways. First, the two preceding situations of danger and rescue mentioned in the Psalm *are* punishments, either for rebellion against God's spoken words (v. 11) or for unspecified iniquities (v. 17). The absence of the punitive element with the sailors is also highlighted by several intertextual links with Job 12. In Psalm 107, the sailors are made to "stagger like drunken men."[29] Similarly, Job accuses God of making the heads of the people "stagger like a drunkard" and "wander in a void (תהו) without a path" (Job 12:24-25). Job makes no mention of any dereliction of duty or corruption on the part of these leaders. The noticeable absence of the sailors' culpability in Psalm 107 is further emphasized later in the Psalm, when, echoing Job 12:21, the speaker claims that God pours contempt on nobles, who must also "wander in a void (תהו) without a path" (v. 40).[30] Given the unpredictable universe in which these sailors and earth-bound leaders do their business, human means of self-protection must be sought—but can they be found?

5 Death—and birth—as shipwreck

For Brown, the *Chaoskampf* "lies below the billowing surface" of poems such as Psalm 107 (2002, 107; cf. Mejía, 1975, 57–58; 63). According to Brown, the psalmists employ "water imagery ... to channel chaos to target various conditions of human and divine distress" (2002, 112). He also cites Psalm 88 as illustrating both fear of drowning and watery chaos. Brown believes that this Psalm gives a "radical twist [to the] combat mythos," because it is God himself who is the embodiment of chaos and the psalmist's enemy (2002, 112–13).

While I agree that some biblical sea imagery points to what Brown calls "conditions of human and divine distress," the fundamental aspect of the human condition expressed by the texts under discussion has nothing to do with chaos, let alone a battle against chaos. The individuals who feel themselves overwhelmed, if not entombed, by God-sent waters or human enemies are not experiencing their world dissolving into chaos, or meaning disintegrating into meaninglessness. They may be painfully aware of their vulnerability and their

---

29. Kartje (2014, 154) characterizes the sailors' staggering and their "souls 'melting'" as an "internal impediment" caused by the "external impediment" of the storm. He wisely refrains from concluding that these reactions are an indication of guilt, as opposed to despair.

30. If the "nobles" mentioned in v. 40 are the agents of the "constraint" (מעצר) inflicted on the people mentioned in the preceding verse, vv. 39-40 may be implying that these leaders *are* being punished for their abuse of power. If so, their plight forms a contrast with the innocent suffering of the sailors described earlier in the Psalm.

inability to control their fate, but they view the threatening external forces as purposeful and expressive of God's will and emotions, including his failure to rescue them from their enemies.

In Psalm 44, the speakers believe themselves to be innocent. But even though they cannot fathom the meaning of their suffering, they do not conclude that it is meaningless or haphazard. Instead, they want God to "awaken" and explain the meaning of their affliction to them (vv. 24-25). They are overwhelmed by the meaning of their God forgetting and abandoning them. Their present reality has two disconcerting aspects: inability to consistently protect themselves from forces wielded by the same God who created those forces and the realization that they cannot always count on the deity to shelter them from the storms of life. It is this which Job finds so troubling when he describes the naked, cold victims who must embrace the rock for lack of shelter in the storm (24:7-8). In such a universe, we vulnerable human creatures must be prepared to keep building and re-building our protective ships and *sukkoth* in case our divine father and suzerain rejects us, becomes inattentive, or is sleeping as soundly as Jonah when our ships are breaking up.

In the face of these realities, what defensive measures *do* humans take in order to survive on the world-sea and avoid shipwreck? In his version of the sea voyage of life metaphor, Schopenhauer describes the individual's life span as a journey through "a sea full of crags and whirlpools," which inevitably leads to the ultimate "shipwreck" of death (1819, 450). In his view, we defend ourselves against awareness of our vulnerability and our inevitable extinction by fostering the illusion that the individual can trust the frail little skiff of the self during her brief life voyage.[31]

Schopenhauer was familiar with a much earlier—and more extreme—use of this metaphor by the Roman poet Lucretius. At one point, Lucretius compares the human infant to "a sailor tossed out from the fierce waves" (*DRN* 5.222-34). In contrast to the wild beasts, human babies are helpless and vulnerable from the moment they are "shipwrecked," that is, brought forth from the womb, the "mother ship."[32] The idea of likening birth to shipwreck forms a striking contrast

---

31. This "flotation device" serves the same function for individuals that Ortega's "raft" of civilization serves for societies. Schopenhauer's metaphor is discussed more fully in Chapter 6 §3. This image echoes the message of the Dutch and Flemish storm and shipwreck paintings described by Judson: "Man is often likened to a ship sailing through life on unchartered waters, constantly in danger forever changing his course and finally, through drowning, achieving release" (1964, 144-45).

32. In Schiller's *The Robbers*, the villain Franz expresses a Lucretian view of humans as "castaways" at birth, combined with confidence that he, the speaker, is one who can survive: "[Nature] gave us an inventive spirit and set us naked and destitute on the shore of this great ocean, the world—swim, whoever can swim, and who is too clumsy, go under!" (I. i.; 1953, 18). This "sink or swim" attitude is not unfamiliar, but here it is based on the idea that only some humans are equipped—or able to equip themselves—to stay afloat as castaways.

to the more common image of life as a sea voyage ending in shipwreck, whether that wreck is understood as divine punishment[33] or as an admission that life inevitably ends in our annihilation. Why does Lucretius employ the shipwrecked mariner metaphor to describe the implications of human existence from birth? After all, shipwrecked sailors are adults who have already been socialized and presumably learned survival skills such as those developed by the stranded Robinson Crusoe.

The idea of shipwreck from birth makes sense if the passage registers the lived experience of those who grow up feeling neglected, uncared for, and utterly alone within a family or society. Sophocles's Philoctetes is one "castaway" who illustrates the points made by both Lucretius and Schopenhauer. He is intentionally deposited on a forbidding and uninhabited island because the terrible odor from his ever-festering foot and his excruciating cries make him an unbearable shipmate. Sophocles has Odysseus employ the usual term for child exposure when he refers to his earlier abandonment of Philoctetes (ἐκτίθημι; *Phil.* 5; see Schein 2013, 117–18). Later, the Chorus describes the suffering hero as being so isolated and helpless that he must "crawl along like a child without his beloved nurse" (*Phil.* 703). As Schein points out (2013, 207), Philoctetes asks for pity from the visitors to his lonely island by explaining his situation "in terms of the human condition generally": "All things are full of terror (δεινά[34]) and dangerously disposed for mortals to fare well or to fare the other way" (*Phil.* 501–03).[35] Therefore, we must always be on guard, so that we can avoid being destroyed when dangers escape our notice (*Phil.* 504–06).[36] In sum, Philoctetes is the quintessential lone sufferer, abandoned without human companionship or even the possibility of death as an escape from his misery, pain, and toil (*Phil.* 797–98).

No matter how much one's father or mother might care for them, all children must eventually be "vomited out" not merely from the womb but from the fantasy of infantile omnipotence.[37] As I will discuss later, many psychologists argue that no infant can totally avoid the experience of parental unreliability and feelings of

---

33. See Goedde (1989, 38–39) and Landow (1982, 16–17, 183).

34. Contrast the use of this multivalent term in the *Antigone* ode, where it can be understood as denoting either "wonderful," "terrible," or both. See Chapter 1 §2.

35. Rose (1976, 58) contends that Sophocles "is primarily offering an image of the human condition" only in "the primitive, presocial stage." One could argue, however, that Philoctetes feels much more isolated and helpless after Odysseus and Neoptolemus arrive on his island than he did prior to their appearance—at least until Neoptolemus and the *deus ex machina* Heracles aid the sufferer at the end of the play.

36. Schein suggests another sense in which Philoctetes is typically human when he notes that the "frailness and vulnerability" of the castaway's body "would presumably have horrified a fifth-century Athenian audience as it horrifies modern spectators and readers, who all have similar bodies and are similarly vulnerable" (2013, 25).

37. This sheltering fantasy is fostered by parents who treat their child as "His Majesty the Baby," to use Freud's shorthand expression (see Lasine 2001, 5–6, 237–38).

annihilation anxiety. These feelings are also acknowledged and addressed in the many myths and fairy tales involving infant exposure on, and rescue from, water. As we approach adulthood we all must recognize—or attempt to deny—that, in one sense, each individual in her little "self-boat" is, and has always been, utterly alone and marked for death, once she has been cast out of the womb. We must also learn that our formerly idealized mother and father are also vulnerable—and too often helpless—and equally doomed to die. No wonder, then, that the sage in Wis. 7:6 cites the fact that newborns enter the world crying. No matter how much anyone might be nursed with care and go on to exercise power like a king, the fact remains that "for all there is one entrance into life and the same way out." Lucretius's metaphor of the shipwrecked baby-sailor makes no mention of a human caretaker on the shore who is ready and able to aid the survivor, as does the girl Nausicca for Homer's castaway Odysseus (*Od.* 6.127–7.347).

Returning to Psalm 107, one commentator believes that the audience of this poem should learn that "it is entirely possible that the least morally culpable may suffer the most hopeless plights." However, "even when one's situation appears so hopeless that no degree of human effort can provide relief, salvation is available solely from Yhwh, *if* he is sought out" (Kartje 2014, 155). Forti goes further, claiming that while Psalm 107 expresses "the idea of human vulnerability," both the Psalms and Jonah present a "caring and merciful God, who controls all human beings in a fair way," illuminating God's cosmic providence (2011, 359, 369–70, 373).[38] Such generalizations exclude the biblical voices who do *not* find Yahweh's control to be reliably caring or fair, as well as the unique voice of Jonah, who recognizes his God's control and compassion but still insists upon asserting his own will and sense of fairness. Put differently, the "lesson" Kartje derives from Psalm 107 requires a second "if" clause: salvation is available solely from Yahweh if he is sought out *and* if he chooses to acknowledge and respond to the petitioner's plight.

---

38. More generally, Brueggemann understands providence in the OT to mean that "the world is under Yahweh's powerful care"; his "inscrutable ways . . . are reliable but not evident" (1997, 353). Arthur Koestler offers a different—and provocative—perspective when he employs the life as a sea voyage *topos* to illustrate how a human being might experience the role of divine providence in his or her life: "The captain of a ship sets out with a sealed order in his pocket which he is only permitted to open on the high seas. He looks forward to that moment which will end all uncertainty; but when the moment arrives and he tears the envelope open, he finds only an invisible text which defies all attempts at chemical treatment. Now and then a word becomes visible, or a figure denoting a meridian; then it fades again. He will never know the exact wording of the order; nor whether he has complied with it or failed in his mission. But his awareness of the order in his pocket, even though it cannot be deciphered, makes him think and act differently from the captain of a pleasure-cruiser or of a pirate ship" (1979, 285–86).

6 Coping with the storms of life in Yahweh's world

Here someone might rightly object that I mentioned only one divine action in the preceding section: putting people in danger and then rescuing them. That much can also be said of gods such as Marduk, whose moods are also described with storm and sea imagery.[39] As I have discussed elsewhere, Yahweh's personality is multifaceted, as are his various roles as divine parent, king, and husband. His interactions with humans are therefore extremely complex (Lasine 2010, 52–57, 2016a, 472–76). The nautical metaphors examined here point to yet another factor causing human life in Yahweh's world to be so complex, if not unpredictable, anxiety-ridden, and fragile. This factor is the extent to which God has—and has not—equipped us to cope with our evanescent existence in his threatening world.

This aspect of the human condition can be summed up by returning to the device of the sixteenth-century Calvinist Philips van Marnix and contrasting Marnix's use of the sea voyage metaphor with John Donne's nautical imagery. Marnix's extremely compact visual representation of the sea voyage of life *topos* recalls Jonah's experience. Marnix employs an image which is almost identical to contemporary depictions of the "Jonah cast over the side" motif (Judson 1964, 145). His sketch typically portrays a ship at sea, with rocks on one side and a sea monster on the other.[40] In the example from Ortelius's *album amicorum*, the Tetragrammaton is written in Hebrew letters in the sky above the constellation Ursa Minor (the "Little Dipper"), with light streaming down to the ship (Goedde 1989, 62, 220, n. 45; Judson 1964, 145).[41] Like the drawing described in my Preface, this version also has the motto *repos ailleurs*—rest elsewhere—written across the scene. Under the sketch is an epigram in Latin, advising us to seek our rest where "the reliable Pole Star of the Gospel calls" us.[42] In the Ortelius volume and elsewhere, Marnix employs this device as part of an emblem with various biblical texts and commentaries underneath it.[43] If we take scripture as our guide when we navigate through life, we will be rewarded with "rest elsewhere," that is, in the

---

39. Marduk is the god whose anger is "like a tempest" or "violent storm" (*meḫû*) and a flood, but whose mind and mood turn back and relent (*Ludlul* I. 5, 7-8; cf. I. 10; Annus and Lenzi 2010, 15, 31).

40. In some versions of his device, Marnix draws rocks on both sides, rather than including a sea monster.

41. In some cases (e.g., the device in the portrait of Marnix by de Gheyn and Marnix's drawing in the album of Janus Dousa), Christ's monogram accompanies the Hebrew יהוה. See the Preface and Russell (1983, 77–78).

42. It is unclear whether Latin *cynosura* here refers to the Pole Star (North[ern] Star) or to the constellation of which it is the brightest member.

43. For example, Ps. 119:1-16; Heb. 13:13-14. See Kreuzberg (1960, 47–48) and Judson (1964, 145; cf. Goedde 1989, 220, n. 46).

afterlife. Calvin himself describes the alternative: those who investigate God's plan without his Word "engulf themselves in a deadly abyss" when their ships are dashed against this "rock" (*Institutes* 3.24; Calvin 1960, 969).

John Donne also employs the metaphor of the "Northern Star" as a navigational guide in his poem entitled "Annuntiation":[44]

> As by the Selfe-fixd Pole wee never doe
> Direct our Course, but the next starr thereto,
> Which showes where th' other is, and which wee say
> (Because it strayes not farr) doth never stray:
> So God by 'hys Church, neerest to him, wee knowe,
> And stand firme, if wee by her Motion goe;
> His Spiritt, as hys fierye Pillar, doth
> Lead, And 'hys Church as Cloude, to One Ende both. (ll. 25–32; 2015, 149)

In this poem the Northern (or Pole) Star stands for the Church of England, which "strayes not farr" from the North Pole, the unmovable God (see Stubbs 2008, 239). By guiding ourselves in accord with the motion of the Church, we stand firm with God. Donne then likens God's spirit to the pillar of fire and his Church to the pillar of cloud, which together guide the Israelites through the wilderness (Exod. 13:21-22).

Donne views life as a sea voyage which necessarily ends in the shipwreck of death.[45] As he emphasizes in one of his sermons, "The world is a Sea in many respects and assimilations" (1955, 306).[46] Donne desperately attempts to use his hope for resurrection to stave off his fear that death means annihilation of his self and, thereby, his world. Like the narrator Qoheleth, Donne has often been described as obsessed with death (e.g., Patrides 1989, 101, 111, 114), if not "gripped by a tremendous fear of death" (Targoff 2006, 217).

Several aspects of Donne's view of life as a dangerous sea voyage are evident in his early verse letter, "Storme" (2001, 132–34). This poem was occasioned by his participation in the ill-fated Essex-Raleigh naval expedition in 1597 (the so-called

---

44. This 1608 poem is also known as "Upon the Annunciation and Passion Falling on One Day."

45. On a personal level, Donne once described his family's situation as "a sea, under a continual tempest, where one wave hath ever overtaken another" (qtd. in Stubbs 2008, 45). Donne insists on fighting death until he is overcome: "When I must shipwreck, I would do it in a Sea" rather than in "a sullen weedy lake" (1839, 321). For more on Donne's simultaneous fear of, and longing for, death and its relation to Donne's focus on Romantic love, see Targoff (2006, 217–31) and R. Watson (1994, 156–252).

46. The good news of this sermon is that the world is most like a sea because it is "no place of habitation, but a passage to our habitations" (1955, 307), a view with which Marnix would surely concur.

"Islands Voyage").[47] The poet envies Jonah who sleeps through the storm and then pities him for having been awakened:

> *Jonas*, I pitty thee, and curse those men
> Who, when the storm rage'd most, did wake thee then.
> Sleepe is paines easiest salve, and doth fulfill
> All offices of death, except to kill.
> But when I wakt, I saw, that I saw not.
> I, and the Sunne, which should teach mee'had forgot
> East, West, day, night, and I could onely say,
> If'the world had lasted, now it had been day. (ll. 33–40)

Once awake, Jonah had to face what Donne had to face in his life-threatening storm, namely, possible extinction.[48] Donne describes those awake in the ship's cabins wanting—and not wanting—to learn their fate, like the dead who leave their graves at the Last Judgment or like husbands who suspect their wives of infidelity:

> Some coffin'd in their cabbins lye', equally
> Griev'd that they are not dead, and yet must dye.
> And as sin-burd'ned soules from graves will creepe,
> At the last day, some forth their cabbins peepe:
> And tremblingly'aske what newes, and doe heare so,
> Like jealous husbands, what they would not know. (ll. 45–50)

The poet sees sickness, death, and punishment everywhere on the endangered vessel. The ship suffers from "sicknesses"; the mast shakes with "an ague" and from the tattered sails "ragges drop downe so, as from one hang'd in chaines a year agoe" (ll. 53–58). Whether one reads Donne's poems, sermons, or letters, one must be prepared to read about death and be reminded of one's own mortality. In my next chapter, I will consider the possible effects of increased mortality salience on readers of biblical texts which feature illness, death, and human vulnerability.

---

47. On these events, see Mentz (2013, 357–59) and Stubbs (2008, 63–85).

48. Donne ends his poem by returning to the idea that shipwreck means the end of the sailors' world: "Darknesse, lights elder brother, his birth-right Claims o'er this world, and to heaven hath chas'd light . . . so that wee, except God say another *Fiat*, shall have no more day" (ll. 67–74). On one's world ending when one dies, see Chapter 7 §3. Donne also refers to Jonah in a letter written shortly after the end of the first expedition: "Jonas was in a whales belly three dayes but hee came not voluntary as I did" (2001, 377). On what Orwell calls "the essential Jonah act of allowing himself to be swallowed" (1981, 245), see Chapter 7 §1.

7 Conclusion

> The *Great Eastern*,[49] or some of her successors ... will perhaps defy the roll of the Atlantic, and cross the seas without allowing their passengers to feel that they have left the firm land. The voyage from the cradle to the grave may come to be performed with similar facility. Progress and science may perhaps enable untold millions to live and die ... without an anxiety. They will wonder that men ever believed at all in clanging fights and blazing towns and sinking ships and praying hands; ... But it seems unlikely that they will have such a knowledge of the great ocean on which they sail, with its storms and wrecks, its currents and icebergs, its huge waves and mighty winds, as those who battled with it for years together in the little craft, which, if they had few other merits, brought those who navigated them full into the presence of time and eternity, their maker and themselves, and forced them to have some definite view of their relations to them and to each other.
>
> —James Fitzjames Stephen (1862, 318–19)

If we consider all the images of enclosure and exposure examined so far, including the dangers faced by human beings in both modes of experience, an urgent question arises: Do Yahweh's words and actions within the Hebrew Bible provide a reliable navigational guide for our lives to the same degree that the Little Dipper and its star Polaris do for seafarers, and the Christian Gospels and Church do for Marnix and Donne?

This question will continue to be pondered as this investigation proceeds. For now, we should keep in mind that "storms" occur when one is in terrestrial enclosures as well as when one is traveling by sea. As the poet Philemon puts it, "Wintry storms do not strike only those sailing the sea, but those who walk around, ... under porticos in the street, and those who stay indoors in the home. ... I experience storms not just for a day, but my whole life long" (Pickard-Cambridge 1900, 106–07). We have already noted cases in which our rocky life voyage—even sleeping below deck in the vessel—can lead to shipwreck whether or not we assert our own wills or attempt to evade God's control. Texts such as Job, Jeremiah, and Psalm 44 carry an even more unsettling message: life can become *even more* stormy and painful for those who most fervently desire to be guided by Yahweh. For these loyal followers of their God, *repos ailleurs* means only the rest provided by nonexistence (see Job 3:3-19; Jer. 20:14-18).

It should therefore be no surprise that Holocaust survivor Richard Glazer used storm and shipwreck metaphors to express the need for constant vigilance against the next "wave," or threat, when he arrived at the Treblinka concentration camp in 1942: "It's a hurricane, a raging sea. We're shipwrecked. And we're still alive. We must do nothing. ... But watch for every new wave, float on it, get ready for the next wave, and ride the wave at all costs. And nothing else"

---

49. The *Great Eastern* was a huge steamship launched the year before Stephen's essay was first published.

(Lanzmann 1985, 48). Here the metaphor expresses a strategy for physical and mental survival. In this respect, the traditional *topos* of life as sea voyage fits Glazer's extreme life experience just as well as it fits the situation of Philemon's character—or the situation in which we are all immersed.

The epigraph for this section is taken from an 1859 essay by judge and author James Fitzjames Stephen. This excerpt combines confidence in progressive human ingenuity with the assumption that human life is analogous to a sea voyage. The passage may strike us now as naive because it seems to accept the myth of human progress and the shelters provided by "science," as well as the idea that a human being might go through life without any care or anxiety. These notions serve to obscure the fact that everyone—including those who are hedged in by prosperity like Job or Qoheleth—is always battling the waves and winds of the life-sea, if only in the sense that Schopenhauer describes in relation to the individual in her frail boat of the self.

Stephen uses the sea voyage metaphor to justify the condition of those who are not privileged to cruise on a great ocean liner. He claims that the exigencies of exposure grant these suffering individuals knowledge, by making them aware of "the presence of time and eternity, their maker, and themselves" (1862, 319). In other words, when humans are exposed to all of these forces they live most fully and become most aware of reality. What is missing in Stephen's view of the human life voyage is an acknowledgment that belief in the shelter offered by metaphorical ocean liners is also one way to obscure awareness of our fundamental vulnerability. Stephen did not live to witness the fate of the RMS *Titanic*, which helped to reveal the folly of belief in unsinkable protection from the dangers of the unbounded sea.

We are now in a position to ask whether the biblical motif of life as a sea voyage expresses the same attitude of pessimism which we found in other strands of the Hebrew Bible. Earlier I noted Crenshaw's definition of pessimism, which includes the idea that "chaos has the upper hand." This investigation has located no evidence that "chaos" is implied by biblical nautical metaphors or by biblical accounts of sea voyage or shipwreck. Insofar as these metaphors point to universal features of the human condition in the Hebrew Bible—including vulnerability, evanescence, and irreversible death—they convey a *realistic* portrait of human life in Yahweh's universe, including the fact that individuals may experience life in the world-sea as "chaotic."

We must also take into account the theodic implications of Yahweh's governance over the human world. Yahweh can be the Rock who shelters us or the rock against which our aspirations shatter. As I discussed in the previous chapter, for Job, Qoheleth, Jonah, and others, it becomes impossible to wrestle with their human vulnerability and mortality without questioning the fairness of their condition. The castaway Jonah refuses to accept Yahweh's proffered shelters, including the sheltering effect of a theodicy based on Yahweh's professed compassion, when that divine attribute is used as the reason not to execute justice. Jonah will not betray his perception of reality and his own sense of justice, even though this refusal leads to him becoming more constricted *and* more exposed than most mortals, as I will discuss in Part Two of this book.

Chapter 4

READING ABOUT DEATH IN BIBLICAL NARRATIVE

Earlier we heard from sages who stress the negative aspects of the human condition. They highlight our fragility, our lack of control over our circumstances, and our evanescence. Some suggest that our mortality may make life seem not only brief but also pointless, if not terrifying as well. We also discussed prophets whose divinely given tasks are so unbearable that they prefer death to life. One question remains to be asked: Can reading about human mortality in the Bible lead modern readers to become more aware of their own inevitable demise? If so, does the Hebrew Bible provide an effective way of coping with that unsettling awareness? These are the issues with which I will deal in this chapter.[1]

In order to address this problem, I will focus on the prophet whose career immediately precedes that of Jonah in the books of Kings. That figure is Elisha, a character whose personality and behavior contrast significantly with that of Jonah. For example, Elisha never wishes to die.[2] Although Elisha goes to a foreign country and utters a prophecy, as does Jonah, he goes without having been ordered to do so by Yahweh (2 Kgs 8:7-13). While the king of Aram seeks out Elisha and asks for a prophecy, no such action is made by the king of Nineveh in the book of Jonah. In addition, Elisha is already well known in Aram when he travels there in 2 Kings 8, while the book of Jonah gives no indication that this prophet (or the Jonah of 2 Kgs 14:25) is already known to the Ninevites. And while the king of Aram had earlier attempted to capture Elisha (2 Kgs 6:13-23), no such attempt is made by the king of Nineveh when Jonah arrives there. Finally, Elisha utters a prophecy which spells doom only for the reigning monarch (and for Israel, whom the next king will defeat). He does not proclaim that Aram will be "overthrown," as Jonah predicts will be the fate of Nineveh.

The proximity of the stories of Elisha and Jonah within 2 Kings probably led to the rabbinic tradition that Jonah was Elisha's disciple, if not the "son of the

---

1. The issue of coping with mortality without expectation of an afterlife is discussed further in Chapter 7 §5.
2. Nor does Elisha take measures to save himself when he is mortally ill, as do King Hezekiah and those who ask prophets about the outcome of their illness or the fate of their ill loved one (see, for example, 1 Kings 14; 2 Kings 1, 8, 20).

prophet" whom Elisha dispatched to anoint Jehu as king in 2 Kings 9.³ The Elisha narratives, together with the stories involving Elisha's mentor Elijah, present readers with an unusual concentration of stories involving death, human fragility, and illness. Elijah wants to die, but God responds by making sure that he never dies. Elisha dies after an ordinary illness, but his bones later bring a dead man to life. By resuscitating dead boys, both prophets show that death is not always irreversible. In addition, Elijah personally kills over five hundred fifty people, and Elisha curses his servant with a skin disease after he has helped to cure a foreign commander who has been a deadly enemy of Israel (1 Kgs 18:40; 2 Kgs 1:9-15; 2 Kgs 5:1-14, 25-27). Rather than attempting to investigate how readers might react to this entire series of stories,⁴ I will focus on Elisha's fatal illness and the report of his bones revivifying a corpse, both in 2 Kings 13.

1 The psychology of reading about death

First, it is necessary to consult current psychological theories about the ways in which people (including readers) may deal with such death reminders. TMT holds that mortality salience can lead some subjects to increase the rigidity of their worldviews and reinforce their other "buffers" against awareness of their mortality (see, for example, Solomon et al. 2004, 20–34).⁵ However, one recent experimental study found that this effect is *not* present when the increased mortality salience is generated by reading literature. Van Peer and his colleagues conclude that "MS in literature has as its effect not a defence mechanism, as predicted by TMT, but a psychological valve, that makes us accept our biological vulnerability" (2017, 39).⁶

Van Peer's findings can also be regarded as evidence that literary presentations of mortality can function as "buffers" in the TMT sense. Freud already points us in this direction in an early essay, stressing that "the feeling of security with which I accompany the [fictional] hero through his dangerous destiny is the same as the feeling with which an actual hero throws himself into the water to rescue someone drowning: . . . 'Nothing can happen to *me*!'" (1941, 220).⁷ Rather than

---

3. *Seder 'Olam* 18–19; Guggenheimer (1998, 160–62; cf. *Gen. Rab.* 21.5).

4. For analyses of these themes in 1 Kings 17–18 and 2 Kings 1, 4, and 5, see Lasine (2004, 117–25, 132–38; 2011, 3–6, 9–15; 2012, 67–76, 115–43; 2016b, 9–20).

5. These subjects may also become more harsh in their judgments of those who disagree with their views, depending upon personality factors such as attachment style. Individuals reacting to mortality salience may also attempt to bolster their self-esteem or seek closer personal relationships. A book-length treatment of TMT for a general audience has recently appeared; see Solomon et al. (2015). On TMT studies, see further in §3 of this chapter.

6. Van Peer seems to be referring to literature "making us accept" our vulnerability while we are reading the work, rather than causing a permanent attitudinal change in the reader.

7. On this quotation from Anzensgruber, see Lasine (2012, 136–37).

increasing our fear of death, reading about vulnerability and mortality in popular novels actually reinforces our unconscious belief in our own immortality.[8] Readers can feel protected by the same "special providence" (*besondere Vorsehung*) which seems to shield the hero (1941, 219).

Freud returns to this subject in his 1915 essay on mortality. We "die in identification with the death of a hero, but we nevertheless survive him," unscathed and ready to die a second time with a different hero (1946a, 344). Earlier in this essay, Freud had noted that however often we attempt to imagine ourselves dead, we continue to remain present as a spectator (1946a, 341). Whether we "die" by identifying with a seemingly invulnerable literary hero or by trying to imagine ourselves dead, in reality we live on in serene safety, like Lucretius's detached spectator on the shore watching ships flounder in the storm (*DRN* 2.1-12).

While Freud stresses that his focus is not on "high" literature, psychologists such as Nell (2002, 22-23) have asserted that even classic works on life's "dark side" do not instill readers with terror or morbidity. Rather than "buffering" or obscuring readers' awareness of their human vulnerability, literature functions as a kind of "safe space" within which readers can explore harsh realities and feel negative emotions without reacting in the same way as they would if they experienced these emotions in their daily lives.[9]

We must then ask whether we should expect similar results when readers respond to accounts of human fragility and mortality in biblical texts. Experts on the psychology of reading find that readers are more affected when information and ideas are presented in artistic narratives rather than in expository prose (see, for example, Oatley 2011, 160-62, 171-75). Are the effects of death reminders consequently any different when they are embedded in narrative rather than in the wisdom literature we discussed in Chapters 1 and 2? After all, narratives usually include characters with whom we might identify or for whom we may feel empathy. We can address this question by focusing on one Elisha narrative.

2 Reading about death and resuscitation in 2 Kings 13

In addition to offering revivification stories which explore the boundary supposedly separating life and death, 2 Kings includes a highly unusual concentration of cases in which the bodily vulnerability of key figures is highlighted. In 2 Kings 13, King Joash visits the sick prophet Elisha. The fact that the man of God "fell sick with

---

8. As Freud notes in "The Uncanny" (1947a, 262-65), while adults have long since "overcome" the belief that death is not final, such beliefs can be recalled both when reading literature and when certain unexpected events occur in daily life.

9. See, for example, Keen (2007, 4, 131): "Fictional worlds provide safe zones for readers' feeling empathy without experiencing a resultant demand on real-world action.... Novels can provide safe spaces within which to see through the eyes" of very negative characters. Cf. Oatley (2011, 125).

his sickness from which he died" (2 Kgs 13:14) led some rabbinic commentators to conclude that Elisha had been ill on previous occasions[10] and is the first person to have been ill and recovered from the illness (*b. B. Meṣiʿa* 87a; *b. Sanh.* 107b). Three other cases in the book describe the opposite situation. In these cases, the incapacitated individual is the king (Ahaziah, Ben Hadad, and Hezekiah) and the prophet's role is to announce the outcome of the disease or injury, either in person or through a messenger. None of these monarchs is said to have become ill or injured in war or as a divine punishment, although royal war wounds are also reported in 2 Kings (e.g., 2 Kgs 8:28-29; 9:14-28).

After reminding readers of the sick prophet's bodily vulnerability and his demise, the narrator of 2 Kings 13 informs us that the dead Elisha's bones are so invulnerable that they could restore another corpse to life. A burial party is forced to deposit a man's corpse in Elisha's grave and the dead prophet's bones revivify the corpse, which then stands up (2 Kgs 13:20-21). The same bones which had not kept Elisha alive on his deathbed now raise a stranger's corpse back to life by mere contact.

Several aspects of this terse account raise psychological questions. First, neither the narrator nor characters within the textual world express astonishment at the corpse returning to life when it contacts Elisha's bones. Nor does awe or amazement lead others to mark Elisha's burial place as unapproachably sacred, let alone build a shrine there, in contrast to ancient Greek texts which report people's reactions to the death and translation of wonder-workers (see Lasine 2016b, 12–13).[11] In addition, neither the narrator of 1–2 Kings nor any of the characters in these books remark upon the unusual frequency of royal illnesses and injuries.

Cohn (2000, 88) assumes that the reader of 2 Kgs 13:20-21 "is surprised at the resurrection of the dead man when he touches Elisha's bones." This may be true of many first-time readers and hearers. But can we take for granted that this has been true of everyone who has read or heard the story? According to Meyer (1988, 143, 136), surprise is elicited by unexpected events which are "discrepant with" or "contrary to" the schemata by means of which we make sense of our everyday surroundings. This prompts us to focus our attention on the schema-discrepant event and, if necessary, to revise the relevant schemata in order to increase the effectiveness of our actions and attributions.[12] The reviving of the corpse through

---

10. Specifically, on two former occasions, both of which were triggered by dubious behavior on Elisha's part: the cursing of the young boys with she-bears and "repulsing Gehazi with both hands" (*b. Sanh.*107b; cf. Ginzberg 1968, 240, 245–46).

11. Shemesh (2008, 34) explains this apparent absence by arguing that such details go beyond the "constricted narrative horizon" of brief saints' legends. On holy sites associated with Greek wonder-workers and heroes, see Lasine (2016b, 13, n. 27).

12. Meyer (1988, 136, 144–46). Meyer describes this process as having several stages. The first involves the interruption of normal processing of schemata in order to focus on the discrepant event. The second is examining and evaluating the event's cause. Finally, when necessary, it leads to the updating or revision of the relevant schemata in order to

contacting bones is certainly "discrepant" with the reality-concept operative in the world of most modern Western readers. The same is true of the world in which biblical characters live prior to 1 Kings, in the sense that these books give no hint that a living prophet could resuscitate a dead person, let alone that a dead prophet's bare bones could accomplish this feat.[13]

Elisha's wondrous acts are often described as the result of power which he himself controls, whether or not Yahweh is assumed to be the ultimate source of that power (see Moberly 2011, 64). Should his deeds challenge readers to revise their "relevant schemata" about divine power? Phenomena similar to Elisha's "miracles" also feature prominently in other narrative genres. Tatar (2003, 61) points out that in "wondertales . . . the supernatural is accepted as part and parcel of everyday reality"; a figure such as a witch "never evokes the slightest degree of surprise or astonishment."[14] The same can also be true with sophisticated literary narratives. Commenting on Kafka's *Metamorphosis*, Todorov (1970, 177) notes the character Gregor Samsa's lack of surprise at being transformed into a kind of enormous vermin, citing a comment by Camus: "One shall never be sufficiently astounded about this lack of astonishment."[15] Todorov adds that Kafka is one

---

more effectively direct one's actions and, in some cases, the manner in which one makes attributions. Meyer, Reisenzein and Schützwohl (1997, 253) add that the first two steps of this process "can be identified with the workings of the surprise mechanism proper, which we take to be an evolutionary old mechanism."

13. Todorov notes another case in which readers may not experience a miraculous event as uncanny; this is when the text belongs to the genre of the "marvelous" (1970, 46–51). In this fictional world, characters and events are not expected to obey the laws and limitations of ordinary reality and therefore do not elicit the feeling of tension which, for Todorov, characterizes the fantastic and the uncanny. The marvelous "characterizes itself by the mere existence of supernatural events, without implicating the reaction those events provoke in the characters" (1970, 52).

14. Nor do genuine *Märchen* evoke anything "uncanny," according to Freud (1947a, 260). The story of Elisha's bones has been called a "wonder story" (e.g., Cogan and Tadmor 1988, 150), an "anecdote . . . about a wonder" (Würthwein 1984, 366), and a "saints' legend" (Shemesh 2008, 32–36). Even if we accept one of these genre designations, the fact is that these stories have now become integrated into the body of scripture, an entirely different genre. As part of scripture, they can no longer be expected to be received in the same way as typical wonder tales and legends. On scripture as an overarching genre designation, see Lasine (1984a, 24–29, 34–35, n. 3).

15. Camus (1942, 171) had actually written that "he" (*il*) shall never be sufficiently amazed, not that "one" (*on*) would be. Camus is describing the naturalness with which the absurd is experienced both by the author of *The Trial* and his character Josef K. For K., being surprised or astonished means that he has lost control of his situation and is therefore vulnerable. After being arrested out of the blue and interrogated at home for unspecified crimes, the inspector in charge comments, "You must be very surprised by this morning's proceedings?" K. answers that he is certainly surprised, but by no means very surprised.

modern writer whose narrators also report seemingly fantastic facts without the characters sharing the readers' experience of astonishment or uncanniness (1970, 181–83). Should we readers of the Bible be equally amazed by the lack of amazement on the part of characters—and the narrator—of the Elisha narratives, if not by our own lack of amazement as readers?

Characters in the Hebrew Bible—including Yahweh—do express surprise or amazement elsewhere.[16] So why not here?[17] Are readers of these narratives assumed to "expect the unexpected"?[18] Are they expected to believe that these miracles *really* occurred? Does the narrator assume the reality of these miracles and take for granted that his target audience shares his assumption? Pinker seems to think so, arguing that "the *casual* description of a dead man's revival upon touching Elisha's bones . . . would be inconceivable if it were not believed that some holiness and magic are retained by the dead" (2007, 77; emphasis added).[19] Alternatively, the narrator could be reporting a change in the structure of reality in the biblical life-world, as he had earlier when recording the entry of holiness into the terrestrial world in Exodus 3 (see Lasine 2010, 32–42).

Or might these narratives be rhetorically designed to evoke a feeling of the uncanny in some readers? According to Freud, "Whatever is associated with death, corpses and the return of the dead, . . . appears uncanny (*unheimlich*) to the very highest degree [to many people] . . . . Our unconscious has as little room

---

The inspector asks, "Not very surprised?" to which K. replies that he is indeed very surprised, but when one has been in the world for thirty years and had to fight his way through alone, he becomes hardened against surprises and does not take them too seriously (Kafka 1994, 19).

16. For example, in Gen. 43:33; Jer. 4:9; 14:9; Hab. 1:5; Ps. 48:5; Qoh. 5:7; cf. Isa. 59:16; 63:5 (of Yahweh being astonished) and Dan. 3:24. The verbs used to express astonishment in these verses include תמה, שמם, and דהם.

17. In Washington Allston's painting, *The Dead Man Restored to Life* (1811-14), all attention is drawn to the emotional reactions of a number of bystanders, while the prophet's bones are hardly visible in the dark background; see Johns (1979, 79 [Fig. 1], 82–83, 87 [Fig. 6]).

18. Whether ancient listeners and readers would be equally surprised by Elijah's ascension would depend upon their interpretation of the cryptic notice about Enoch in Gen. 5:23-24 and their familiarity with the many figures from other cultures who have been favored by a god with some form of immortality.

19. Pinker apparently accepts the Shunammite's view that Elisha is a holy man. While Moberly concedes that the unusual power displayed by Elijah and Elisha is envisaged as "'in their possession,' 'under their control,'" he also notes that the narratives sometimes include something which allows readers to "make sense of what is happening in categories familiar elsewhere in the HB," such as Elisha telling Gahazi that God had not informed him about the Shunammite's distress (2011, 64–65). While these stories "stand in their strangeness," such additions tend to "conform them somewhat . . . to the 'normal' understanding of life with YHWH as attested elsewhere in the HB."

now as it did in the past for the idea of its own mortality" (1947a, 254–55).[20] From this perspective, readers might be expected to view the story of Elisha's bones as uncanny and simultaneously "realistic," in the sense that it reflects the reality of our "immortal" unconscious minds. From this perspective, 2 Kgs 13:20-21 may be reminding readers of their childhood hopes that mortality may not be inevitable *for themselves*. This attitude is well illustrated by a note written by Wordsworth in reference to his "Immorality Ode": "[As a child] I used to brood over the stories of Enoch and Elijah, and almost to persuade myself that, whatever might become of others, I should be translated, in something of the same way, to heaven" (Wordsworth 1947, 463).

Freud does qualify his assertions by noting exceptions to his rule, such as the miracle stories about the reawakening of the dead in the New Testament; these call forth feelings which have nothing to do with the uncanny (1947a, 260). Freud is often understood to mean that potentially uncanny elements within the "generic world" of the NT "testify to the laws of a supernatural or magical universe" (Fletcher 1999, 125).[21] However, some NT resuscitation narratives do report witnesses' emotions of surprise or astonishment. In the story of Jairus's daughter (Mk 5:42; Lk. 8:56), "they" or the "parents" are astounded or amazed (ἐξίστημι). In the case of the widow's son at Nain (Lk. 7:16), fear seized all of them and they glorified God. Elsewhere in the Gospels people are said to be amazed, or wonder, at Jesus's miracles (Mt. 8:27; 9:33; 15:31; Lk. 5:9),[22] and Acts 3:10 reports this reaction to a healing by Peter.

In contrast, stories about the return of the dead which do generate feelings of the uncanny resonate with abandoned childhood fantasies and beliefs and play upon any lingering doubts adults may have about the firmness of the line separating life

---

20. In "The Motif of the Choice of Boxes" (usually called the "Theme of the Three Caskets"), Freud observes that "the creation of the Fates (*Moiren*) is the result of an awareness which warns humanity that it too is a part of nature and therefore subject to the unalterable law of death. Something in humans must struggle against this subjection, for it is only with extreme reluctance that a human relinquishes his exceptional position" (1946c, 33–34). On the child Wordsworth and Tolstoy's child-character Seryozha dreaming about being exceptions to the rule of death as were the biblical Enoch and Elijah, see Lasine (2012, 135–37).

21. Todorov (1970, 46) understands the uncanny in a somewhat different way from Freud. The "fantastic" only lasts as long as the reader (and characters within the story) hesitates in deciding whether what is occurring in the story world conforms to "reality" as commonly defined. If the reader decides that the laws of reality remain intact and are able to explain the phenomena, although the events are still incredible or shocking, the story belongs to the genre of the uncanny (*l'étrange*). For a comparison between Freud and Todorov on the concept of the uncanny, see Fletcher (1999, 124–27).

22. All three passages in Matthew employ θαυμάζω, while Lk. 5:9 has θάμβος.

and death in their life-world.²³ By bringing together our adult sense of reality and our childhood wishes and beliefs within the safety of a narrative world, readers need not be threatened by this clash of realities as they would be if the same things occurred in "real life."²⁴ A final reason why no one within the narrative world of 1–2 Kings is reported to be nonplussed by these wondrous happenings could be that the narrator is allowing readers to give full rein to their own amazement or shock, as in other cases.²⁵

3 Power and immortality: Exalting Elisha's bones

The miraculous powers apparently wielded by Elisha have led many scholars to conclude that 2 Kgs 13:20-21 and the rest of the Elisha narratives are designed to praise this man of God. A smaller number criticize this prophet figure and/or his "prophetism" (e.g. Bergen 1999). Shemesh (2008) is the most ardent advocate for Elisha's greatness. She interprets the prophet's actions in the same way as the Shunammite in 2 Kgs 4:9. That "great woman" calls Elisha a "holy man of God," a phrase not used in reference to any other individual in the Hebrew Bible.²⁶ Shemesh concludes that the Elisha stories are "saints' legends" and attempts to "rebut" any reading of these stories which does not "exalt" the prophet.

However, if the Elisha narratives are viewed as offering little reason to admire this prophet as an ethical or religious figure, then exalting him means bowing down to sheer amoral power.²⁷ We must therefore ask what it is about Elisha and his reported actions which might be considered to exalt him. When discussing 2 Kgs 13:20-21, many commentators speak as if Elisha's bones themselves had the properties of personhood, retaining the identity of the individual they had propped up when he was alive. Among ancient sources, Sirach declares that "from where he lay buried his body (בשרו) prophesied" (Sir. 48:13; NABRE) and Josephus notes that after Elisha's death "*he* still had divine power" (*Ant.* 9.8.6.; emphasis added). Shemesh asserts that "even after his death the man of God could perform miracles." Cohn (2000, 88–89) concludes that "death did not totally defeat" the prophet. Bodner calls this event "Elisha's encore performance" (2013, 150 cf. 147).

---

23. Freud (1947a, 268) believes that children's anxiety is never entirely extinguished. It is usually tied to aloneness, stillness, and darkness, qualities which are all associated with childhood fears of annihilation and abandonment; cf. Piven (2004, 10–12).

24. Because they now reside in what many readers consider to be "scripture," such biblical "folktales" take on a special stamp of reality and authority for those readers.

25. The manner in which the shocking rape and murder of the Levite's concubine are reported in Judges 19 is one such case; see Lasine (1984b, 44–50).

26. On the Shunammite's understanding of "holiness," see Lasine (2016b, 3–9).

27. On Elisha's religious and ethical conduct in 2 Kings 2–6, see Lasine (1991, 42–49, 2011, 9–15, 23–25, 2016b, 11–20). On scholars who view Yahweh and his holy power as amoral, see Lasine (2010, 32–48).

For Hamilton (2001, 451), "Elisha dead is more effective than most people alive!" Brinton claims that the bones "were still so replete with [Elisha's] miraculous individuality, that the corpse revived" (1890, 19). Bergen is more critical of the bones: "If Elisha's bones really wanted something to do, why did they not stop the [Moabite] raids?" as if the bones themselves had desires and were capable of feeling bored.[28]

For all these scholars, the body of the dead prophet remains the *person* Elisha, and "his" effectiveness in performing miracles is no different in kind from that of the living prophet. To imply that Elisha himself resurrected the corpse is to reduce Elisha's self to a concentration of power stripped of all personality.[29] The seeming perdurance of Elisha's identity could be described in the same way that Becker characterizes wealth as a means of symbolic immortality: it "radiates its powers even after one's death" (Becker 1975, 81). Another form of symbolic immortality recognized by Becker is transference, in the sense of participating vicariously in the apparent invulnerability of a hero or group leader (1973, 148–50). Elisha certainly fits the bill for readers who view him as an exalted saint. On his own—both during his life and after his death—Elisha seems to wield power and perform "great deeds" (גדלות; 2 Kgs 8:4) which otherwise are achievable only by Yahweh himself. From this point of view, Elisha is the kind of hero with whom others might identify in order to enjoy a respite from their actual powerlessness and vulnerability.

The narrator of 2 Kgs 13:20-21 shows no interest in the identity or fate of the character who benefits from Elisha's posthumous power, namely, the revived corpse. However, later rabbinic commentators *are* interested in the personality of this very minor character. According to one tradition, the corpse is the virtuous, kindly, and well-loved Shallum, the husband of Huldah the prophetess, whose son Hanamel was a cousin to Jeremiah (*Pirqe R. El.* 33; Friedlander 1916, 244). According to another, it is the son of the Shunammite whom Elisha had resuscitated earlier. The son had died again, only to be revived by the bones of his former healer. However, his third and final existence was very short in duration; after standing up on his feet, he died yet again and was buried in another sepulcher, because he was a sinner.[30] Yet another view is that the man was Ahab's prophet Zedekiah.[31]

---

28. I want to assume that this question is asked with tongue in cheek, but Bergen draws a serious conclusion from it, taking failure to stop the raids as yet another "flaw[ed] performance" by Elisha.

29. In contrast, Overholt (1996, 57) obliquely acknowledges this weak notion of "individuality" when he appeals to Hill's study of the "local hero" in order to make sense of "this otherwise bizarre account." Overholt quotes Hill's statement that "the local hero, being dead, is completely depersonalized, and it is social forces that provide his power" (Overholt 1996, 56; Hill 1992, 63).

30. *Midr. Tehillim* Bk. I, 26, 7; Braude 1959, 363; cf. *b. Sanh.* 47a.

31. *Qoh. Rabb.* 8:10; Cohen (1939, 222; cf. Dray 2006, 105). For Zedekiah ben Kenaanah, see 1 Kgs 22:11-24.

What all these suggestions have in common is that they are *moralizing*; that is, they are interested in the identity of the revived corpse insofar as the identified individual had been a good or an evil person, who did or did not deserve this unique chance to continue living. While we are told enough about Elijah for readers to form their own opinions about whether Elijah merited ascension, 2 Kings 13 provides absolutely no information on whether this particular corpse deserved to live again—or whether Elisha did *not* merit translation.

The most surprising and intriguing of the rabbinical suggestions about the corpse in 2 Kings 13 is the notion that it is the body of the old prophet of Bethel, whose deception led to the death of the man of God from Judah in 1 Kings 13 (Rosenberg 1989, 341). It is surprising because we know that the old prophet wanted his own bones to be laid next to the bones of the man of God after he died (1 Kgs 13:31). Much later, Josiah is informed that the two are in fact buried together (2 Kgs 23:17-18). Rashi's view seems to imply that the old prophet was first buried in Elisha's grave and only later laid to rest in the same grave as the man of God from Judah. The suggestion is intriguing because it links two cases in which there is contact between a corpse and a previously buried prophet's body or bones. Although 2 Kgs 13:20-21 has been used to ground the talmudic rule that an unrighteous person cannot be buried with a righteous one (*b. Sanh.* 47a), 1 Kings 13 and 2 Kings 23 report cases where this does in fact take place—if one accepts that the old prophet of Bethel is wicked and the man of God is an innocent dupe.[32] In 1 Kings 13, laying one corpse's bones against another's ensures that the wicked prophet's bones will remain undisturbed even when Josiah conducts his purge hundreds of years later. It would be quite ironic if that same wicked man's corpse was expelled from Elisha's grave by that true prophet's bones, only to live long enough for his bones to be placed beside those of another true prophet, one whose death had been both miraculous and bizarre.[33]

4 Readers' fear of death and the prospect of an afterlife

Given the extent to which some biblical wisdom and narrative texts heighten mortality salience, one question calls for our attention: Why does the Hebrew Bible generally withhold from readers the most desirable psychological buffer against death anxiety, namely, the prospect of immortality?[34] In their TMT analysis

---

32. On this issue, see Lasine (2012, 94–106).

33. While in 1 Kings 13 the dead man of God's body is repeatedly referred to as a נבלה (carcass, corpse), the corpse in 2 Kings 13 is consistently called the "man" (איש). Could that be due to the fact that the narrator knows that this body will soon turn out *not* to be irreversibly dead?

34. Daniel 12:2 is sometimes cited as an exception to this rule ("and many of those asleep in the dust of the ground shall awake, some to everlasting life and some to disgrace

of religion and mortality salience, Vail and his colleagues assume the "pervasive presence of afterlife beliefs in religions, past and present."[35] They argue that "mortality salience produces increased belief . . . in literal immortality," because this is an "especially powerful means of buffering death anxiety" (2010, 86, 88, 91). Other studies have found a more complex relationship between belief in an afterlife and fear of death. In one, participants "who scored high on belief in a rewarding afterlife but relatively low on religiousness reported the *highest* fear of death" (Wink and Scott 2005, 212; emphasis added).[36]

While such studies rarely mention William James, they tend to support James's view that "religion, . . . for the great majority of our race, means immortality, and nothing else" (1920, 524). Freud also recognizes that hopes of immortality have a buffering effect. In a 1915 address to the B'nai B'rith entitled "We and Death"—that is, "we *Jews*" and death—Freud describes how religions have attempted to "rob death of its significance as the annihilation of life" by making the "life enclosed

and everlasting abhorrence"). Dahood believes that he has found other examples in the book of Psalms: "Since you will not put me in Sheol, nor allow your devoted one to see the Pit" (Ps. 16:10) and "but God will ransom me, from the hand of Sheol will he surely snatch me" (Ps. 49:16 Heb.; Dahood, 1966, 86, 296). In his view, both speakers "firmly believe that [they] will be granted the same privilege accorded Enoch and Elijah; [they are] convinced that God will assume [them] to himself without suffering the pains of death" (1966, 91, 301). Geiringer calls this maneuver the method of self-exception: "We except ourselves from the common laws of mortality whilst readily acknowledging them as far as others are concerned" (1952, 179; cf. Lasine 2012, 139–40). The question remains whether ancient Israelites would interpret Elijah's ascension (and, for that matter, Jonah's rescue from the fish) in terms of their own fear of death or share the certainty of the unconscious mind that it cannot die. Biblical scholars such as Crenshaw contend that "lacking a view of life beyond the grave, . . . Israelites accepted death as inevitable, sometimes, to be sure, with *slight tinges of resignation*"—except in "instances when death came out of season and violently" (1983, 4; emphasis added).

35. Although Vail and his team assert "the *ubiquitous* nature of afterlives in *virtually all* religions," at times they are more cautious, stating only that "*most* religions address the problem of death anxiety . . . through the promise of literal immortality" (2010, 86, 88; emphasis added).

36. According to Wink and Scott, "The presence of a firm view in regard to religion and the afterlife, irrespective of whether it emanates from a secular or sacred ideology, tends to buffer against fear of death" (2005, 212). Individuals with this view "fear death the least because they construe death as personally meaningful." This study focused on American Christians; for observations on Jewish attitudes on the afterlife and religious practice, see Cohen et al. (2003, 293), Cohen et al. (2005, 320–21), and Florian and Kravitz (1983, 605–06). For a survey of several recent studies of afterlife belief and death anxiety, see Jong and Halberstadt (2016, 128–30).

by death into a mere preparation" for a better afterlife (1990, 137).[37] Freud finds it "extremely curious (*merkwürdig*) that our holy scriptures have made no allowance for the human need for a guarantee of continued existence" after death (1990, 137).[38] He considers this to be one of the factors which made it "impossible for the Jewish religion to replace the other ancient religions after their downfall" (1990, 138). On the eve of the next world war, Freud (1950, 117) repeats this assertion more emphatically (and less accurately), claiming that ancient Jewish religion completely dispensed with immortality;[39] the "possibility of a continuation of existence after death is nowhere and never mentioned" in ancient Jewish sources.[40] He also finds this to be "*merkwürdig*."[41]

If James, Freud, and TMT theorists are correct, what are we to make of the fact that the Hebrew Bible does not offer its readers what would seem to be the best of all death anxiety buffers? From their perspective, biblical death reminders would seem to *invite* reader anxiety.[42] In spite of Vail's insistence that virtually all religions offer the prospect of an afterlife, the Hebrew Bible is not the only ancient work which negates any hope of a meaningful existence after death, as Freud was well aware (see n. 42). At times Vail and his colleagues expand their notion of the afterlife to include consciousness persisting after death. One could argue that this idea is reflected in biblical depictions of Sheol,

---

37. A revised version of this address was published in *Imago* later that year; see Freud (1946a). For differences between the two versions, see Solmes (1993, 11–39).

38. Freud removed this observation from the published version of the lecture, which was not directed to a Jewish audience.

39. Post-biblical Judaism is not so ready to dismiss an afterlife as are the vast majority of texts within the Hebrew Bible. For example, in *b. Sanh*. 90a, all Israel is said to have a portion in the world to come, except for individuals who assert that resurrection (המתים תחיית) is not in the Torah. While resurrection is not mentioned in the late-Hellenistic Jewish work known as the Wisdom of Solomon, the souls of the righteous are at peace and "their hope is full of immortality" (Wis. 3:1-4; cf. 2:23; 5:15-16).

40. Freud contrasts the Jews with the ancient Egyptians, who sought to deny death by predicating an existence in the "Beyond." He then proposes that Atenism is the source of the biblical attitude toward personal extinction. This is stressed by Freud in order to bolster the supposed parallel between Mosaic religion and Akhenaten's this-worldly monotheism. As noted by Bernstein (1998, 30–31), Freud also used *merkwürdig* as a keyword to describe his fascination with the fact that ancient Israelites eventually returned to monotheism after having rebelled against Moses and, in Freud's opinion, having murdering the prophet.

41. On the implications of Freud's view, see Chapter 7 §4.

42. Yet, in spite of Vail's insistence that virtually all religions offer the prospect of an afterlife, the Hebrew Bible is not the only ancient work which removes any hope of a meaningful existence after death. Freud, for one, is fully aware of this; in "We and Death," he cites Heine's version of the speech given by the shade of Achilles in Homer's "Odyssey" (9.489-91), in which the hero declares that the lowest life on earth is better than being king over all the decayed dead in Hades (Freud 1990, 137).

if not by Homer's Hades and Babylonian Irkalla[43] as well. The shades in Isaiah and the *Odyssey* do have some sense of their former identity and memories of their past life.[44] However, I would argue that these texts are not designed to offer readers the hope of consciousness after death. Rather, they are a literary means of conveying nonexistence by draining from these locales everything which readers would consider worthy of being called "life." They do so in a way which simultaneously expresses a vague sense of personhood on the part of the shades. As a result, these depictions show the finality of death at the same time as they illustrate Freud's assertion that one cannot imagine oneself dead without remaining present as a spectator.[45]

One reason why Freud may find the Jewish Bible's view of death to be remarkably strange is that he views the personal God Yahweh as a buffer against human vulnerability and lack of control. The Bible shows the external and internal forces of nature to be expressions of a personality with whom we can "negotiate," so that we may feel ourselves at home in the uncanny—*heimisch im Unheimlichen* (1948, 338).[46]

Experts on ancient Greece and Mesopotamia have labeled both cultures "pessimistic," in part due to their lack of a positive afterlife vision.[47] Does that judgment say more about what modern historians believe to be the cause of pessimism than it does about the attitude of ANE cultures? Do modern scholars assume that the main point of religion is to offer its adherents the buffer of immortality? In Chapter 2, I differentiated between pessimistic resignation as a response to death reminders and realistic coping with the unpleasant fact of our

---

43. For example, *GE* VII, 185, Parpola (1997, 97). "Irkalla" ("the Great City") is one of a number of names for the underworld in Akkadian literature; see, for example, Bottéro (1992, 273–74).

44. See Isa. 14:9-20; *Od.* 11.29-635. In the *Odyssey* none of the shades (except for unburied Elpenor and the prophet Teiresias) can converse with Odysseus until they have drunk blood from a sacrifice. The descriptions of the underworld in *Gilgamesh* do not include words spoken by the shades of humans, although they are said to eat clay, see darkness, wear feathers like birds, and tremble (*GE* VII, 184-93, XII, 20; Parpola 1997, 97, 115). As for Egypt, Groenewegen-Frankfort (1987, 30–36) points out that many Old Kingdom private tomb paintings depict scenes from daily life but the dead tomb owner is not portrayed as participating in any of those activities. He merely sees or watches (*m33*), passively. His watching is his only "tenuous link with life" (1987, 35).

45. In this sense, "Hades . . . is the ultimate human experience," as Sourvinou-Inwood says of the Greek underworld (1996, 72).

46. Freud's own attitude toward death is complex. While he believes that it is "better to grant death its place in reality and in our thoughts, to which it is entitled" (1990, 142; cf. 1946a, 354), he does not always take his own advice; see Chapter 7 §5.

47. Jakob Burckhardt claims that "Greek consciousness . . . probably exceeds anything in other literatures in its total pessimism and despair" (1998, 94). On pessimism in ancient Mesopotamia and Egypt, see Chapter 2, n. 3.

inevitable extinction. In the latter case, reading about death within the safety of the scriptural world can itself act as a buffer against the kind of anxiety which might lessen our ability to cope with life in the world of the Hebrew Bible, a world in which Yahweh's human children must deal with the often unpredictable psychology of their never-dying—yet emotionally vulnerable—divine Father.[48] How Jonah copes with life in Yahweh's world—and how we might do the same—is the subject of Part Two of this study.

---

48. On the psychology of the personal God Yahweh, see Lasine (2001, 177–263, 2002, 38–50).

Part Two

JONAH AND THE HUMAN CONDITION IN YAHWEH'S WORLD

Chapter 5

JONAH AS A LITERARY CHARACTER

The next two chapters of this investigation focus on the "human condition" of one biblical character, Jonah. This prophet has often been viewed as an "Everyman" figure. Gaines asserts that Jonah "becomes Everyone" in the sense that he "endures what feels to him like an unbearable burden." He is a "profoundly *human being*" whose "follies are ours" (2003, 9; cf. Ostriker 2007, 117). P. -E. Lacocque believes that Jonah is "very human" in a more general sense: "His struggles, ambivalence, and existential issues are easily identified as our very own as well" (1984, 228, n. 39).

The most influential understanding of Jonah's similarity to ourselves is that offered by psychologist Abraham Maslow: "So often we run away from the responsibilities dictated (or rather suggested) by nature, by fate, even sometimes by accident, just as Jonah tried in vain to run away from *his* fate" (1971, 35). For Maslow, Jonah's running away is a strong indicator that the prophet displays a "Jonah complex." A number of other psychologists (and philosophers) have also used the term "Jonah complex" to denote a variety of psychological phenomena, usually based on only one or two of the events reported in the biblical book. Many biblical scholars have also analyzed Jonah's personality, but without employing, or creating, a diagnostic label; in most cases, they too have no difficulty making judgments about the prophet's defining traits.

In this chapter, I will argue that the book's forty-eight verses do not furnish us with sufficient data to support *any* definitive psychological profile of the prophet, whether complex or simple, idiosyncratic or universal. In fact, the biblical Jonah gives no more indication of having any sort of "Jonah complex" than Sophocles's Oedipus shows signs of having an "Oedipus complex."[1] At the same time, the book's plot, informational gaps, quoted speeches, and network of intertextual allusions

---

1. See C. Segal (2001, 41). Paul (1991, 268–69) notes that when Freud alludes to Sophocles's Oedipus in *The Interpretation of Dreams*, he is showing "how the play serves as a collective, publicly constituted fantasy that corresponds to the unconscious . . . fantasies harbored by each member of the audience as repressed residues of childhood," rather than asserting that the character Oedipus has this complex. This chapter will ask whether the same may be true for readers of Jonah's story.

make this text uniquely capable of evoking readers' fundamental fantasies and fears about their condition as human beings. As a result, readers may interpret Jonah's personality in ways which express more about their own personalities, expectations, values, academic paradigm, and group identity than they say about this elusive biblical figure.

1 Psychological judgments on Jonah's character

A literary character is usually thought to be "coherent" if he or she seems to possess robust personality traits and is consistent—or consistently inconsistent—in behavior, although some literary theorists argue that the concept of a coherent character or self is obsolescent, illusory, or a tool of ideology (see Lasine 2012, 5–19). For some observers, Jonah is consistently presented as an "anti-hero,"[2] or, more specifically, as an "anti-Moses," an "anti-Elijah,"[3] an "anti-Noah" (Kim 2007a, 503), or as Jeremiah's "antitype" (Wolff 1986, 120). Negative traits often attributed to Jonah include self-pity (Blank 1955, 29–31), self-centeredness,[4] petulance,[5] and "know-it-all hubris" (U. Simon 1999, xxii). He has also been accused of arrogance (e.g., Bickerman 1967, 13) and "arrogant dogmatism" (Zornberg 2008, 166), as well as "colossal egocentrism" (Trible 1994, 202), excessive concern with his self-image (Robinson 1991, 533), hypocrisy, and self-love.[6] Kassel (2012, 414) views Jonah's behavior as resembling "that of a boy in the midst of puberty . . . recalcitrant, stubborn, egotistical, uncommunicative and lazy." For Gaines, the Jonah of ch. 1 is even more immature: "Like a two year old child, Jonah throws a temper tantrum" (2003, 38). For others, Jonah shows signs of psychological disorders such as acute depression (Zornberg 2008, 275; McCarthy 1980, 62–63), a "paranoid-schizoid position of isolation" (Salberg 2008, 327; cf. 320), and "craving narcissism" (Capps 1992, 153).[7]

A second group of commentators consider Jonah's character flaws to be typically "human." Ostriker takes Jonah to be an "Everyman" who exhibits "our stubborn

---

2. For example, A. LaCocque (2004, 83), D. Marcus (1995, 96), Gaines (2003, 112–13), and Capps (1992, 149). Cf. Sherwood (2000, 27, 110, 243).

3. Kim (2007, 503); cf. LaCocque and Lacocque (1990, 150) on Jonah as an anti-Elijah. Gaines (2003, 111) contrasts Elijah's supposedly "noble" reason for seeking an end to his life to Jonah's "puny" statement, "for I would rather die than live." On Elijah's desire to die, see Lasine (2012, 123–24) and Chapter 2 §4.

4. For example, Craig (1993, 140), Neil (1962, 967), and Hays (2010, 306).

5. For example, Michaels (1987, 236), Sasson (1990, 297), and Capps (1992, 157).

6. For example, Holbert (1996, 438) ("self-centred, lazy, hypocritical").

7. A. Lacocque (2007, 169) detects signs of a "narcissistic complex of inferiority" and "fear of success" in Jonah's reaction to the repentance of the Ninevites. On similar "diagnoses" of other biblical prophets, see Chapter 2 §4.

fear of change, our rejection of connection and love, our secret death wish" (2007, 117).⁸ A third group observes a much more positive Jonah; here the prophet is at times presented as "a man of faith" driven by "zeal for divine integrity" (Ackerman 1987, 240), a "fundamental[ly] serious" prophet who is characterized by "his utter fidelity to himself" (U. Simon 1999, xxi, 35), or a victim who has been given an "unbearable mission" and is then forced to "defend his dignity" in face of Yahweh's attempts to use him as a "robot" or "guilt offering" (Frolov 1999, 92–93, 97).

2 What we are, and are not, told about Jonah's situation and character

If we are to evaluate these remarkably diverse views of Jonah and the theological and historical assumptions upon which they depend, we must first appreciate how *little* the narrator tells us about the prophet's personality, motivations, and emotions.⁹ At the very start, readers are not told what Yahweh specifically wants Jonah to proclaim against Nineveh.¹⁰ Our only textual clues to God's intent are his statement that Nineveh's "evil" has come up to him, the narrator's later report that Yahweh did not do "what he said he would do" to the Ninevites, and the Ninevite king's reference to his people's "evil ways" and the "violence that is in their palms" (3:8).¹¹

In stark contrast to the furious and jealous Yahweh of Nah. 1:2-3, in Jonah, we are not told that God was angry at the Ninevites, even though the Ninevites

---

8. Cf. Gaines (2003, 9, 111), P. -E. Lacocque (1984, 228, n. 39), and the other commentators quoted in Chapter 1 §5.

9. Landes (1999, 274) finds "no fewer than 63 places in the text where the author's deliberate or inadvertent withholding of information poses at least some interpretive issue for the reader."

10. Sasson (1990, 66, 72-75) renders the expression קרא על (1:2) with "declare doom upon," while Limburg (1993, 37) chooses "preach." Both translations interpret this rather vague negative expression in terms of the translator's understanding of Jonah's mission and his proclamation in 3:4. When comparing this passage with similar verses, Sasson concedes that all of the examples with על imply only "imposing an (unpleasant) fate upon something." Limburg's rendering of "preach" leaves open the possibility that God wants Jonah to urge the Ninevites to repent before it is too late. Sasson (1990, 236) and U. Simon (1999, 4) both seem to accept Jonah's actual words in 3:4 as reflecting God's original order to Jonah. Admittedly, Jonah's use of הפך in 3:4 and the expression קרא אל/על employed by God in 1:2 and 3:2 preclude certainty here (see, for example, Ben Zvi 2003, 34; on הפך, see n. 22 in this chapter). In Jon. 1:2, God could simply be telling Jonah to indict, condemn, or denounce Nineveh for its wickedness. Ironically, Jonah's harsh words in 3:4 follow God's use of אל in 3:2, which is *less* harsh than the word על which God had used in 1:2.

11. The root for "evil" (רָעָה/רַע/רָעַע) has a variety of nuances in the book, depending upon the situation and the character in relation to whom the word is applied. See, for example, Sasson (1990, 76).

themselves later assume that this is the case (3:9).¹² Dozeman (1989, 214) takes the Ninevites' assumption as fact. However, divine anger is not always said to accompany divinely ordered destruction. For example, Yahweh is not said to be angry when he sends the Flood,¹³ although the LXX removes the divine emotions of pain and regret felt by Yahweh in the MT (Gen. 6:6-7) and replaces them with the emotion of anger (ἐθυμώθην; 6:7). In the book of Jonah, it is only Jonah himself who feels anger (4:1, 9). One of Jonah's complaints about Yahweh's personality is that Yahweh is "long to anger" (4:2), that is, that he does not get angry quickly enough when anger is called for.

Such gaps continue through the chapter. For example, we are not explicitly told why Jonah fled from Yahweh's presence by heading in the opposite direction. Some commentators take Jonah's flight as an indication that he foolishly thinks that he could escape Yahweh's "reach." In Roth's formulation, "Jonah assumes that he can escape God by the normal human device of going away and leaving no address" (1969, 71).¹⁴ Limburg (1993, 89, n. 152) compares Jonah with Cain: "Cain, too, ran away 'from the presence of the LORD.'" However, Cain is not "running away from" God; Cain knows that he has been driven from the face of the earth and will be hidden from Yahweh's face (v. 14). Genesis 4:16 reports that Cain "went out from the face of Yahweh and settled in the land of Nod." This does not imply that Cain is (or thinks he is) outside the sphere of Yahweh's control. Rather, he is away from the direct presence in which he had conversed with Yahweh. One might compare this to a courtier who is dismissed from the royal court. He may be distant from the presence of the king who sits on his throne in the palace, but not from that king's power or influence (see Lasine 2001, 9–12). For a prophet such as Jonah, the notion that he could successfully evade Yahweh would indicate an abysmal ignorance of the nature of the God whose messages he is supposed to transmit.¹⁵

When the captain implores Jonah to call to his god (v. 6), Jonah is not said to reply, let alone call to Yahweh. There is no mention of Jonah asking God for instructions before he tells the sailors to heave him overboard (v. 12). Nor can we answer Magonet's question: "Why does not Jonah just jump overboard instead of

---

12. On Nah. 1:1-3, see Chapter 6 §4.

13. In fact, God is *never* said to be angry in the book of Genesis; the first time he is said to feel this emotion is when he is angry at Moses's repeated attempts to evade *his* prophetic commission (Exod. 4:14; see Lasine 2010, 48–49).

14. Cf. Redditt (2008, 261) and Wolff (1986, 139). According to *Mek. Pisḥa* I, 88–99, Jonah's motivation for his initial flight from his mission is a case of "honoring the son" (i.e., Israel) rather than a concern for his own reputation or a desire for vengeance against Gentile outsiders. Since Jonah knew that the Gentiles were close to repentance, he did not want recalcitrant Israel to be condemned by contrast. See Sherwood (2000, 90–91) for examples of scholars who do "emphatically Mainstream things, like converting the narrative into diatribe against the narrow-minded Jew."

15. For an interpretation of Jonah's flight based on the motif of the runaway slave/servant, see Ben Zvi (2003, 66–73; cf. Gaines 2003, 38).

making them throw him and thus become guilty of 'shedding innocent blood'?" (1992, 143).[16] Furthermore, there is no evidence that Jonah offered a sacrifice and performed what he vowed, even though he, as speaker of the psalm in ch. 2, claims to have done both.

In addition, the narrator never attributes fear to the prophet, although Josephus (*Ant.* 9. 10. 2) and many modern readers assume that Jonah flees God out of fear.[17] Moreover, ch. 1 is the only part of the book in which *any* character expresses or displays fear. In Jon. 3:5 the Ninevites are said to react to Jonah's prophecy not with "fearing" but with "believing," and the same is true of the king's reaction in vv. 6-9. Similarly, in ch. 4, the emotions at issue are anger and pity, not fear. Finally, Jonah never expresses or displays a fear of death, in spite of the circumstances, an absence highlighted by its contrast with the "great" fear of the sailors (1:5, 10).

The prayer Jonah utters in the belly of the fish would seem to offer an ideal opportunity to learn about his character. Abela agrees, calling the prayer "the most important outpouring of Jonah's spirit." However, the prophet could simply be reciting an existing psalm, or portions of different existing songs which come closest to fitting his unique and bizarre situation and which express typical expectations concerning God as protector and rescuer.[18] This would account for the ways in which Jonah's prayer clashes with his situation. Most strikingly, the psalm makes no mention of Jonah being in the fish. In addition, Jonah refers to the danger as already past, speaking as someone who has already been saved from Sheol. And while the rescued swimmer of the psalm was surrounded by the expanse and depth of the waters with his head wrapped in seaweed, nothing was said in ch. 1 about Jonah struggling in the boundless sea. In fact, the sea calmed when Jonah entered it.

Nor had ch. 1 given any indication that Jonah had been thinking about God's "holy temple,"[19] which figures prominently in his prayer. We were not even told where Jonah was located within his "own country" (4:2) when God first commanded him to go to Nineveh, let alone that he had been in Jerusalem. In fact,

---

16. The fact that Jonah's motive is unstated leaves open the possibility that the prophet could be seeking to transform his situation into a scenario in which he plays the role of a sacrificial victim who is "innocent blood," as the sailors believe would be the case if they hurled him overboard.

17. For example, in Melville's *Moby-Dick* Father Mapple gives a sermon in which Jonah's motive for flight *was* fear of the Ninevites: "Jonah, appalled at the hostility he should raise, fled from his mission" (2002, 53). A. Lacocque assumes that the book of Jonah allows us to gain a quite complete understanding of the prophet's personality and emotions, including his fears—even on the most abstract level: "What Jonah dreads most is to become Jonah, for to become Jonah means to be committed to other(s)" (2004, 86).

18. Whatever the poem's origins, Hunter (2001, 152) is correct to conclude that, as it stands, the psalm "is far from mere pastiche."

19. Guillaume (2009, 1) believes that "it is far from obvious that the 'palace [היכל] of your sanctity' in Jon. 2:4 and 7 refers to the temple of Jerusalem."

the name "Israel" never appears in the book, although Jonah does identify himself to the ship captain as a "Hebrew" (1:9). Finally, in the psalm, Jonah claims that it was Yahweh who threw him into the heart of the seas (v. 4). If we assume that Jonah is speaking "after the fact" in ch. 2, this statement implies that his own call for the sailors to throw him overboard was a way of enacting what he perceived to be Yahweh's will.

Thus, there is no basis for Landes's assertion that Jonah's psalm refers to "his near-death-by-drowning that Yahweh has punitively instigated" and that the distress to which Jonah refers is "from what he encountered in the sea" after being thrown overboard (1999, 283). Nothing in the text indicates that Jonah nearly drowned in the calm sea in the moment[s] before the fish swallowed him. Landes supports the idea that Yahweh is punishing Jonah with the fish by noting that the verb בלע ("swallow") regularly has a pejorative connotation in the Hebrew Bible. Stories involving sea monsters devouring humans regularly present such events as negative in nature, as I will discuss later. In the case of Jonah, however, readers' initial expectation of negativity is being prompted only to be reversed by the fish's unexpected salvific function.[20]

Jonah's role in ch. 3 is restricted to the first four verses. Jonah now obeys God's renewed order to proclaim against the great city of Nineveh, although the reason why Jonah obeyed is left unclear. According to Ingram (2012, 148), Jonah then "blasted the Ninevites with a hell-and-damnation sermon, instead of following God's command to proclaim grace to them." Yet this "sermon" consists of only five words, and there is no clear evidence that God had told Jonah to proclaim grace to the Ninevites.[21] For readers conversant with other biblical confrontations between a prophet and a king, the fact that Jonah does not proceed to make his doom proclamation directly to the king is surprising, but not as surprising as the fact that the prophet disappears from the scene after this.

---

20. Landes adds that Jonah himself "has no sense of being punished by the fish"; in fact, he "seems to be quite happy inside the fish." Neither conclusion is supported by the text; the narrator gives us no hint that Jonah is ever aware of being in (or having been in) a fish's belly.

21. While Hebrew הפך ("overthrow") usually implies a turning upside down from safety to destruction (e.g., in 2 Kgs 21:13), it can also signify a reversal in a positive sense, from sinfulness to repentance (see, for example, Sasson 1990, 234–35, 267–68). In the case of the *niphal* feminine participle נהפכת in Jon. 3:4, the negative sense is much more likely. The same verb is used consistently in the Hebrew Bible for God's destruction of Sodom, and the prophet Jeremiah employs the verb in an entirely different context to remind readers of the Sodom story (Jer. 20:16). U. Simon (1999, 29) calls "dubious" the notion that "alongside the primary negative sense, to which the prophet overtly refers, there is also the subliminal possibility that the city will *turn* from evil to good." He points out that the narrator does not call our attention to this latent ambiguity and that the moral alternation of the Ninevites in v. 10 is expressed by שוב, not הפך. Finally, the Ninevites themselves take Jonah's use of הפך in the negative sense (see, for example, Sasson 1990, 267, 295).

Chapter 4 begins with the narrator telling us that something ("it")[22] was greatly evil to Jonah and angered him. This verse immediately follows our being told that God "repented of the evil" and did not do to Nineveh what he said he would do to them (3:10). This suggests that Jonah's reported feelings in v. 1 are a response to God's decision concerning Nineveh, even though we have heard nothing about the prophet's emotions since he was expelled by the fish (and little prior to that).[23] Much is left unsaid here. Has Jonah already waited forty days and then realized that the destruction will not occur or did Yahweh somehow make Jonah aware of his decision concerning Nineveh as soon as he had made it?

In the next verse, the prophet complains to Yahweh by quoting Yahweh's self-characterization as merciful in Exod. 34:6. If Jonah's oracle in 3:4 did express Yahweh's intention toward Nineveh, the prophet's objection in 4:2 is that Yahweh had committed himself to destroying the city—with no possibility of remission of punishment—and then remitted punishment anyway. It is often noted that Jonah lists only Yahweh's merciful attributes, omitting mention of Yahweh's vengeance, jealousy, and punishment of the guilty, which accompany the attribute formula in Exod. 34:6-7, Nah. 1:3, and other passages. The formulation in Joel 2:12-14 is uniquely similar to Jon. 4:2 except in one crucial sense: "'Yet even now,' declares Yahweh, 'turn to me with all your heart,' ... for he repents of the evil. Who knows whether he will not turn and repent?" Joel[24] seems to be assuring Israel that God will certainly "repent from the evil" if they repent, only to go on and suggest that Yahweh *might* repent. In contrast, Jonah's position is often taken to be that once an unconditional doom oracle has been given, Yahweh should not turn and repent, whether or not the guilty parties turn and repent after hearing that oracle. In this case, the guilty Ninevites have no covenant relationship to Yahweh and speak only of "Elohim."

Readers must also decide what to make of Jonah's claim that he had made these objections to Yahweh when he was still in his own country. No such statement is mentioned in ch. 1. The question "Was this not the/my word?" appears only here and in the Israelites' rhetorical question to Moses in Exod. 14:12. In that verse,

---

22. As Trible (1994, 197–98) points out, the referent for "it" in 4:1 is not clearly demarcated. Perry eliminates this vagueness in a way which leaves readers with the most negative impression of the prophet, by translating v. 1 with "Now Jonah sinned a great sin, and he was distressed" (2006, 143).

23. In general, Jonah's words tend to feature what he claims to know (1:12; 4:2), not what he feels. Von Rad (1965, 292) and Sasson (1990, 349) both describe Jonah as "aloof" from others. At times, he also seems detached from *his own* situation. Rosen and Michaels point out that when the storm overtakes his ship, Jonah is "perfectly unsurprised and unfrantic," sleeping "as if indifferent to the general terror" (1987, 224; Michaels 1987, 232). However, these observations say less about Jonah's personality than about the kind of information which the narrator has chosen to impart to readers.

24. If we assume that it is the prophet Joel who is listing Yahweh's attributes here, and not Yahweh characterizing himself in the third person.

the people claim that when they were still in Egypt, they told Moses to leave them alone, since it was better for them to do slave labor for the Egyptians than to die in the wilderness.[25] In both verses the question ends with a reference to the country in which the questioner claims to have been located when he/they made the alleged statement. Do these parallels imply that Jonah may not have made these objections at the start? In other words, is his question merely a way of saying "I told you so," as some commentators have suggested?[26] The wilderness wandering narrative in Exodus-Numbers tells us enough about the mentality of the murmuring Israelites for readers of the Hebrew Bible to strongly question the people's veracity when they claim to have objected to leaving Egypt. Whether a given reader will suspect that Jonah is also offering a "revisionist history" will largely depend upon that reader's prior judgments about Jonah's character. If the Israelites in Exodus 14 are merely saying "I told you so," the likelihood increases that the function of this intertextual allusion is to prompt readers to consider the same possibility for Jonah.

Jonah then departs from the city and makes a *sukkah* ("booth" or "hut") for himself there, so that he can observe what becomes of the city, while sitting "under/beneath it in the shade" (v. 5). Next God "prepares" a *qiqayon* plant to provide shade for the prophet. The narrator does not explain why extra shade would be needed; nothing had been said about Jonah's *sukkah* being inadequate to that task. Nor have we been told that Yahweh (or a phenomenon like the later "cutting east wind")[27] destroyed Jonah's booth, making it necessary for the plant to come to the prophet's rescue.[28]

---

25. U. Simon (1999, 36) notes that "the same expression is used by Reuben in Egypt (Gen 42:22)." However, in that verse, the phrasing is different (הלוא אמרתי אליכם). More importantly, in the Genesis passage, we have evidence from both the character and the narrator that Reuben really did say what he claims to have said (cf. Gen. 42:22 and 37:21-22).

26. For example, Sasson (1990, 296). Wolff interprets the verse in terms of his extremely negative assessment of the prophet's personality. He calls Jonah's question "the 'I told you so' of the arrogant dogmatist," observing that it "reveals the fact that the know-all ends up in hopeless despair" (1986, 166). Wolff notes the verbal similarity between Exod. 14:12 and Jon. 4:2 but does not ask whether the Israelites' question is also a case of "I told you so."

27. For "cutting" as the meaning of the *hapax* חֲרִישִׁית, see Tucker (2006, 98–99).

28. Commentators attempt to explain this seeming inconsistency in a variety of ways. Sasson says the plant gives "welcome shade . . . when a booth *may* not have been enough" (1990, 317; emphasis added). Gunn and Fewell (1993, 141) assume that "the booth has proved inadequate." U. Simon (1999, 35) takes for granted that Jonah's booth is "rickety." Good (1962, 455) asserts that the *sukkot* mentioned in Isa. 1:8 and Job 27:18 denotes "flimsy" objects. Yet even in those cases, there is nothing necessarily "flimsy" or "rickety" about temporary structures which successfully fulfill a protective function like a hut in a vineyard or an insect's cocoon. The *sukkah* in Isa. 1:8 is also paralleled to a besieged city, that is, a structure which is still standing and capable of resisting siege. On a cocoon as

God[29] then prompts Jonah to experience a series of emotional ups and downs. First Jonah feels "evil" from the sun and then faint (vv. 6, 8). Next he feels greatly happy or glad (שמח) about the shade-giving plant, only to become so angry when the plant withers that he renews his death wish. Yahweh then characterizes Jonah's anger as being driven by "pity."[30] The book concludes abruptly, without readers having a chance to hear Jonah's response—if any—to Yahweh's closing question (if it *is* a question[31]) concerning the appropriateness of Jonah's anger and God's implied pity toward Nineveh.[32] Thus, while we are allowed to hear Jonah's complaint about Yahweh's characteristic mercy and the prophet's repeated wish to die, the book's final chapter does not supply a definite reason for Jonah finding divine mercy to be inappropriate here or the exact reasons for his initial request to die.

Given the absence of information about Jonah's family situation and his life after the journey to Nineveh, it is hardly surprising that we are told nothing about the prophet's death or his feelings about dying. Did he still believe that it was better for him to die than to live? Several later expansions of his story attempt to fill in these blanks. *3 Maccabees* claims that Jonah "returns," presumably to his own home.[33] The first-century work *The Lives of the Prophets* claims that Jonah is the

---

shelter, cf. Modell (1976, 296): "A cocoon is also similar to a fortress, where nothing leaves and nothing enters."

29. In 4:4, it is "Yahweh" who is said to ask Jonah if it is appropriate for him to be angry. In v. 6, "Yahweh Elohim" prepares the plant. In vv. 7-8, "Elohim" prepares the worm and the wind. In v. 9, "Elohim" asks whether it is appropriate for Jonah to be angry about the withering of the plant. And in vv. 10-11, it is "Yahweh" who asks the book's final question. On the variation in the use of divine names in the book, see, for example, Limburg (1993, 45).

30. Is Yahweh intentionally *mis*characterizing Jonah's reaction? After all, losing the benefit of the plant about which he had been "greatly" glad is hardly the same as "caring" or "feeling pity" for it. See Chapter 6 §4 for other views of Yahweh's motives in this scene.

31. Guillaume (2006, 244) and Cooper (1993, 158) both contend that Yahweh may be declaring "as for me, I will not have pity over/do not care about Nineveh." However, both admit that the verse can be read both as a question and as a declaration, pointing to Job 2:10 as a similarly ambivalent utterance. Guillaume also notes that the LXX takes אחוס לא "at face value and renders it with the future indicative of φείδομαι: 'I will not spare . . . .'" On the debate over the better understanding of v. 11, see Ben Zvi (2009, 2–13).

32. Cooper (1993, 156) points to other gaps in ch. 4: "Even assuming that Jonah resented his prophetic 'loss of face,' there is not the slightest indication that he begrudged the Ninevites their salvation, nor does he express any opinion about the proper divine response to human initiative." In addition, God never says "that he was merciful to the Ninevites because of their repentance."

33. According to *3 Macc.*, the divine father watched over Jonah, when he "wasted away in the belly of the sea monster [κῆτος] raised in the depths," and then "revealed him to all his relatives unscathed" (6:8; NETS; on κῆτος in Jonah and Greek heroic tales, see Chapter 6, n. 22). Cf. Josephus *Ant.* 9.10.2. "After giving them this message, he returned [ὑποστρέφω]"

son of the old widow who is resuscitated by Elijah in 1 Kings 17. In this version, Jonah's mother accompanies the prophet on his journeys after his proclamation against Nineveh until she dies and is buried by her dutiful son. Later, Jonah himself dies and is buried (10:1-11; Hare 1985, 392–93). In contrast, *Midr. Tehillim* 26 reports that Jonah entered the garden of Eden without having died, since God had tested him both in the fish and in the depths of the sea (Braude 1959, 363). In this tradition, Jonah becomes the second biblical prophet who wants to die but is permanently prevented from dying by the God who had commissioned him.

Together, these traditions underscore the lack of personal information about the prophet in the Hebrew Bible, including his parents and his childhood. The claim that Jonah is the son of the non-Israelite widow of Zarephath calls our attention to the fact that Jonah never refers to Israel and only identifies himself as a "Hebrew" to his shipmates. The lack of a nurturing maternal figure in the life of the biblical Jonah is underscored by the contrasting report in *The Lives of the Prophets*, which stresses how Jonah's widowed mother accompanies him on his travels both before and after the time of the biblical book.

Viewed as a group, both the biblical and the post-biblical traditions also call our attention to the absence of a male parental figure in the book of Jonah, unless we take God to be that figure when he converses with Jonah in ch. 4. As I will discuss in the next chapter, Yahweh can be, and has been, viewed both as a caring and patient father and as a harsh and manipulative parental figure in the book. Jonah's apparent detachment from all human support systems in the Bible makes his relationship with Yahweh even more crucial for his survival. This, in turn, emphasizes how risky it is for Jonah to resist being submissively dependent upon Yahweh. The fact that Jonah is not more severely punished by his God is a testimony to Yahweh's tolerance toward prophets who give him a hard time (see Chapter 2 §4). Those of us who are *not* prophets cannot assume that Yahweh will have the same tolerance for our own attempts at asserting our autonomy and independence.

3 *"Jonah complexes" and our own*

Some readers base their conclusions about Jonah's character on the book's many metaphors of enclosure. After sleeping in the recesses of the ship (ירכתי הספינה), Jonah is encased in the innards (מעי) of the fish. From this location, he speaks of being in "the belly (בטן) of Sheol," "the heart of the seas," the "deep" (תהום), and the "pit" (שחת) and longs for Yahweh's "holy temple." And in ch. 4, Jonah himself builds the sheltering *sukkah* and receives temporary shelter from the *qiqayon* plant.

According to some commentators, this series of enclosures indicates that Jonah consistently *chooses* to be "embedded," as a psychological defense against risk.

(Marcus 1937, 112–13; trans. modified). In the Hebrew Bible, however, readers are not even told whether Jonah has a family, let alone how old he was when God commanded him to go to Nineveh.

In support, several point to Maslow's version of the "Jonah complex." Maslow bases his professedly "non-Freudian" concept on Jonah's flight to Tarshish (1971, 35). Although the biblical narrator supplies no motivation for Jonah's action, Maslow knows what it is; like Jonah, "many of us evade our constitutionally suggested vocations" (1971, 35).

Philosophers Bachelard and Sartre, on the other hand, base their "Jonah complexes" on Jonah's being swallowed by the big fish, rather than on his flight. For Sartre, "Jonah in the stomach of the whale," like "the stone in the stomach of the ostrich," is the "symbol of the 'digested indigestible'"; the known object "is entirely within me, assimilated, transformed into myself, . . . but at the same time it is impenetrable. . . . It remains outside" (1943, 625).[34] For Bachelard, "the Jonah complex is a psychological phenomenon of deglutition" (1948, 144). Jonah in the "whale" symbolizes a primitive urge to gluttonously swallow nutriment without the necessity of chewing it first. The fear of being swallowed, or being digested after being ripped apart by teeth, can indeed point to fear that one's individual self or identity might be engulfed or annihilated. But this is *not* a danger which is faced or feared by the biblical Jonah, as it is by literary characters who have been compared to Jonah, such as Robinson Crusoe.[35] Moreover, if Sartre and Bachelard's notions were actually applied to the book of Jonah, the figure with the "complex" would have to be the big fish, not the prophet!

All these versions of the "Jonah complex" focus on the topological dimension of human existence. This involves, among other things, our experiences of enclosure and exposure, as well as the kind of metabolic exchange between inside and outside described by these French philosophers. The same is true of Fromm's contention that Jonah's "going into the ship, going into the ship's belly, falling asleep, being in the ocean, and being in the fish's belly" are all symbols which "stand for the same inner experience," namely, "a condition of being protected and isolated, of

---

34. Sartre is contrasting his "Jonah complex" with ordinary assumptions about knowing. As he writes in a 1939 essay, the expression "he devoured her with his eyes" and "many other signs sufficiently mark the illusion common to both realism and idealism, according to which to know is to eat. . . . We have all believed that the Mind-Spider (*l'Esprit-Araignée*) drew things into its web, covered them with a white spittle and slowly swallowed them, reducing them to its own substance" (1947, 29). Contrast Nietzsche's idea that the modern person drags around with her "an immense multitude of indigestible stones of knowledge" (1964b, 127–28; see Lasine 2012, 24–55). While Sartre himself points to the undigested stone in an ostrich's stomach, Nietzsche alludes to the stones clattering inside the body in *Märchen*. Nietzsche is probably alluding to "The Wolf and the Seven Young Goats" tale rather than "Little Red Cap," since the former emphasizes the element of the noise made when the wolf tries to walk with the stones inside him. On "Little Red Cap"/"Little Red Riding Hood," see the essays in Dundes (1989).

35. For example, Fisch (1986, 218), who suggests that Jonah's many trials "may be used as a kind of midrash on *Robinson Crusoe*." On Crusoe's fear of being swallowed up, see Heims (1983).

safe withdrawal from communication with other human beings," like "the fetus in the mother's womb" (1951, 22). Biblicists Gunn and Fewell (1993, 130) also view Jonah in this fashion, as I noted in Chapter 2. Following Ackerman, they "see Jonah seeking security in 'enclosure' . . . to escape the challenges and . . . the contradictions of the . . . 'outside' world."

The opposition between enclosure and exposure is also central to Maslow's Jonah complex. In practice, not risking change and growth is a form of what Schachtel calls "secondary embeddedness," a preference for the seeming safety of enclosure over the risk of exposing oneself to the dangers inherent in change and exploration. The "danger of separation from embeddedness" triggers anxiety (1959, 44, 185–212). According to Schachtel, long after passing through the intrauterine phase of life, people continue to seek womblike shelter, first in the parental home and ultimately in the habitat they create for themselves through their habitual attitudes and behaviors (1959, 176, 185, 193).

In contrast, psychologist James McCarthy understands the book in terms of *escape* from embeddedness, illustrating "the mythological abundance of the struggle of the embedded self for autonomy" (1980, 191). The story represents the "first recorded symbolic dramatic treatment of the connection between depression, the fear of death, and separation anxiety" (1980, 62; cf. 63). According to McCarthy, "The flight . . . the casting of Jonah into the sea, and the swallowing . . . by the whale all reiterate the theme of the child's fear of death via being devoured by angry parent figures" (1980, 62).

Jung's version of the "Jonah-and-the-whale complex" attempts to assimilate the biblical story to the pattern of "the night-sea journey" (Jung 1967, 210; cf. Steffen 1982, 20–27). The typical night-sea journey proceeds from east (darkness and death) to west (light and life), thereby expressing the process of individuation which a person may undergo during the second half of life. Being swallowed by a monster represents regression "back to the intra-uterine, pre-natal condition" (Jung 1967, 419; cf. Eliade 1960, 218–23). In fact, one travels further back beyond the mother, "leaving the sphere of personal psychology altogether, irrupt[ing] into the collective psyche where Jonah saw the 'mysteries' . . . in the whale's belly" (1967, 419–20). In "the parable of Jonah . . . a person sinks into his childhood memories and vanishes from the existing world. . . . [He] finds himself apparently in deepest darkness, but then has unexpected visions of a world beyond." For Jung, the "beyond" is *within*; it is "the stock of primordial images which everybody brings with him as his human birthright" (1967, 408).

Jung's claim that Jonah saw a form of "mighty mystery" in the fish's belly is based on the view of the sixteenth-century physician Paracelsus (Jung 1967, 330). The biblical book itself does not even provide a basis for asserting that Jonah even knew he had been swallowed by a "monster," let alone that he witnesses mysteries when he was near death in "the belly of Sheol" (2:3). And while the directions of east and west do play a role in Jonah's flight from God and Nineveh in ch. 1, we are not told the location of either the dry land on which the fish vomits up Jonah (2:11) or the spot where Jonah is located when God calls him the second time (3:1).

More importantly, the biblical Jonah shows no sign of having been transformed by his experience in the fish, whether in terms of Jung's notion of the life-task of "bringing together 'conscious' and 'unconscious'" (Jung 1967, 301) or Bettelheim's parabolic Freudian reading, in which "Jonah discovers his higher morality, his higher self, and is wondrously reborn, now ready to meet the rigorous demands of his superego" (1989, 53). In fact, we cannot take for granted that Jonah has learned any kind of life-lesson—or even that he *needed* to learn such a lesson.

One might object that Jonah does obey Yahweh's renewed command after his emergence from the fish and goes to Nineveh. However, we are not told *why* he obeyed this time. We have no evidence that Jonah heeding Yahweh's call represents an acceptance of his "vocation" in Maslow's sense of the term. As I will discuss below, Jonah could simply have learned the futility of trying to evade Yahweh's directives. If so, by going to Nineveh, he is accepting his powerlessness, just as Job's recantation of his case against God could simply be an admission by Job that trying to reason with such a God is futile, because only power and unquestioned obedience matter to this deity (Job 42:6).

Jungian literary critic Terence Dawson laments that Jungian analyses of narrative often "explore the parallels in myths while ignoring the differences" and focus on isolated incidents or details rather than on the work as a whole. He also notes that Jung's concern was with trying to identify a hypothetical *Ur*-text that might have determined the surface narrative, rather than with explicating the "surface narrative" itself.

The most recent Jungian studies of Jonah continue to illustrate the problems which can occur when one does not avoid these pitfalls. Ingram's 2012 study of Jonah applies Harold Ellens's "three laws of psychological hermeneutics" to the book.[36] As I have discussed elsewhere (Lasine 2013), Ellens's "psychological lens" has actually been crafted according to theological principles rather than

---

36. According to these "laws," it is "necessary to separate the garbage from the gospel" when analyzing biblical texts (Ingram 2012, 142). Anything in the Bible which is not "a word about grace" is "psychospiritually destructive" and "not the divine word" (2012, 147). The garbage is "the cultural-historical matrix" (2012, 143). In effect, Ellens's gospel/garbage law is a very extreme example of a "canon within the canon." It therefore contradicts Mosaic law, specifically, the so-called "canonical formula" which declares that one should not add or subtract one word from God's *torah*. Later in Deuteronomy, Moses states that this *torah*, the totality of *all* the words he is transmitting, is "no vain thing (רק) for you; for it is your life." This verse gave rise to the rabbinic dictum that "if it seems vain, it is from you"—that is, it's your fault, not the text's; that is, you may need to polish, or switch, the lens through which you're viewing the problematic text, rather than dismissing that text as garbage. If the Hebrew Bible were abridged strictly according to Ellens's laws, it would be even shorter than the *Olive Pell Bible*. Pell removed 80 percent of the Christian Bible, retaining "only those passages that offer the greatest consolation and healing to the distressed in body or soul" (Pell 1952, vi).

psychological ones.[37] Ingram contends that viewing Jonah through Ellens's lens makes the book's "puzzling aspects disappear," enabling us to recognize that "the spiritual message in the book is of God's universal, unconditional, and radical grace." Anything in the book—in fact, anything in the entire Bible—which "runs contrary to this message is worthless" (2012, 140).

Ingram assumes that Jonah "knows" from the start "that God will not destroy the city that was a threat to the Israelites." In contrast, the way that the sailors and Ninevites perceive God is destructive, unconsciously creating "sick archetypes in our psyches" (2012, 148). Like many other critics, Ingram paints Jonah's personality in very harsh terms, without considering the strong arguments that can be made for a more positive appraisal of Jonah's character and motives, as we have seen. The Jungian assumptions behind her approach allow Ingram to speculate about the unknown author's unknowable "unconscious drives" and personal experience of cognitive dissonance. Her Jonah is irrational and manipulative and experiences "the fear, anxiety, and feelings of inadequacy which come with dysfunctional core metaphors" (2012, 149) even though the narrator never attributes fear to Jonah.

Later Ingram refers to "Jonah's long-held worldview of legalism," an astounding claim considering that we know absolutely nothing about Jonah's *Weltanschauungen* before the time of the book. According to Ingram, the only thing that "pleases [Jonah's] heart is a desire for justice or vengeance," which she considers to be "contrary to God's grace" (2012, 151, 149). Jonah's feelings of hatred are so strong that a conversion would mean he would have had to confront them; therefore, his life is a farce and his way of living somewhat hypocritical. This Jonah is not only legalistic and consumed by hatred but particularistic as well. Ingram calls him a "rigid 'works righteous' kind of guy" who may want God to be concerned only for Israel (2012, 152). In short, through her "psychological" lens, Jonah is reduced to a familiar Jewish stereotype.[38]

Jongsoo Park's 2004 study of Jonah is an exclusively Jungian analysis. Like Ingram, Park believes that the book gives us access to the unknown author's unconscious mind. Park assumes that "Jonah is the psychological projection of the author," who "had to live with his enemies" (2004, 277, 280). Even if Nineveh was "almost forgotten" by the book's original readership, it still "elicited strong emotion" because it "continued to exi[s]t in the unconscious." Jung's theories allow us to determine that the author's intention was a desire "to share his psychological journey with the reader," by using "mythological motifs . . . [to draw] out the

---

37. See Van Heerden (2003) for a survey of some of the psychological interpretations of Jonah up to his time of writing.

38. For example, Oesterley and Robinson contend that the author of Jonah "sets forth Jonah as the type of the narrow-minded, exclusive Jew, who not only despises all non-Jews, but conceives of the Almighty as the God of the Jews only, and as a God who has no care for the rest of His creation" (1934, 375). See Sherwood (2000, 21–32, 56–87, and *passim*) for many other examples, both ancient and modern.

collective unconscious of the readers who had similar experiences to those of Jonah" (2004, 276–78, 281).

This approach allows Park to interpret Jonah's behavior as "outward expression[s] of his unconscious." Even objects like the "mythical" *qiqayon* plant "reflect [Jonah's] unstable psyche." Like Ingram, Park feels free to predicate various emotions and motivations to Jonah which are not mentioned in, or implied by, the biblical text. Thus, Park's Jonah is "terribly upset" at the beginning and flees because he "sees his shadow" (i.e., the dark side of his personality). Later, he is shocked by the Ninevites' contrition and becomes suicidal, due to "the loss of his familiar belief system."

Park also assumes that the message Jonah delivered was not intended to destroy Nineveh. This "confronts Jonah with another image of God. . . . The two Gods in Jonah made him torn; one God is in the consciousness of the law, and the other God is hidden in the unconscious." Jonah had two choices: keep "his conventional way of thinking," the Ego, or "hear the inner voice, the Truth"; this is the "Self" (2004, 279). Jonah is "caught between the existential reality and the demand of the divine (unconscious)."

Avivah Zornberg's 2008 *Psychoanalytic Dialogues* article on Jonah makes little reference to psychological theories; however, she, like Ingram and Park, describes Jonah as clinging to a conventionally rigid and myopic worldview. Her Jonah insists on "always already knowing"; this is the key to understanding "his flight from the enigma of his humanity" (2008, 271).[39] He cannot bear to remain in a situation of "essential uncertainty," and therefore "flees into a compulsive knowingness" so that "nothing . . . can surprise him" (2008, 284–85). His "knowingness acts as camouflage for fear. A dangerous world . . . makes him cling to his certainties." While ascribing fear to Jonah is even more important for Zornberg's interpretation than it was for Ingram's, the fact remains that the biblical narrator does not describe the prophet as afraid. In the end, Zornberg's judgment of the prophet echoes that of many commentators: Jonah is an "arrogant dogmatist," a "know-all [who] ends up in hopeless despair" (2008, 166).[40] Zornberg's respondent Jill Salberg goes further, diagnosing Jonah as suffering from a "paranoid-schizoid position of isolation."[41]

---

39. Zornberg's evidence for Jonah's "knowingness" is Jonah's statement that he knows the storm has come upon them on his account and that he knew all of Yahweh's compassionate traits. She concedes that Jonah's knowledge is accurate in both cases. But what Jonah knows is merely "knowledge to die by, not to live by," and he "wears his knowledge [of God's character] with bitterness and cryptic rage, to justify his flight and his death" (2008, 284).

40. Nor does Zornberg investigate the sources of *her own* "knowingness" about Jonah, even though the book's narrative rhetoric seems designed to frustrate interpreters' attempts to pin down and "know" its meanings.

41. Salberg describes her approach as "British Object Relations and Relational." Her Jonah "is in a state of agitation" at the start, and God is "angry" at Nineveh. Her Jonah "needs a God who is rigidly consistent." Jonah is "unaware of how his own internal split

However, Salberg also resembles the others in making Jonah's behavior entirely a function of his internal mental problems, not a possibly accurate perception of intractable external situations in the world governed by Yahweh, a world often characterized by ambiguity and contradiction. This precludes taking seriously the possible validity of Jonah's attitude toward justice and the problematic nature of the mission he has been given.

Attempts to assimilate the plot of the book of Jonah to a heroic journey, involving separation, initiation, and return[42] meet with similar problems. We do not learn anything about Jonah's situation within the society from which he is "separated." The three days in the fish give no indication that Jonah has become an enlightened "liminar" and "human total,"[43] even though the legendary claim that Jonah emerged from the fish naked and bald suggests a rebirth (see, for example, Ginzberg 1968, 252). Nor is there any mention of a final phase of reintegration into his society; in fact, we are not told that Jonah returns to his "own country," let alone that he returned with a boon for his unmentioned people, as is the case for heroes such as Gilgamesh, Moses, and the Egyptian shipwrecked sailor.[44]

However, the Jonah narrative does evoke a different aspect of hero stories. As I will discuss in the next chapter, heroes such as Perseus and Heracles defeat sea monsters by intentionally allowing themselves to be swallowed by the monster in order to save a princess who is threatened by the beast. Once inside, they kill the beast from within, emerge from their state of embeddedness, and save the princess. This plot-element can even be found in films such as *Men in Black* (1997), where the swallowed hero "K" slays the monster from within, saving not only a woman but a galaxy as well.[45] The big fish swallowing Jonah may briefly evoke such heroic

---

world of good and bad is projected outward onto the external world" (2008, 320–21). Like a good therapist, God recognizes that "the movement that Jonah needs to make" is an "internal shift from the paranoid-schizoid position of isolation to the depressive position space of engagement" (2008, 327).

42. See, for example, E. L. Smith (1997, 56–60) and Steffen (1982, 109–14). Campbell (1968, 91–92) understands being in the belly of the whale in terms of the hero journey "monomyth."

43. On Victor Turner's understanding of the liminal process, and the application of his ideas to biblical texts, see Lasine (1986, 59–61, 67–68).

44. As I will discuss in Chapter 6 §2, the Egyptian sailor is a sole survivor who washes up on a soon-to-be-submerged island. Here he is aided by a species of deity and then manages to reach home with the boon of tribute as well as an awareness of realities unknowable in his home world.

45. In this film, the gigantic alien "bug" swallows the weapons of the human agents, after which agent "K" baits the monster to eat him. The beast complies, and "K" blows the beast apart from inside using his previously swallowed weapon, freeing himself in the process. While there is more than a hint of attraction between the rescued young woman and agent "J," she becomes "J's" new partner rather than his spouse.

exploits for some readers, but the situation in Jonah is obviously very different. The big fish is not threatening anyone, including Jonah, and there is no need for the prophet to fight his way out of its belly.

The defensive posture denoted by the terms "embeddedness" and "Jonah complex" are also characteristic of Norbert Elias's modern Western "*homo clausus*" (1997, 52). Here too self-enclosure functions as an illusory way of sealing oneself from the perceived danger of being exposed to uncontrollable external forces.[46] The biblical Jonah shows no evidence of being an ancient *homo clausus*.[47] Nor do his actions suggest that he is attempting to avoid risk through embeddedness, let alone that his "fear of engulfment . . . is vividly, if ironically, depicted" when "he is gulped in by a 'whale'" (A. Lacocque 2004, 90).

In fact, Jonah consistently displays a readiness to *expose himself* to danger, rather than striving to avoid it. If we take Jonah's words in 4:2 at face value, it is conceivable that Jonah might not have viewed his avoidance of the divine commission as being very risky, considering that Yahweh is so merciful and forgiving. However, readers of the entire Hebrew Bible know that gambling on Yahweh not showing his wrathful side is itself quite risky. Jonah chooses to flee onto the open sea, which naturally requires that he embark on a ship.[48] When he asks to be thrown overboard, he shows no sign of expecting anything other than exposure to the unbounded sea. His later entry into the great city of Nineveh also exposes Jonah to possible danger. Once outside the city again, he exposes himself to the heat of the sun and copes with this problem on his own by erecting the *sukkah*. Rather than representing an attempt to seek safety in a womblike shelter, building the *sukkah* may be nothing more than an attempt to make his exposure on the landscape more tolerable.

The sailors and the Ninevites had achieved safety from God-caused danger by submitting their wills to him, once again making their ship and city into havens of safety. In Berger's terms, they accept Yahweh's "sheltering canopy," which for the moment protected them from fear of death and the danger of being "swallowed up" by chaos (1969, 27, 55). In contrast, Jonah chooses to remain outside such canopies, even though this exposes him to divinely caused suffering.

This survey of "Jonah complexes" demonstrates that any persuasive psychological study of Jonah must take into account *all* the features of the text, both what is—and is *not*—said by the narrator and *how* it is said, if the pitfalls illustrated

---

46. A pathological form of this strategy is illustrated by the patients of Modell who feel themselves to be encased in a "plastic bubble" or "behind a sheet of glass," as though they were "not 'really in the world'" (1976, 294).

47. Elsewhere (Lasine 2012, 53–55), I have argued that such supposedly modern self-conceptions can also be found in other periods, depending upon the social figuration which characterizes a specific society in a specific historical context.

48. Given the lack of information about the size of the ship and the number of its crew, the "recesses" of the ship in which Jonah sleeps could merely be the area of the ship's hold in which the sailors routinely slept.

by these studies are to be avoided. Such an analysis must also acknowledge the rhetorical function of the book's many intertextual allusions and the patterns formed by *Leitwörter*. In addition, the psychological optic through which one views this elusive narrative must not be allowed to obscure important aspects of the text which clash with the principles by which that optic was designed. Finally, interpreters must resist making premature judgments about the personalities of the book's characters, a different sort of pitfall about which social psychology has much to teach us.[49]

Clearly, psychological analyses will never produce a personality profile of the character Jonah which will seem accurate or persuasive to all readers. Nor should this be their goal. However, psychological insights can help to explain how and why readers differ in their assessments of the prophet or why a specific reader may assess Jonah differently at different times. The branch of social psychology known as attribution theory can be especially helpful in this endeavor. Attribution theory alerts us to our tendency to interpret the behavior of other people (and literary personages) as a function of character alone, without adequately taking into account the constraints on their behavior caused by the situations in which they find themselves. Once we become aware of this bias,[50] we can correct for it by focusing on the interplay between character and situation when assessing reported behavior.

This interplay is complicated by the fact that people sometimes "seek situations that will 'push' them in the same direction as do their own dispositions" (Gilbert and Malone 1995, 33). Consequently, "situations are largely of one's own making and are themselves describable as a characteristic of one's own personality" (Wachtel 1973, 330; cf. Lasine 2012, 78). Within the world of the Hebrew Bible, another complicating factor must be considered, namely, the possibility that God may choose to place his human subjects in situations of *his* own making, including no-win situations such as those into which he places characters such as Saul and Jeroboam.[51] In the case of Jonah, God initially chooses to place Jonah into a potentially perilous situation in the great city of Nineveh. However, the prophet quickly puts himself into an even more difficult position by fleeing his mission and boarding the ship. At this point, God quickly takes over and manipulates the prophet's situation by preparing the big fish and, later, the plant.

These bizarre situations go far beyond the political catch-22s faced by Saul and Jeroboam, because they confront readers with fundamental—and disquieting— aspects of the human condition per se. Readers who wish to assess Jonah's character are thus invited to do so in terms of their own attitudes toward the most profound

---

49. On this problem, see Lasine (2012), *passim*.

50. Gilbert and Malone's term for this mechanism is "correspondence bias" (1995, 22–27); it is more commonly referred to as "the fundamental attribution error" (see Lasine 2012, 7–19).

51. On these cases, see Lasine (2001, 39–50, 2012, 147–58).

human vulnerabilities,[52] vulnerabilities with which Jonah chooses to cope without passively surrendering his will to God or succumbing to paralyzing fear. In the next chapter, I will ask whether focusing on the *plot* of the book of Jonah rather than the protagonist's perceived personality can tell us anything more about the human condition in the Hebrew Bible.

---

52. These vulnerabilities are discussed further in Chapter 7 §3.

Chapter 6

THE PLOT OF JONAH, CHILDHOOD CRISES, AND THE PERILS OF ADULTHOOD

If Jonah's reported actions do not conform to the psychological profiles presented by the theorists discussed in the previous chapter, how do we explain what Orwell calls the "hold that the Jonah myth has upon our imaginations"? (1981, 244). In light of all the versions of the tale transmitted over many centuries in words and images and the continuing popularity of Jonah's story in children's literature[1] and videos, it is difficult to deny that the story has indeed had a powerful effect on a wide variety of readers.

One part of the answer is immediately evident: the plot of the book evokes crucial challenges faced by children and the continued relevance of these issues for adult life, especially when they have not been resolved successfully during one's early years. In the first two sections of this chapter, I will focus upon psychological dangers faced by children, including the ways in which these crises are expressed in fairy tales, myths, and the book of Jonah. In the next two sections, I will track the perils faced by adults, in part by analyzing the ways in which the epic heroes Gilgamesh and Homer's Odysseus deal with their human vulnerability and mortality. Together, these analyses will help to explain why some readers tend to view Jonah as a pouting child with a protective divine father, while others find him to be a principled adult struggling to establish his autonomy[2] in face of opposition from the paternal God who seeks to frustrate Jonah's efforts at maturation.

---

1. Dalton (2007, 299, 307–08) surveyed hundreds of children's storybook versions of Jonah and found that many deviate from scripture most dramatically when it comes to the prophet's angry complaints in ch. 4. Some eliminate the final chapter completely, ending the story with Nineveh's repentance or as early as Jon. 3:3, when the prophet goes to this great city. Over twenty other children's books replace Jonah 4 with a fabricated conclusion in which the prophet is redeemed or even happy about Nineveh's change of attitude.

2. The meaning and value of "autonomy" are highly debated in moral and political philosophy as well as in feminist theory. In this study, the term refers only to being independent of parental control when surviving as an adult.

1 Fears of being swallowed and eaten

You [Father] enhanced the ranting with threats and even now that has its effect on me. For example, this was horrible to me: "I'll rip you apart like a fish," even though I knew that nothing worse would follow after it (of course as a little child I didn't know that), but it nearly corresponded to my imaginings of your power that you would have been capable of it. It was also horrible when you ran around the table screaming in order to grab someone, whom you obviously didn't want to grab, but did it anyway, and whom mother seemingly rescued in the end. Once again—as it seemed to the child—one remained alive through your favor, and maintained it as your undeserved gift.

—Kafka, "Dearest Father"[3] (1953, 177)

"Hold your noise!" cried a terrible voice. . . . "Keep still, you little devil, or I'll cut your throat!" A fearful man, . . . who limped, and shivered, and glared, and growled; . . . "You young dog," said the man, licking his lips, "what fat cheeks you ha' got." . . . "Darn me if I couldn't eat em," said the man, with a threatening shake of his head, "and if I han't half a mind to't!"

—Dickens, *Great Expectations* (1861, 2–3)

I was at ease, but he smashed and smashed me;
seized my neck then bashed me and bashed me;[4]
he set me up as his target;
his archers surround me.
He splits open my kidneys and does not pity;
he pours out my gall on the earth.

—Job 16:12-13

For a developing child, a threat to the integrity of one's self or identity can lead to (at least symbolic) flight, in order to avoid annihilation or self-dissolution at the hands of an ambivalent or hostile parent. Psychologists have noted that an ambivalent symbiotic mother-child relationship and inadequate parental protection can prompt a mortal fear of being swallowed and eaten up, and thereby "reengulfed." It can also trigger "storm-rage reactions" by the child (Mahler 1952, 1979, 177–78). Some go further, asserting that children fear being killed by their parents (e.g., Ehrensaft 2008, 102–07).

In recent years, many psychologists have ventured estimates of the age when children first become aware that death is irreversible, inevitable, and universal (see, for example, Beit-Hallahmi 2011, 48; Talwar 2011, 100; Corr 1997, 220–27).

---

3. Usually called "Letter to his Father."

4. This is Habel's rendering of the assonance created by the use of the *pilpel* form of פרר and פוץ in v. 12 (1985, 262, 264–65).

Yet annihilation anxiety can precede such full awareness. Winnicott notes that "babies who have been significantly 'let down' once or in a pattern of environmental failures (related to . . . the mother or mother-substitute) . . . carry with them the experience of unthinkable or archaic anxiety" (1992, 260). He emphasizes that this is one extreme on a spectrum tracking a child's experience of parental unreliability. Piven (2004, 10) also acknowledges the young child's inchoate awareness of personal death. He notes that "the annihilation anxiety incubated and moulded in infancy is an immanent threat throughout adult life, to which the psyche responds with defensive evasion, fantasy, and the construction of belief systems which render death nonthreatening." Such threats include "separation from the protecting caregiver, helplessness, and abandonment," all of which involve exposure of some sort.[5]

In the case of Jonah, it is not the caregiver's absence which makes the prophet feel the most helpless but his oppressive presence. Some readers might conclude from the abrupt ending of the book, with Jonah still exposed to sun and wind and possibly no longer in dialogue with God, that Jonah feels abandoned as well. If one accepts the common view that Jonah acts childish in the book[6]—both at sea and on dry land—his actions can be interpreted as a struggle for power and control. Difficulties in the process of separation between mother and child can result in a relationship of dominance and submission, a struggle about who will control whom (see Lasine 2001, 230–35). A parent who demands submission and mirroring from the child might read the book of Jonah as teaching that a child must unquestioningly submit to the parent's demands, not least because resistance is futile. When ch. 4 of Jonah is viewed from this perspective, Yahweh resembles a father who is patiently leading his pouting child toward the recognition that the father's course of action was correct, and that the "child's" anger and sense of moral outrage were inappropriate.

The fear of being swallowed, or being digested after being ripped apart by teeth, can point to fear that one's individual self or identity might be engulfed or annihilated. Children's fears of being swallowed up, torn open, or eaten by parents are consistently reflected in fairy tales and other children's literature.[7] In some, the threatening parent is represented by a monster. In others, the parental figure remains idealized, while the threatening qualities are displaced onto the monster. Figures such as Colloti's Pinocchio and the Grimms's Little Red Cap are swallowed

---

5. Piven (2004, 10–11) also includes punishment, confusion, the child's rage and unsatisfied wants, and lack of control of bodily functions in his inventory of anxiety-causing threats. In a sense, the child's consciousness is a type of enclosure, within which she may feel exposed to powerful negative emotions which she is not yet able to fend off.

6. For examples, see Chapter 5 §1.

7. This is true no matter what psychological theories are imported to explain the details of a specific story. Interestingly, in the medieval poem *Patience*, Jonah threatens the Ninevites with being swallowed up by the abyss (ll. 359–64; Finch 1993, 198–99; cf. Sobecki 2008, 131–34).

by the monster. A terrible huge shark ingests Pinocchio "the way you might gulp down an egg" (Colloti 2010, 72). Little Red Cap is swallowed by a wolf. Yet both she and Pinocchio remain alive and conscious in the beast's belly, as is Jonah in the great fish. Even Yahweh's favorite child Israel is still able to speak about the way in which Nebuchadrezzar has swallowed her like a sea monster (בלענו כתנין, *qere*) and vomited her out (Jer. 51:34, 44). In all these cases, engulfment refers to living entombment rather than to annihilation or nurtured growth in the womb.

In this mode of engulfment, the "child" is prevented from developing her self through interaction with other people and the world at large. The child remains in a state of eternally halted gestation, a condition for which Jeremiah actually yearns after he has been battered and enticed by his God, his close friends, and the citizens of Jerusalem (Jer. 20:14-18). Similarly, Job wishes that Yahweh would entomb him alive in Sheol until the storm of his parental rage has passed (Job 14:13; see Chapter 2 §4). Jeremiah and Job are both adults who had once been sheltered and hedged in protectively by God, only to be exposed to horrible suffering by this same ambivalent parental figure. Even though Jonah expresses no desire to be sheltered in the big fish and does not experience the fish's belly as a welcome shelter, once he has been swallowed, it is still possible that readers of Jonah's story might find *themselves* reminded of the primal threat to selfhood evoked by being swallowed, even if that fear has long since sunk down into the depths of their psyche.

The emphasis on violence, suffering, and death in fairy tales does not necessarily imply that such tales inhibit children's ability to come to terms with their mortality. In the 1805 edition of *The Prelude*, the poet Wordsworth expresses gratitude that his parents had not raised him to be a vain and conceited child prodigy, even though "fear itself, natural or supernatural alike, . . . touches [such children] not" (5.315-18; 1979, 168). He prefers that a child read about Fortunatus and Jack the Giant Killer (1979, 170). Having been "exposed to fairy stories and romances," the child Wordsworth felt "no vulgar fear," even when confronted by the sudden appearance of an actual drowned man (1979, 176). Psychologist Beit-Hallahmi would agree; he argues that an "unprotected" child is better able to handle seeing a dead body than a child such as Siddhartha, whose father attempted to insulate from unsettling realities, another form of failed protective enclosure (2011, 45-49).

While the epigraphs to this section are not taken from fairy tales, they too point to parents who "playfully" threaten to eat or rip open their children and the terror which this behavior can cause for the child. These parallels support Tatar's view that "the hard facts of fairy-tale life offer exaggerated visions of the grimmer realities and fantasies that touch and shape the lives of every child and adult" (2003, 192). All the epigraphs describe an adult male's seemingly boundless power over an individual. Kafka is talking about his biological father, whom he consistently describes as though he were the possessor of the divine attributes of wrath, unaccountability, and near-ubiquity. Here, the child feels that his very life is an undeserved gift of favor by the father who might otherwise dismember and annihilate him. As Sokel puts it, Kafka indicts his father's "utter disrespect for the autonomous personality of his child," as well as his father's "capricious, self-righteous arbitrariness" in the father's "treatment of the world" (2002, 311). The threat of ripping up the child as one does with an edible fish also hints at the threat of cannibalism.

A few years before Kafka wrote this long indictment of his father, Freud published his famous "Wolf Man" case study. In this essay, Freud refers to the characteristic of "affectionate abuse" (*zärtlichen Schimpfen*) which "so many people display in their interaction with their children," specifically, "the facetious threat to gobble up" the child (Freud 1946b, 9; cf. 1947b, 58). Freud cites one patient whose children could never become fond of their grandfather because of his "affectionate game" of frightening them with the threat to cut open their stomachs (1947b, 58). In Kafka's case, however, it is clear that as a child he felt his father's threat to "rip him apart like a fish" to be anything but facetious.

In some cases, the monster is *both* threatening and benign. In their analyses of the psychological functions of exposure myths and fairy tales, both Rank (2004, 47–92) and Tatar (2003, 10, 50, 60) note the copresence of nurturing and hostile parental images in these narratives.[8] In other stories, the monster turns out not to be a true monster after all. In the epigraph from *Great Expectations*, the child Pip is appropriately terrified by the cannibalistic threats of the ogre-like Magwitch. Yet as an adult, Pip discovers that Magwitch has been his protective benefactor, just as readers who expect a sea monster to annihilate and assimilate Jonah learn that this monstrous fish is actually a benign rescuer.[9]

The situation of Job in the final epigraph is more ambiguous. When he describes God ripping him open and spilling his innards, he is experiencing the parental deity as a predatory beast which is in the process of annihilating him. Readers of the entire Hebrew Bible know that this is the same God who elsewhere threatens that parents will eat their children if they do not follow his rules, a grisly outcome which in fact occurs several times (see Lasine 1991, 29–35). Yet most readers understand Yahweh's rewarding of Job in the epilogue as a cue that God has really been Job's reliable protector all along, including during his God-caused ordeal. Nevertheless, Job's response to God's speeches 42:6 can also be understood to be his acknowledgment of God's uncaring or even demonic side (see Lasine 2016a, 472–73).

2 Fantasies of being swallowed and killing the monster from within

So far I have mentioned a number of individuals who are swallowed by a beast but who remain alive in the monster's belly and emerge basically intact. This plot

---

8. As R. Segal points out, in Rank's opinion, heroes are creative persons who "vaunt their independence by setting themselves against the community" (2004, xvii–xviii). Commenting on his *Myth of the Birth of the Hero* years later, Rank explains that one "becomes a hero because he does not want to owe anything to his parents, but has to justify this independence by achievements" (qtd. in R. Segal 2004, xxvii).

9. On Magwitch as an ultimately benevolent "ogre," see Ostry (2002, 69).

is also found in hero stories and Hollywood films, the most famous of which is probably the Heracles and Hesione myth, first compared to Jonah in the fifth century CE by Cyril of Alexandria (2008, 160–61).[10] The most striking differences between the Heracles story and the fairy tales discussed earlier are that the hero *intentionally* has himself swallowed in order to destroy the sea monster (κῆτος, as in LXX Jonah) from within, either by hacking at his sides or by "carving" his liver.[11] In so doing, Heracles saves the young woman who would have been eaten by the beast.

As with Jonah, Little Red Cap, and Pinocchio, Heracles being swallowed by the monster does not lead to irreversible death by mastication. Here, the one swallowed saves himself without needing a parental helper such as the hunter who rescues Red Cap from the wolf's stomach or the God who speaks to the great fish which then vomits out Jonah at the shore (Jon. 2:11). The Heracles myth offers a fantasy of adult autonomy, rather than infantile dependence. The "much-toiling" hero[12] can extricate himself from this primal nightmare scenario. In this way Heracles is birthing himself, as opposed to being vomited out by the monster, as is the case with Jonah. Interestingly, Hesione, the endangered woman, is not saved because Heracles has fallen in love with her. However, this is an element in the parallel myth of Perseus and Andromeda, who later marry and become parents themselves. In most variants of the latter tale, Perseus slays the sea monster without first being ingested.[13]

Letaldus of Micy's late-tenth-century story called "About a Certain Fisherman Whom a Whale Swallowed" is also instructive in this context. The shipwrecked fisherman (named "Within") is explicitly likened to Jonah, while the whale

---

10. In Lycophron's *Alexandra*, the monster is dubbed the "grey hound"; instead of "the young woodpecker (πῖπος), he swallowed in his throat a scorpion" (i.e., Heracles; ll. 475–78). Not all variants of this myth have Heracles kill the sea monster from within (e.g., Valerius Flaccus, *Argonautica* 2.451-578; D. Ogden 2013, 157–59). The fish swallowing Jonah may briefly evoke heroes such as Heracles, but the similarities are quite limited. The big fish in Jonah is not threatening anyone—including Jonah—and there is no need for the prophet to fight his way out of its belly. For an amusing discussion of Jonah, Perseus, and Heracles as ancient members of the "clan" of whalemen, see Melville's *Moby-Dick* (2002, 284–88).

11. See, for example, Lycophron, *Alexandra*, line 35.

12. Euripides, *Her.* 1192; see Chapter 1 §3.

13. While ancient Greek literature does not mention Jason being swallowed and disgorged by a monster in his pursuit of the golden fleece, six images have been thought to refer to such an occurrence. The most famous is an Attic red-figure kylix often attributed to Douris. Jason's head and arms hang limply off the dragon-like monster's lower jaw, while the hero's hips and legs remain unseen in the monster's throat (see Mackie 2001, 10–11). Mackie concludes that Jason had descended into the dragon's belly and is then disgorged, pointing to Jonah as one of several parallels (2001, 12 cf. Hamel 1995, 349). E. Simon (1981, 119–20) disagrees. She speculates that the hero has climbed into the dragon's gullet and cut off its tongue, which is why the dragon cannot gulp him down all the way.

is said to be like Scylla and Charybdis in its "maw and eyes," thereby recalling Homer's shipwrecked Odysseus as well (Ziolkowski 2007, 247, 244). Within is a well-known and experienced fisherman who wears a twin-edged sword when "he entrusts himself alone to the open sea." But he cannot prevent the monster from swallowing both him and his coracle, leaving him "shut up in a dark cave." Within remains courageous and sets parts of his wooden vessel and his oars on fire from within the beast's "greedy belly." Now the roles of eater and eaten are reversed. The whale cannot flee because it "bears its enemy within itself." Within then hacks at the beast with his sword, ultimately eating its organs, restoring "his body with its body" (2007, 244–45). Yet he cannot escape the whale even after it lies dead on the shore. The townspeople use swords and axes to harvest the creature's meat, until they hear Within calling to them from inside its belly.

Within is a mature individual who has both wife and children. Far from being risk-averse, as is often said of Jonah, he trusts his ability to survive on the sea. At the same time, he needs his fellow townsman to complete his escape from the "lightless prison" of the whale's innards. Scylla and Charybdis each represents a primal danger, the former of being torn apart and the latter of being swallowed forever. Within not only evades these threats but goes on to be the one who tears and swallows the flesh of *his* prey. While he does undergo an ordeal in the whale's belly, he returns to his fellow townsmen with the boon of food. In these respects, the story is both a fantasy of autonomy and an illustration of the role of one's peers in escaping from fatal entrapment.

The fascinating and enigmatic Egyptian *Tale of the Shipwrecked Sailor* deserves mention here. According to Goedicke, in this story, "the image of the sea journey symbolizes, ... earthly existence" (1974, 82). While the sailors have "the intellectual capacities" to prophesy a storm, "the surprise remains of being exposed to the storms of life. In the crisis, the well-equipped ship is wrecked, the metaphor for life-experience" (1974, 83). The Egyptian tale also combines several elements relevant to both the Jonah narrative and primal childhood fears. These include the motifs of shipwreck in a storm and being a sole survivor who initially fabricates a shelter for himself. The castaway is later aided by a benign monstrous serpent who transports him in his mouth, but does not swallow or injure him (ll. 38–42, 77–80).

The speaker tells his story in order to hearten his present ship's commander, whose mission for the Pharaoh has apparently failed. The sailor's experiences seem to illustrate the serpent's view that we should keep calm and carry on with endurance and self-control,[14] because disasters inevitably occur during our

---

14. The sailor recommends that his captain speak with stout-heartedness (or self-possession; *ib-k m-ꜥk*; line 16; Blackman 1932, 42) when appearing before the king to report on his mission, and the serpent later counsels the sailor to make his heart stout (*rwḏ ib*; line 132; Blackman 1932, 45).

life-voyages and cannot be controlled even when they are foreseen (ll. 31-39).¹⁵ In addition, the commander has not lost one of his crew members on this failed voyage, whereas the narrator is the lone survivor of a shipwreck and the divine serpent is the lone survivor of a fiery disaster which struck his kin on land.

In ancient Mediterranean literature, the importance of endurance is exhibited, above all, by Homer's shipwrecked Odysseus, one of whose epithets is "much-enduring" (πόλυτλας). However, the way in which the Egyptian sailor's story is framed can lead readers to ask whether his shipwreck report is actually a "tale of Alcinous" (Plato, *Resp.* 614b), that is, a fantastic and undisconfirmable story such as those Odysseus tells his hosts on the island of the Phaeacians (*Od.* 9-12). How a reader understands the sailor's tale depends upon how she or he interprets the commander's terse response to his "excellent" (or "skillful"; *iqr*) friend: "Who gives water to a bird at the dawn of its being slaughtered in the morning?" (ll. 183, 185-86; Blackman, 1932, 48). The commander's evocation of this "I'm a dead duck" or "my goose is cooked" proverb suggests that he is unmoved (and perhaps annoyed) by the sailor's tale. Does he find the sailor's means of encouragement to be trite and/or fanciful? Is he being sarcastic when he calls the sailor "excellent"? Like the book of Jonah, this tale ends abruptly, thereby precluding definitive answers to such questions.

3 Jonah and other mature ancient heroes

As on the raging sea, which, unbounded on all sides, raises up and plunges . . . howling cresting waves, a mariner sits in a skiff, trusting in his frail vessel, so the individual person sits calmly in the middle of a world of torments, propped up and trusting in the *principium individuationis*.

—Schopenhauer (1819, 507)

Threats to one's self—in its various historical and cultural figurations—continue throughout one's adult life. In the epigraph, Schopenhauer appeals to the "life as a sea voyage" metaphor in order to communicate how we cope with our continual vulnerabilities. The fragility of our "skiff" as a defense against forces, both external and internal, is not a fact which people are especially eager to acknowledge. Instead, we attempt to create the illusion of safety from potentially destructive forces in the enveloping world by trusting in the principle of individuation. Without the aid of this illusion, we would have to admit that the life of the individual consists of a journey through "a sea full of crags and whirlpools." No matter how much

---

15. Cf. Parkinson (1998, 89-90, 99, n. 20) and Baines (1990, 60, 66). Parkinson (1998, 89) takes this to be the "universal" lesson of the text as a whole. Baines is less certain; he notes that this moralizing message is delivered only in the sailor's and the snake's "rather sententious proverbial utterances" (1990, 60).

exertion and skill one puts forth to avoid these obstacles, the voyage unavoidably ends in the "shipwreck" of death (Schopenhauer 1819, 450). In psychologist Ernest Becker's later formulation, "life can suck one up, . . . take away his [sic] self-control, . . . [and] expose him to new contingencies," until death, the "total submergence and negation" (1973, 54).

Likening adult life to navigating a dangerous world-sea while bailing out our awareness of unpleasant realities which might sink our little craft would seem to make ordinary existence an heroic enterprise. As we have discovered, some commentators have viewed Jonah as undergoing a hero journey, while others regard him as an Everyman. Here, it is instructive to compare Jonah with Homer's Odysseus, another journeying hero who has been called an "Everyman."[16] It would be more accurate to say that Homer presents Odysseus as a quintessential mature adult male (an ἀνήρ); in fact, this is the first word of the epic. Historically, Odysseus's adventures have been influential as "a symbol of man's [sic] voyage through life" (Rutherford 1986, 146). Horace (*Ep.* 1.2.22) describes him as "unsinkable" by the "waves of adversity" which afflict him. Odysseus manages to protect his heroic self from annihilation even when he is threatened by the flesh-rending Scylla on her crag and Charybdis's whirlpool. Scylla eats her victims with the three rows of teeth in each of her six heads, while Charybdis swallows and sucks them down (*Od.* 12.73-110, 235-59, 430-46). Rutherford (1986, 152) rightly notes that description of Scylla rending Odysseus's comrades "speaks clearly in the language and images of men's nightmares." However, he could have added that visions of being ripped apart, eaten, and swallowed also express children's primal fears.

In addition, Odysseus chooses to reject the safety of eternal embeddedness with the goddess Calypso—the ultimate fantasy of infantile omnipotence—for an adult life of risk which will inevitably terminate with his own death. In pursuing this goal of a successful mortal life, Odysseus must constantly evade the dangers of being engulfed, dismembered, devoured, or imprisoned in enclosures such as Calypso's "womblike cave" (Taylor 1963, 96), all of which would obliterate his fame (κλέος) and his ability to protect his family. Ultimately, Odysseus succeeds in ensuring that his glorious deeds will remain famous and that his son will live to continue his family line with his wealth intact.

---

16. More precisely, Stanford (1967, xii–xiii) calls Odysseus "a symbol of the Ionic-Greek Everyman in his eloquence, cleverness, unscrupulousness, intellectual curiosity, courage, endurance, shrewdness . . . a realistic mixture of good and bad." Dougherty (2001, 175) disagrees: "This archetypal man, . . . is not Everyman; he has a distinct set of qualities—qualities that have made his return possible." However, what makes Odysseus like every Ionian Greek—and like everyone else—are the universal situations in which he finds himself, not his unique ability to survive in those situations. Stanford's description of the Ionian-Greek self-image does not assume that every individual in that group will be as clever, courageous, or unscrupulous as Odysseus, and therefore as successful at remaining alive.

The theme of family is absent from the book of Jonah (see Chapter 5 §2). Jonah shows no interest in fame, although many readers view Jonah as being concerned over being known as a false prophet. While Jonah, like Odysseus, finds himself in a "frail vessel on the raging sea," he shows no sign of being concerned for the preservation of his individual identity, let alone his future fame. He is not warned ahead of time about the danger of being sucked down by the storm or swallowed by a big fish, as Odysseus is warned by the goddess. Nor does Jonah need to be warned, because the sea calms when he enters it and the fish serves a salvific purpose rather than a destructive one.[17] In short, the book of Jonah is *not* about the "man" Jonah, in the sense that the *Odyssey* is about the ἀνήρ Odysseus.

The same is true of Jonah's relation to the hero of the *Epic of Gilgamesh*. While Gilgamesh is fleeing personal death when he begins his risky and unprecedented journey through the "waters of death," we are given no evidence that Jonah is fleeing death when he embarks on his sea voyage to Tarshish. We are also informed about a wider range of Gilgamesh's emotions, from his fear of personal death to his mourning over the loss of a loved one. The theme of embeddedness is also prominent in this work, most conspicuously with the female figures Ninsun and Siduri,[18] who advocate for risk-avoidance by urging the hero to remain embedded in an enclosure, as do Penelope and Calypso in the *Odyssey*.

When heroes such as these take flight, they do so as adults who have already established their autonomy and transcended their desire to please a dominating parental figure at the cost of their own will and integrity, even if that figure is a god. From this perspective, Jonah's flight and later quarrel with his divine parent express his refusal to obey divine dictates if he believes them to be unreasonable, even if his refusal results in his annihilation or being entombed alive. Here, Jonah becomes a rebel in the sense of Dostoevsky's Ivan Karamazov, a principled (although flawed) young man who wants to "return his ticket" to his God's unjust world (Dostoevsky 1976, 226; cf. Frolov 1999, 102).

At the same time, Jonah's *sukkah* and the raft (σχεδία) built by Homer's Odysseus both express the continuing need for a safe enclosure to protect oneself from a hostile surrounding world. Such enclosures may also be employed to express our continuing epistemological vulnerability. Plato's Simmias alludes to Odysseus's raft when he suggests that if it is impossible for us to learn the truth about basic life problems, one should take arguments which are "the best and most difficult to refute" and "risk sailing through life" (*Phaed.* 85c-d; cf. Burnett 1911, 81). For Simmias, this is a *deuteros plous* or "second sailing," that is, the

---

17. The same is true of the dolphin in Herodotus's report concerning Arion. Sailors plan to throw Arion overboard in order to acquire his wealth. Arion chooses to die by throwing himself overboard rather than being killed by the sailors. He is then saved by the dolphin, but without being swallowed by the beast (*Hist.* 2.24).

18. Ninsun famously laments that the sun-god Shamash has placed in her son "a sleepless heart" (ŠÀ-*bi* [=*libbi*] *la ṣa-li-la te-mid-su*; SE III, 45; Parpola 1997, 79). On the cautionary speech by the barmaid Siduri in the OB version of the epic, see Chapter 2 §2.

knower's "next-best" option. Many centuries later, Hume described his trepidation at launching "out into those immense depths of philosophy, which lie before me," by likening himself to "a man, who having struck on many shoals, and having narrowly escaped shipwreck in passing a small frith, has yet the temerity to put out to sea in the same leaky weather-beaten vessel" (2007a, 171–72). The core danger expressed with these metaphors is the unavoidable risk involved in navigating our way through life in our frail bodily—and mental—vessels, without adequate navigational information and without the prospect of a rescuer when danger nears.

The symbolic force of Odysseus's raft is increased by Homer's continued emphasis on the dangers faced by the human individual. On the sea, these can range from being swallowed up or torn apart to being entombed in pleasure in a seductive goddess's cave.[19] Odysseus did not begin his journey home on a flimsy raft. He captains a seemingly sturdy ship, only to be forced by the gods to build a raft in two different crisis situations,[20] ultimately ending up naked on the Phaiacean shore. This plot structure illustrates the fact that even the sturdiest of vessels commanded by the "many-turning" Odysseus is no more effective than a supposedly flimsy *sukkah*[21] when it comes to self-built—or collectively built—human enclosures, especially when a deity is set on destroying that shelter.

Plato's Simmias is aware that to make our life voyage more steady and danger-free requires "some divine word" (*Phaed.* 85d). In Homer's epic—and in the book of Jonah—the "divine" is the cause of the hero's danger as well as being the hero's rescuer. In Homer's world, Odysseus has to contend with gods such as Poseidon, whose will is adverse to his own, but he also has divinities such as Athena and Ino aiding him. Even after Odysseus approaches the seeming safety of the Phaiacian shore, he is aware that primal dangers from Poseidon still threaten him (*Od.* 5.415-22). A "great wave may snatch me up and throw me against stony rock" if he tries to land. Yet if he swims on in search of a harbor or beach, he knows that the squall may snatch him up again and bear him along the fish-filled open sea. Some divine power "may even set upon me some great sea monster."[22] Odysseus

---

19. On the degree to which ancient Greek sailors tended to "hug the coast" out of fear of the open sea, see Morton (2001, 143–45).

20. The first is the "makeshift raft" which Odysseus binds together from the keel and mast of his ship, which Zeus has wrecked in a storm (*Od.* 12.423-25; Stanford 1967, 418). The second is the sturdier raft which Odysseus constructs with the help of the goddess Calypso (*Od.* 5.162-79, 234-62).

21. Jonah's "booth" is on dry land, but the dynamics of exposure and enclosure are the same.

22. The kind of sea monster Odysseus fears is a κῆτος, the same term used to denote Jonah's "big fish" in the Septuagint (cf. Mt. 12:40; κοιλίᾳ τοῦ κήτους). This is also the term used to describe the various sea monsters which threaten heroes such as Heracles and Perseus, as well as the gigantic beast which swallows Lucian's narrator and his ship in *A True History* (Bk. 1 §§30-31).

knows all this is possible because the "renowned Earth-shaker is filled with hate[23]" against him (*Od.* 5.423).

In Homer and later Greek literature, Poseidon is god of both sea and earthquake. The *Homeric Hymn to Poseidon* (line 22) calls this deity "the great god, mover of the earth and barren sea, of the deep." We have already noted the dangers of engulfment and being torn apart to which Poseidon exposes the hero Odysseus, when he took to the sea in his attempt to reach the land of Ithaca.[24] At the symbolic center of Odysseus's homeland is the marital bed which he had fashioned out of an olive tree firmly rooted in the earth, around which he built his palace (*Od.* 23.183-204). In the *Odyssey*, Odysseus ultimately reaches this solid and reliable form of "embeddedness" and is seemingly content. In his retelling of the story, Dante has the restless hero feel compelled to return to the dangers of the sea yet again, only to die when a whirlwind strikes his ship and the sea closes over Odysseus and his old shipmates (*Inf.* 26.141-42).

As noted by Burkert (1987, 139), "Poseidon remains an embodiment of elemental force; sea storm and earthquake are the most violent forms of energy directly encountered by man [sic]." Aristotle makes the same point without reference to this god when he is discussing fear, courage, and rashness: "We should call someone mad, or incapable of feeling pain and danger, if he feared nothing, 'earthquake nor swelling waves,' as they say of the Celts" (*Eth. nic.* 1115b23-28). These are phenomena which should frighten even the most sane and courageous person. Put differently, they are the most extreme examples of what evokes (or should evoke) deep fear in humans. In the Hebrew Bible, on the other hand, the same God may oppose or help the adult who has ventured out on his own—or do both at different times. Yahweh's power is not limited to the sea. One need only recall the epiphanies which portray Yahweh as a gigantic divine warrior marching on the earth (e.g., Judg. 5:4-5; Hab. 3:3-15; Isa. 63:1-3) or causing an earthquake to display his power to Elijah (1 Kgs 19:11-12).

---

23. The term used here (ὀδύσσομαι) for hateful rage sounds similar to the name "Odysseus." Homer implies that the hero's name means "the hated one" or "the object of rage"; cf. *Od.* 1.62, 5.340 and Stanford 1967, 215. Similarly, Job plays on his own name (אִיוֹב) when he charges that Yahweh considers him a hated enemy (אוֹיֵב; Job 13:24). Both recipients of apparent divine hatred are "men"; in fact, "man" is the first word of each story (אִישׁ; ἀνήρ). The difference is that the God who treats Job as his enemy is the sole all-powerful deity, whereas Poseidon, who hates Odysseus, is just one deity, whose intentions and powers are countered by other gods who are more sympathetic to this human hero.

24. Seneca deflates the drama of Poseidon's enmity toward Odysseus in an amusing fashion. He suggests that the sea-god's anger was not the primary reason why Ulysses was shipwrecked so many times. The hero was simply prone to seasickness, which led him to attempt reaching the lee shore no matter how great the danger (*Ep. mor.* 53 §4).

4 Yahweh's character and his relationship with Jonah

The parent-child relationship can become a struggle for dominance or control (see Lasine 2012, 230–35). Control is also a key factor if one views Jonah as a mature adult who is attempting to keep his integrity in Yahweh's world. Dempsey notes that "with respect to power, God is the one who is in full control of Jonah" (2000, 123; cf. Fretheim 2007, 127–28). Yet Jonah *is* able to flee his mission. Admittedly, this merely grants Jonah temporary and ultimately illusory control over his actions. But, as suggested earlier, his flight may also express a refusal to let God's command control his behavior, even if his refusal results in his annihilation or being entombed alive. On the ship, Jonah controls what the sailors do with him, once he has told them that he had fled from Yahweh (1:10, 12). The book's final chapter shows that the prophet's resistance to God's authority remains even after he has completed his mission. His words imply that his resistance stems from moral objections to the task, while his twice-repeated request to die expresses both the futility of resistance and a desire to—at least—control when and how he will escape his untenable situation.

Psychologist Jerry Piven (2004, 11) points out that the adult conception of death contains within it the residues of infantile terror and trauma, although it also continues to evolve with the development and experiences of the individual. If we view Jonah as a mature adult, what should we make of his attitude toward death? From this point of view, Jonah's death wish stems from a refusal to live on Yahweh's terms, rather than being an expression of wounded narcissism or a desire to protect himself from being viewed as a false prophet. Readers of the entire Hebrew Bible know that full submission to Yahweh's will does not always prevent his faithful followers from being devastated and traumatized, as we discovered when examining Psalm 44 and the God-fearing sailors of Ps. 107:23-30.[25] Readers must decide for themselves whether to assume that Jonah also has this knowledge and is reacting to it in his conversation with God.

From this perspective, Yahweh is being patronizing to his prophet in ch. 4, rather than displaying paternal nurturance. God exposes Jonah to the elements as a way of showing him that he cannot make it through God's world on his own. In this scenario, God is talking down to Jonah and toying with his emotions in a way which makes Jonah appear infantile, if not *feel* infantile.[26] In addition, readers who view Jonah as childish do not have to take seriously the prophet's complaint about Yahweh's excessive compassion or his repeated death wish. Elsewhere I have argued that Yahweh is at times portrayed as a narcissistic parent in the Bible, a parent who does all he can to keep the "children of Israel" from gaining

---

25. See Chapter 3 §4 and §5.

26. Of course the character Jonah does not express such feelings or accuse God of trying to make him feel infantile. However, readers who view Yahweh as browbeating the prophet in this scene may still impute this motive to the deity, especially if they have observed a similar interpersonal dynamic in their own experience.

6. The Plot of Jonah, Childhood Crises, and the Perils of Adulthood 111

the separation from parental control necessary for them to gain an adult sense of autonomy (Lasine 2002, 39–43).[27] From this standpoint, readers who view Jonah as infantile may be viewing the prophet in the way that the character Yahweh views him—or would want us to view him—in ch. 4.

We may also have clues to how Yahweh views himself. As we discussed in Chapter 5 §2, the prophet cites Yahweh's self-description in Exod. 34:6 when he objects to God's acceptance of Nineveh's repentance (Jon. 4:2). Exodus 34:6-7 are part of an ongoing debate between God and Moses about covenantal fidelity to a guilty people. After Yahweh agrees to remain with, and work wonders for, his covenanted people (v. 10), he warns the people against making covenants with the inhabitants of the promised land and bowing down to their gods. In fact, they must destroy the cult objects of these gods, for "Yahweh, his name is Jealous, he is a jealous God" (v. 14; cf. Exod. 20:4), who demands exclusive devotion from his people/children.[28]

The fact that Yahweh assigns himself the trait of being "long to anger" (אפים ארך) acknowledges that he can become angry under certain conditions. This also implies that his anger is under his control and will manifest itself only when he is pushed to the limit of his patience. As God says in the Meḵilta, "I am ruler of my jealous anger" (Baḥodesh 6). Does this mean that Yahweh would never have the kind of angry knee-jerk response that Moses exhibits when he breaks the tablets in anger in Exod. 32:19? Earlier in Exodus 32, Yahweh had told Moses to leave him alone so that his anger will get hot against them and consume them (v. 10). In the following chapter, Yahweh seems unsure that he can rule his anger at the Israelites because they "push his buttons." He tells Moses that he cannot continue

---

27. On the divine parent-human child relationship in ancient Mesopotamia, see Jacobsen (1976, 157–60). On Greek gods not being reliable parental figures, see Lasine (2001, 253–54). In classical Greek literature, the negative aspects of total devotion to one protective deity are dramatically illustrated in Euripides's *Hippolytus*. Hippolytus disdains the cult of Aphrodite and even the institution of marriage, due to his devotion to his personal deity, the virgin Artemis. As a result, Aphrodite ensures that Hippolytus suffers a horrible and humiliating death. Hippolytus cannot rely on his personal god to rescue him. As Burkert observes, "In the last, decisive extremity the gods abandon man [sic].... Artemis bids farewell to the dying Hippolytus and goes. 'It would be a grievous matter to rescue the generation and offspring of all humans' [*Iliad* XV.140-41] and so the gods save none" (1987, 188; the rendering of *Il.* XV.141 has been modified). In general, ancient Greek gods do not demand exclusive devotion, but they also do not like their cults to be ignored.

28. Yahweh's list of his own personality traits in Exod. 34:6-7 has been called a "timeless expression of the character of YHWH" (Barton 2001, 81) and "a kind of 'canon'" defining Israel's God (Fretheim 2010, 302). Scholars such as Crenshaw (1995, 136) and Fretheim (2010, 302) take Yahweh's wrath and his intended punishments to be a function of the people's situation and attitude toward him, rather than an indicator of God's own character. See further in Lasine (2016a, 467–69).

to go among his people for even "one moment" lest he destroy them when they begin acting according to their "stiff-necked" nature (Exod. 33:3, 5). Yet Yahweh is not said to get angry when Jonah violates his direct order to go to Nineveh or when Jonah complains and wants to die later on. Nor is God said to be angry at Nineveh. After all, Nineveh is not located in the holy land, and Jonah is not told to address any Yahwists who might happen to be living there.

Interestingly, Jonah is not the only Israelite prophet to directly employ Yahweh's self-characterization in Exod. 34:6-7 in reference to the fate of Nineveh. Nahum does so as well, although in a radically different way. Nahum highlights only the interconnected traits of jealousy, wrath, and vengeance in 1:2-10. He begins by naming Yahweh "the jealous one" and alludes to his vengeance (נקם) three times in the same verse: "God the jealous one (אֵל קַנּוֹא) and Yahweh the avenging one, Yahweh the avenging one and master [or possessor] of rage; Yahweh takes vengeance on his adversaries and reserving wrath[29] for his enemies" (v. 2). Yahweh's anger is mentioned five times in vv. 2-6. In fact, the only trait that Nahum repeats from Exod. 34:6 *also* focuses on Yahweh's anger, namely, his being "long to anger." Nothing is said about divine compassion, graciousness, covenantal loyalty, truth, or forgiveness.[30]

The fact that Nahum views Yahweh's wrath as driven by his jealousy is striking, since this is the only case in the Hebrew Bible where his jealous anger is directed at an external enemy ("Nineveh")[31] rather than at Israel (see Spronk 1997, 34). It is also striking that Jonah does not urge God to manifest his jealousy or anger at the city which Jonah had predicted would be overturned in forty days. Instead, Jonah focuses exclusively on Yahweh's graciousness, compassion, longness to anger, and his mercy, as well as his ability to "repent of the evil." When Jonah goes on to implore Yahweh to take his life, he is interpreting his own situation through the optic of Yahweh's self-characterization—but not in terms of Yahweh's jealousy or wrath. In effect, Jonah explains his desire to die in terms of Yahweh's character rather than his own. In fact, one reason that Jonah sees his situation as both unbearable and unchangeable is his assumption that Yahweh's character traits are robust and unchanging.

If all these characteristics of Yahweh—including wrath and jealousy—*are* robust and unchanging, what does that imply about the "human condition" of all

---

29. On נוטר here, see Spronk (1997, 35–36). He follows Fishbane in regarding the expression לאיביו נוטר as a "dialectical pun" on נצר in the "attribute formulary" of Exod. 34:7 (Fishbane 1988, 347, n. 79).

30. As noted by a number of commentators, Jonah and Nahum are the only books in the Hebrew Bible which end in a question. Nah. 3:19 asks, "Upon whom has not passed your continual evildoing?" Glasson (1969, 54–55) suggests that God's question at the end of Jonah may refute the implication of Nahum's question, by implying the superiority of divine mercy over justice.

31. For examples of how "Nineveh" in this book was later interpreted as standing for other enemies of God's people, see Spronk (1997, 20).

who believe that the biblical God governs their life-world—and who may therefore have to cope with this deity's less congenial personal traits? How does their life-world differ from that experienced by individuals who do not acknowledge a deity as fundamental to their condition? How does the prospect of personal death affect those who do, and do not, believe in the biblical God? These are among the questions that will be dealt with in the final chapter of this study.

Chapter 7

CONCLUSION: LIVING AND DYING IN THE HEBREW BIBLE

Our study of the book of Jonah has shown that the opposition between enclosure and exposure plays an important role in that character's textual world, as well as in the life-worlds of the book's readers. I will begin this final chapter by discussing George Orwell's version of the "Jonah in the whale" motif, which highlights the advantages and disadvantages of embeddedness as a coping device, not only for people who expect that a personal deity will shelter them in "the shadow of his wings" like the "little man in his eye" (Ps. 17:8; cf. Deut. 32:10) but also for those who do not share that belief.

The book of Jonah presents us with a textual world governed by a very hands-on deity. That deity is the cause of, and the cure for, stormy seas, engulfing sea monsters and the rocks which threaten to wreck the ship in which individuals make their sea journey through life. In the larger context of the Hebrew Bible as a whole, this God is also the one who promised Israel the holy land and who caused the earth to open its mouth and swallow the rebels who had been on their way to that land. With this in mind, in the later sections of this chapter, I will ask whether the human condition in Yahweh's world is any less daunting, anxiety-producing, and precarious than living in a godless world thought to be indifferent to humans. Finally, if religion serves to counter the fear of death, as commonly assumed, how should we understand the fact that the Hebrew Bible does not offer its readers the comforting prospect of a meaningful afterlife?

1 Orwell's "essential Jonah act"

As I discussed in Chapter 5 §2, risk aversion has been central theme in some psychologists' ideas of a Jonah complex, even though Jonah takes huge risks and none of the other characters in the book is shown to be living a life free of risk. Jonah, the crew of his ship, the Ninevites, and even the *qiqayon* plant are vulnerable and at risk of being destroyed at some point. How should one live in a world full of risk? While even Qoheleth encourages enjoyment of life's pleasures, the pessimist Schopenhauer makes this sage appear relatively sanguine when he asserts that spending our life journey pursuing pleasures and joys is "the greatest wrong-headedness." For Schopenhauer, it is preferable to behold "this world with a too-somber gaze as a kind of hell," so that "one is only anxious to procure a fireproof room in it" (1963, 485). This image implies that being annihilated by "fire" is always a possibility, if not a continuing danger from which one should insulate oneself, thereby limiting risk. In terms of the enclosure-exposure opposition, the fireproof room is functionally equivalent to Schopenhauer's skiff of the self on the world-sea,[1] in that both are designed to protect one from being overwhelmed and killed by an elemental external force. The fireproof room is the most constrictive form of protection, because it becomes one's entire world for life, rather than being a temporary shelter or "panic room" in an emergency. Quite apart from the fact that spending one's entire life in such a dismal enclosure would be an impoverished sort of existence, everything we have discussed in this study implies that the idea of a risk-proof and lasting haven from disaster is an illusion, whether we imagine such a chamber as a waterproof ship's hull or a fireproof room.

George Orwell's reaction to Jonah in the "whale" envisions a more positive sort of enclosed living. Orwell contends that "countless people have envied" Jonah "in imagination [and] day-dream." Why? The usual reason: "The whale's belly is simply a womb big enough for an adult" (1981, 244). However, Orwell's reference to a "womb" goes beyond the usual use of the metaphor in relation to Jonah's psychology. When you are ensconced in *this* kind of womb you have "yards of blubber between yourself and reality," allowing you to "keep up an attitude of the completest indifference, no matter what happens" (1981, 244). This sort of belly resident is not an unconscious sleeping fetus. Nor is she a child basking in the illusion of infantile omnipotence. She is an adult with developed "attitudes" and feelings, who retains her consciousness of self just as much as Red Riding Hood in the wolf's stomach, Pinocchio in the shark, and Israel after being swallowed by Babylon. This kind of container is more like a castle surrounded by a moat of blubber than a womb.

Orwell singles out the novelist Henry Miller as having "performed the essential Jonah act of allowing himself to be swallowed, remaining passive, accepting."[2] Orwell adds that in Miller's case "the whale happens to be transparent" (1981, 245). His "willing Jonah" wants to obscure the dangers associated with our being immersed in an uncontrollable enveloping world by becoming a detached beholder of that world from inside a safe enclosure. Orwell predicts that good writers "in the remaining years of free speech" will share Miller's passive attitude and "[rob] reality of its terrors by simply submitting to it." He admonishes these writers to "get inside the whale—or rather, admit you are inside the whale (for you *are*, of course)" (1981, 250).

Orwell's use of the "Jonah in the whale" motif cannot be adequately understood apart from his cultural milieu, and the events which took place as the essay

---

1. On this Schopenhauerian metaphor, see Chapter 6 §3.
2. Orwell (1981, 243–44) takes his lead from Miller's comparison of Anaïs Nin to Jonah in the whale's belly, with the help of Aldous Huxley's remark that people in El Greco's pictures look as though they were in the bellies of whales (see Miller 1959, 297).

was being written in 1939–40. It can therefore serve as a historical "case study" illustrating the advantages and disadvantages of supposedly Jonah-like enclosure in response to overwhelming external dangers. When fighting in Spain in 1937, Orwell had developed a growing distrust of communism as an antidote to fascism; "progress and reaction have both turned out to be swindles." Looking back on the literary history of the 1930s and the work produced by his fellow left-wing writers in Britain, Orwell concludes that "a writer does well to keep out of politics" (1981, 240).[3] When Orwell was at work on "Inside the Whale," England declared war on Germany. To Orwell, "what is quite obviously happening, . . . is the break-up of laissez-faire capitalism and of the liberal-Christian culture." And what will follow is "almost certainly" an age of "totalitarian dictatorships" and the stamping out of the autonomous individual. In such circumstances, literature "must suffer at least a temporary death" (1981, 249–50). It is this situation which makes "the essential Jonah act" of passive acceptance so attractive.

According to Sherwood, in this essay, Orwell is arguing that "Jonah-ism . . . becomes nothing less than a dangerous a-political quietism." Orwell's point is "clearly that the intellectual in society should take up his/her post outside the whale" (2000, 139–40). This conclusion is not supported by Orwell's essay. Nor is it how "Inside the Whale"[4] has been understood by Orwell's Marxist critics. E. P. Thompson accused Orwell of writing "an apology for quietism . . . in which the aspirations of a generation were buried" (1978, 223). D. A. N. Jones is even more blunt when referring to all of Orwell's writing during this period: "If you took Orwell's advice, you'd end up doing nothing" (1971, 155). At the same time, the essay hints at the possibility that the need for embeddedness in the "whale" might be temporary. Referring to Orwell's statement that "seemingly there is nothing left but quietism," Marks notes that the qualifier "seemingly" suggests that "there might be something left" (2011, 97).[5]

Orwell's political position in early 1940 was not unique. In the first issue of his literary journal *Horizon* in January 1940, Cyril Connolly declares that "the war is separating culture from life, . . . Left Wing politics is for the time exhausted, . . . and our politics are in abeyance" (1940, 5). The situation may be temporary, but it is also urgent: "At the moment civilization is on the operating table and we sit in the waiting room." E. P. Thompson also acknowledges that "1940 was a

---

3. Yet, as Levenson points out, "even at this moment of radical pessimism, Orwell's instinct is to keep writing" (2007, 74). E. P. Thompson (1978, 223–24) grants that there was reason for Orwell's "profound political pessimism"; he was right to state the problem, but not to "give up" the problem. On pessimism leading—or not leading—to resignation, see Chapter 2 §1.

4. Or Orwell's 1941 broadcast on the BBC in April 1941, printed in *The Listener* a month later with the title "The Frontiers of Art and Propaganda" (Orwell 1968, 123–27).

5. In a letter of January 1940 to his publisher Gollancz, Orwell concedes that he may have been "over-pessimistic" in this essay and that "freedom of thought etc. may survive in an economically totalitarian society" (Davison 2013, 173).

nadir of hope." Like Connolly, Thompson uses a medical metaphor to express the urgency of this moment: "An essay [such as 'Inside the Whale'] is an attempt at instant contemporary diagnosis of the kind which is performed in an emergency ward where there is no time for strict clinical (or in this case historical) discipline" (1978, 224).

It may not have required the outbreak of hostilities for Orwell to suggest that writers should passively accept frightening realities in their world and admit that they are powerless to eliminate those dangers. When Orwell predicts the breakup of liberal-Christian culture, he adds "war or no war" (1981, 249). And when he looks back at the Great War of 1914–18, he calls it "only a heightened moment in an almost continuous crisis." That crisis is "the disintegration of our society and the increasing helplessness of all decent people" (1981, 249). This is why Orwell thinks "that the passive, non-co-operative attitude implied in Henry Miller's work is justified. Whether or not it is an expression of what people ought to feel, it probably comes somewhere near to expressing what they do feel." A good example is Tubby Bowling, the protagonist of Orwell's 1939 novel *Coming Up for Air*, whom Levenson calls "Orwell's Jonah" (2007, 72). This character, one of Orwell's "ordinary chaps," also sees the prospect of totalitarianism in England's future (Orwell 1950, 186).[6]

In sum, Orwell's use of Miller's Jonah metaphor suggests the defensive posture of passive detached beholding from inside the shelter of a fantasized "whale" may be attractive to any individual or group who perceive their world to be overwhelming and dangerous. Feelings of helplessness in the face of overwhelming external forces are not experienced merely during violent periods of social upheaval. However, our study of the book of Jonah makes it clear that the character Jonah is no more an example of "Jonah-ism" than he is of a "Jonah complex." The biblical Jonah does *not* "allow" himself to be swallowed and never acknowledges that he is speaking from inside a fish. And Jonah feels anything but cozy when he is enrobed in seaweed in his metaphorical "belly of Sheol." Nor is he passive and accepting in this situation—or in any of the other difficult situations in which God has placed him.

While the posture of Orwell's whale resident bears some resemblance to the detached spectator described by the Stoics and Epicureans such as Lucretius, it also calls to mind the psychiatric patients who describe themselves as feeling encased in a "plastic bubble" or "behind a sheet of glass."[7] Ultimately, the need for defensive retreat into protective enclosure is something experienced by all of us, long after dreams of intrauterine bliss have retreated to the farthest reaches of our consciousness.

---

6. What soon spurred Orwell to action in fighting the fascists was patriotism, as Orwell understood that term. See Rossi (2007).

7. On Lucretius, see Chapter 3 §5. On these psychiatric patients, see Chapter 5, n. 47 and Vokan (1979).

Joseph Conrad's narrator Marlow alludes to this coping mechanism when he observes that "each of us makes for himself [a shelter] to creep under in moments of danger, as a tortoise withdraws into its shell" (Conrad 1989, 274). The tortoise shell metaphor suggests that we turn a part of *ourselves* into a shelter, even though the sheltering part must be rendered insensible for it to fulfill its function. This recalls Freud's description of the developing individual being bombarded by stimuli, which results in our contact boundary with the external world becoming a "baked-through crust" (1940, 25). As I discuss elsewhere, other theorists take such armoring as characteristic of modern Westerners who have developed personalities which are also as closed and impermeable as the hull of a boat. Certain social formations benefit from their members being examples of Elias's "*homo clausus*" or Weber's individual enclosed in a "steel-hard casing" (see Lasine 2012, 39–40). Berger and Luckmann (1989, 101–03) note that socially constructed networks of meaning can serve a similar protective function for individuals, sheltering us from "anomic terror," the anxiety of uncertainty, and awareness of death.

Within the world of the Hebrew Bible, the need for such a protective "shell" can also arise, even though ancient social figurations and the human place within the natural world differ in some ways from that experienced by people in modern Western societies (see Lasine 2012, 24–55). Whether making our *selves* into a shelter was an option for ancient Near Easterners remains open to debate. Orwell's reaction to the figure of Jonah shows that at least some modern readers may interpret the book's plot in this fashion.

2 Life and death "keeping house together": The end of the book of Jonah

William James notes that while "our sacred books and traditions tell us of one God who made heaven and earth" and saw that they were good, "on more intimate acquaintance," we find that every praiseworthy phenomenon "exists cheek by jowl with some contrary phenomenon." Even "life and death keep house together in indissoluble partnership." Once we acknowledge this uncanny copresence of opposites, "there gradually steals over us, instead of the old warm notion of a man-loving Deity, that of an awful power that neither hates nor loves, but rolls all things together meaninglessly to a common doom" (1962, 10–11; cf. 1920, 139–40). In the book of Jonah, the prophet is very aware of the "notion of a man-loving Deity," but this notion brings him no warmth or comfort. Might readers who have been prompted to think about their vulnerabilities by the book's plot find the world controlled by the loving and hating[8] biblical God even more intimidating than James's indifferent "awful power"?

The passionate God of the Hebrew Bible is rarely indifferent to humans' actions. If he decides to strip an individual or nation of his protection, those targeted by

---

8. The most compact juxtaposition of these opposing emotions is Yahweh's statement in Mal. 1:23: "I loved Jacob and Esau I hated."

his anger or abandonment know that there is a divine will behind their suffering, not some accident.⁹ I ended my earlier discussion of Jonah's psalm by suggesting that God may be exposing Jonah to the elements as a way of showing Jonah that he cannot make it alone. He—and therefore we too—must remain entirely dependent upon Yahweh's favor in order to feel safe in the "very good" cosmos he has created.

As a result, when Yahweh's people experience themselves living in a world bereft of protection, face to face with the prospect of their ultimate annihilation, they should know that this is due to God's intentional abandonment of them rather than the nonexistence of a warm loving deity. For such people, the "awful power" of which William James speaks *is* Yahweh, when he chooses to make us learn the hard way about what can happen if we vex him. We have already noted that the same can be true even when Yahweh's subjects are not said to vex him. With Yahweh's protection removed, his faithful followers can become "sheep for the slaughter" (Ps. 44:23), exposed without a sheltering sheepcote.[10]

The writing prophets repeat this lesson constantly. When the prophets conjure up images of a nightmare world destroyed by Yahweh's wrath, the few survivors must live in deserted cities from which animals have disappeared and humans dwell in utter desolation (see §4 of this chapter). In biblical metaphorical terms, such a life can induce the vertigo of a drunken person, someone who reels like a sailor on choppy seas or someone treading uncertain quaking ground, groping at noonday like a blind person in darkness (Deut. 28:29; Ps. 107:27; cf. Job 5:14; 12:25). Put differently, Yahweh can give us what a Kafka character calls "a seasickness on firm land" (1970, 217). Our last sight of Jonah is also on firm dry land. He is not said to be tottering like a drunken sailor or "seasick," but the sun and wind have made him faint. Yahweh's last question might also make anyone vertiginous. Thus, we leave Jonah when he is still exposed both to the elements and to his God's strange interrogation. He is still allowed no sheltering enclosure and we readers get no closure either.[11] The issues raised by the book remain unresolved.

The book's plot and its conclusion can also be viewed quite positively, especially when Jonah's experiences are compared to those of the castaways we discussed earlier. Jonah escapes the danger of the sea storm. His ship is not wrecked,[12] and he is rescued when he is cast into the sea. Nor does Jonah have to contend with rocks on the lee shore, as Odysseus fears will be the case when he finally sights land after the "earth-shaker" Poseidon has shattered his raft (*Od.* 5.366-70, 406-23).

---

9. See further in §4 of this chapter.
10. See Chapter 3 §4-5 and Chapter 6 §5.
11. On the book's lack of closure and its implications, see, for example, Crouch (1994). According to Trible (1996, 525-26), the fact that the story "stops, but ... does not end" leads the reader to "get the point," namely, that "the reader is Jonah; Jonah is the reader." In this way, "the story subverts the reader."
12. However, one occasionally finds reference to Jonah's "shipwreck," such as the Paul Bris painting of Jonah being thrown overboard, which is entitled "The Shipwreck of Jonah" (*Le Naufrage de Jonas* [ca. 1600]).

Jonah does not even have to fight his way to the shore on an improvised raft or by riding the waves while immersed in the sea.[13] Instead he is conveyed to shore by the miraculous fish. And unlike the stories of the Egyptian sailor, Odysseus, and Crusoe, in the biblical book we receive no information about where Jonah landed on the shore, what his physical condition might have been, what measures he took to survive and recover there, or how he traveled from there to Nineveh. He simply heeds God's second call and proceeds to Nineveh, with no mention of his being exhausted, injured, or traumatized by being hurled into the sea or by being in the fish's belly.[14]

In ch. 4, when Jonah is exposed to the sun and wind on dry land, it is not because he was abandoned there as is the case with Sophocles's Philoctetes; Jonah chooses to remain seated on the east of the city. And while the divine Heracles appears at the end of Sophocles's play to inform and advise Philoctetes about what he must do next, their interaction does not have the intimacy, nuance, or argumentative nature which characterizes the dialogue between Jonah and Yahweh. We leave the prophet alive and in communication with his God, even though our knowledge of their conversation ends abruptly.

In these ways, the plot of Jonah resembles the popular fiction described by Freud in a 1908 essay:

> If the first volume has ended with the sinking of the ship in a storm at sea, in which our hero is situated, at the beginning of the second volume I am certain to read about his marvelous rescue.... The feeling of security with which I accompany the hero through his dangerous destiny is the same as the feeling with which an actual hero throws himself into the water to rescue someone drowning.... It is the true heroic feeling.... "Nothing can happen to *you*!"[15] (1941, 220)

If a reader of Jonah has a feeling of security when accompanying the prophet on his journeys, this could be the result of viewing Yahweh as the hero's "safety net." The fact that the book's hero survives being cast into the sea and lodging in a monster's belly could also prompt a reader to recall her infantile fantasy of omnipotence. The book also challenges egoistic feelings of security and invulnerability by showing readers the difficulties and dangers of dealing with this parental God. Considering what Yahweh makes Jonah endure, one can easily imagine the character Jonah thinking "*everything* happens to me!" rather than "nothing can happen to me!"

In the end, Jonah does not illustrate all aspects of the human condition in Yahweh's world, because readers are given no information about the prophet in

---

13. On Odysseus's two rafts, see Chapter 6, n. 20. On shipwrecked Crusoe being carried by waves to the shore, see Defoe (1994, 34–35).

14. Contrast Jacob limping off after his encounter with God at Penuel (Gen. 32:32-33).

15. Freud is quoting a character in a work by Anzensgruber; the character recommends that one say this to oneself; see Lasine (2012, 137 and 137, n. 55).

key areas of human existence. As noted earlier, we have no way of knowing if Jonah has a wife and children, let alone whether he is in a position to enjoy life with them in the way recommended by speakers such as Siduri in *Gilgamesh* and the biblical Qoheleth. We cannot know whether he values the symbolic immortality offered by fame or reputation, even though it is often assumed that Jonah is angry that his reputation as a true prophet will suffer if Nineveh is not destroyed. Nor do we know whether Jonah takes pride in being an Israelite, let alone being the member of a specific tribe or resident of a specific city. What the plot of Jonah *does* illustrate is the continual and crucial role played by the God Yahweh in this character's life.

Since Jonah's mission is that of a prophet, some readers might conclude that they need not be concerned about Yahweh playing such a direct role in their mundane lives. Then again, since the book does not apply the term "prophet" or "man of God" (איש אלהים; נביא) to Jonah (or anyone else), one cannot exclude the possibility that Jonah represents an "Everyhuman" in the sense that the deity plays an equally major role in everyone's life voyage, whether we know it or not. We must now ask how the human condition has been described and experienced by those who do *not* view themselves as living in a world governed by the God of the Hebrew Bible.

3 Vulnerability and the human condition

When modern authors list the sources of human vulnerability, the same root causes tend to be mentioned. The nineteenth-century political philosopher Benjamin Constant believes that "our sadness" has several sources: "Authority can banish us, lying can slander us; the bonds of a totally artificial society wound us; inflexible nature strikes us in what we cherish; old age advances toward us, a gloomy and solemn time when objects grow dark and seem to withdraw, and something cold and dull spreads on everything that surrounds us" (2011, 267). Freud depicts humans as threatened with suffering from three sides: "One's own body, which, destined to deteriorate and disintegration, cannot even do without pain and anxiety as warning signals, ... the external world, which can rage against us with overpowering, unrelenting, destructive forces, and ... relations to other people" (1930, 25). A somewhat less gloomy situation is sketched by a character in Aldous Huxley's novel, *Island*:

> One third, more or less, of all the sorrow that the person I think I am must endure is unavoidable. It is the sorrow inherent in the human condition, the price we must pay for being sentient and self-conscious organisms, aspirants to liberation, but subject to the laws of nature and under orders to keep on marching, through irreversible time, through a world wholly indifferent to our well-being, toward decrepitude and the certainty of death. The remaining two thirds of all sorrow is homemade and, so far as the universe is concerned, unnecessary. (2009, 101–02)

While these inventories of human vulnerability have items in common, they are not totally identical. Freud points out that the suffering we endure through our relations to others "is perhaps more painful to us than any other" and is no less "fatefully unavoidable" than suffering which has another origin (1930, 25). This contrasts with the position of the old Raja in Huxley's novel, who contends that only a third of human sorrow is "inherent in the human condition"; the other two-thirds is "homemade."[16] In later editions of his novel, Huxley made additions to this paragraph, in which he claims that the homemade portion of sorrow is gratuitous and can be removed through "appropriate manipulations of the human environment" (Nugel 2009, 76). It seems unlikely that the sorrow which humans cause one another should be classified in the part of human life which is subject to environmental manipulation. Is it in fact inevitable that we will cause ourselves and others intense suffering? Inevitable or not, many would agree that the most acute form of suffering occurs when we are betrayed by someone to whom we are bound in a relationship of love and basic trust.

Huxley's character speaks of a "world wholly indifferent to our well-being." As I will discuss later in this chapter, this is not how biblical followers of Yahweh view their world; they feel yoked to their God by ties of parental and spousal love, as well as by loyalty to their divine suzerain. What percentage of their sufferings are not "homemade" but "God-made"? The previous chapters of this study already suggest that Yahweh's people—given their expectation of divine loyalty in return for their loyalty to him—may be shaken to their core when they believe themselves to have been abandoned, let down, or betrayed by their divine husband or father. They also have reason to expect that Yahweh will feel both grief and violent anger when he decides that his human children/spouse have betrayed him, abandoned him, ignored his rules, or showed themselves to be ungrateful for the blessings he has showered upon them.

All three modern authors cite increasing bodily decrepitude as a cause of sadness or suffering, as does Qoheleth (12:1-2, 7; see §4 of this chapter). However, in his list of causes, Constant is speaking of life as it is experienced by those who have rejected the consolations of true religious sentiment. When irreligious people "cast a sad glance on the world" which they have "depopulated" of gods and protective powers, they "see human beings alone on an earth which must engulf them." The universe is "without life: generations fleeting, fortuitous, isolated appear there, suffer, die. . . . No tie exists between these generations whose lot here is pain, thereafter nothingness" (2011, 272; cf. 2013, 117). In both *Principles of Politics* and his lifework *On Religion*, Constant describes the life of these individuals as constricted, arid, and impoverished.

---

16. The protagonist of this novel, who reads the former Raja's notebooks, had been shipwrecked on the Raja's island. In this sense, the wisdom expressed by Raja is analogous to the insights imparted to the Egyptian shipwrecked sailor by the divine serpent (Chapter 6 §2).

Given the threats with which humans are confronted, both universal and "homemade," with a deity and without one, it is hardly surprising that modern individuals have been said to have developed a protective closed self and that societies of any period have developed systems of meaning to prevent themselves from being "swallowed up by chaos" and anomy (Berger 1969, 27). Constant's use of engulfment and containment imagery, together with his references to eternal silence and nothingness beyond, raise the question whether some modern readers of Jonah might tend to overstress the symbolic force of the book's near-shipwreck and engulfment imagery because it resonates with their own time-bound experience of safety in enclosures.[17] In a sense, individuals who encase themselves in a defensive shell in order to survive in a world depopulated of protective powers play the roles of both Jonah *and* the big fish. That is, they have "swallowed" *themselves* in order to remain inside their own imaginary steel-hard Orwellian "whales" before the world can swallow them up.

In their world governed by narrow egoism, self-interest, and "moral arithmetic," Constant's irreligious moderns become disconnected from past generations (2013, 80). When "each is his own center, all are isolated. When all are isolated, there is only dust. When the storm arises, the dust becomes mire" (2013, 81). One might object that all humans are, on the deepest level, always and only "dust," not merely in their earthly origin (e.g., Gen. 3:19) but in terms of isolation. Beneath the consolations provided by a social safety net (if one is available) and the assumption of an irrevocable link with one's caring deity, there lurks a deeper and more disconcerting possibility: every human individual is as profoundly alone, exposed, and bound for extinction as Sophocles's Philoctetes.[18] While Constant is displaying the aridity of life without the consolations of religion, he is also calling our attention to aspects of the universal human condition which cause us the most primal and profound anxiety: engulfment, exposure to threat, and annihilation.

In the first edition of *Principles of Politics* (1806), Constant also points out that it is impossible for justice to be achieved in a universe bereft of protective powers. Some ambitious individuals will "argue, fight over others, hurt and torture them." Their victims "do not even have the consolation of hoping that at some point these monsters will be judged, that they will finally see the day of redress and revenge shine" (2011, 272). This is a conclusion which even religious characters such as

---

17. Of course Constant's vision is also *zeitgebunden*, as are my own observations and the perceptions of all the writers I quote in this book. White argues that Constant is describing one of several Romantic responses to the French Revolution and the Reaction; for these Romantic writers, humans as "awash" in a dangerous "historical sea" (1973, 145). Similarly, Gay includes Constant among the Romantics who attempted to address the *mal du siècle*, in which the "autonomous self" is "adrift in a world from which the divine father has disappeared" (1995, 43, 61). These statements should not be taken to mean that Constant was incapable of noticing ways in which humans have been "awash" and "adrift" in other "historical seas."

18. Philoctetes is discussed in Chapter 3 §5.

Job and Qoheleth can affirm. Yet Constant believes that the human condition should lead those who "regard all the hopes of religion as mistakes" to be "more profoundly moved than anyone else by this universal chorus of suffering beings, these petitions of distress, soaring up toward a sky of bronze from all parts of the earth, to remain without reply" (2011, 267).

Certainly one need not be a skeptical *philosoph* to be moved by, or to empathize with, the suffering of those who still await an answer from their benevolent deity. Constant's mention of the grieving who cast requests "at a stony heaven, to wait unanswered" recalls the despair of Yahweh's human children who call upon him to hear and respond to their cries, even though he has not yet done so. For these sufferers, the most acute anxiety is experienced precisely because their "religious hopes" remain strong. Their core belief in a caring parental deity increases the agony of their protector's silence and/or seeming indifference to their plight.

Constant describes the barrenness of life in a world from which the divine has been removed. In his *Pensées*, Pascal suggests how our awareness of our mortality might be experienced in a world by those who have ceased to seek God. He begins by asking readers to imagine "a number of people in chains, and all condemned to death." Every day the prisoners witness some of their fellows having their throats slit. Those who remain see their own condition in those of their fellows. Looking at one another with grief and without hope, they wait for their turn. This, concludes Pascal, is "the image of the condition of human beings" (1966, 556).

Nothing is said in this vignette about the positive aspects of human existence or religious hopes for a better afterlife. Instead, mortality is characterized as a condemnation and as we serve our "life sentence" we await our turn to be executed. The only emotions Pascal attributes to these imprisoned lifers are grief and despair. Nothing in this sketch alerts readers that for Pascal this condition applies only to those who have decided that death is the end of life and have consequently given up hoping for immortality through God. According to Pascal, such individuals obscure their knowledge of their mortality and wretchedness by devoting themselves to *divertissement*, that is, diversion and distraction (1966, 516–18).

Legal theorist Martha Fineman believes that the sources of human fragility we have been discussing should be considered when one is formulating social and legal policy and practice. When advocating for "vulnerability theory," Fineman "claim[s] the term 'vulnerable' for its potential in describing a universal, inevitable, enduring aspect of the human condition." This aspect arises "from our embodiment, which carries with it the ever-present possibility of harm, injury, and misfortune, . . . whether accidental, intentional, or otherwise" (2008, 8–9). Such events are "ultimately beyond human control," so that "both our personal and our social lives are marked and shaped by vulnerability" (2008, 10). Therefore, the liberal idea of an autonomous, independent individual is not "anchored" in the realities of actual human life, especially the reality of our "dependency and the lack of capacity" (2008, 12–19).

Of course, this does not mean that people have given up the pursuit of such unattainable goals. The aspects of human experience expressed through engulfment, embeddedness, and exposure imagery remain relevant in whatever social figuration one finds oneself and however one attempts to cope with his or her primal anxieties (e.g., by pursuing autonomy). Twentieth-century writers who attempt to determine the defining traits of their own time and cultural milieu often point to these same factors. For example, Simmel locates the deepest problems of modern life in the various external forces which threaten an individual. These include the sovereign powers of society, one's historical heritage, the external culture and technique of life, and the conflict with nature for a person's bodily existence, including the threat of being "levelled out and used up" (1903, 187). Three decades later, Freud boiled down the sources of these fundamental vulnerabilities to three: our own body, the external world, and our relations to others.

Over the centuries, many thinkers have concluded that religions in general have their origin in the same vulnerabilities we have been discussing, especially the threats emanating from natural forces, other humans, our own irrational impulses, and the prospect of personal death. Enlightenment figures such as Hume argue that religious ideas arose due to "the incessant hopes and fears which actuate the human mind," including "the anxious concern for happiness, the dread of future misery, the terror of death, the thirst of revenge, the appetite for food and other necessaries" (2007b, 38, 39). The causes for suffering listed by Freud also menace our self-regard and therefore call for consolation: "The world and life must have their terror removed" (Freud 1948, 337–38).

According to Hume and Freud, one way in which religion seeks to tame these terrors is through envisioning an anthropomorphic deity or deities. Hume describes the process in this way: "Every disastrous accident alarms us, and sets us on enquiries concerning the principles whence it arose: Apprehensions spring up with regard to futurity: And the mind, sunk into diffidence, terror, and melancholy, has recourse to every method of appeasing those secret intelligent powers, on whom our fortune is supposed entirely to depend" (2007b, 42). Whether one deity is viewed as the individual's "peculiar patron" or as "the general sovereign of heaven," his devotees "will endeavour, by every art, to insinuate themselves into his favour," including through the use of "praise and flattery" (2007b, 53). Freud also stresses that when we anthropomorphize the forces of nature, we are able to negotiate with these human-like deities, by attempting to "coax, placate or bribe them" (1948, 338). Once God is envisioned as a single paternal protector, people's relations to him can "win back the intimacy and intensity" of childhood relations with one's father (1948, 341).

Freud (1948, 372–73) concedes that a person who rejects the consolation of religious illusions find himself "in a difficult situation; he will have to admit his complete helplessness, his insignificance in the bustling mechanism of the world." One is "no longer the center of creation, no longer the object of tender care by a benevolent providence." Freud draws an analogy between this situation and that of a child who has left the warm and comfortable paternal household. This is not an argument for remaining embedded in the family womb. Freud asks, "Is it not true that infantilism is destined to be overcome?" After all, "the human being cannot remain a child forever"; one must finally "go out into 'hostile life'"[19] in order to be educated to reality.

Both Hume and Freud find that dependence upon such a God can create new causes for fear and uncertainty on the part of his followers. For Hume, imagining a human-like deity whose nature explains all the disasters and capriciousness which permeate human life means projecting onto God "human passions and infirmities." This leads to the deity being represented "as jealous and revengeful, capricious and partial, and, in short, a wicked and foolish man, in every respect but his superior power and authority" (2007b, 41). And Freud notes that while viewing one's God as a father can lead to father-child intimacy, one also has reason to fear one's parents, and "especially one's father." Freud shows the kind of father he has in mind when he claims that all the traits of "the great man" are traits of the father, including the "vehemence of his deeds" and "godly unconcern which may increase to the point of ruthlessness." The great man/father "must be admired, he may be trusted, but one cannot help being also afraid of him" (1950, 217; cf. Lasine 2016a, 472–75).

Does having a personal or paternal deity protect biblical characters—or the moderns who read their stories—from fear of engulfment by external threats or the fear of being crippled by awareness of their inevitable demise? Jonah's relations with his God are too complex to provide a simple "yes" or "no" answer to this question. Many readers believe that Jonah needs to learn the lesson of overcoming infantilism, in Freud's sense. Yet it has become clear that Jonah is not averse to encountering "hostile life" head on, and that the enclosures in which the prophet finds himself (or creates, in the case of the *sukkah*) do not indicate a fundamental desire to remain embedded in womblike safety. In fact, the biblical Jonah takes the ultimate risk of resisting his overly merciful divine father's will. Readers who assess the prophet's character positively could interpret his resistance as an attempt to achieve the kind of adult autonomy for which Homer's Odysseus is understandably famous.

4 Weltende? *Visions of death, exposure, and enclosure in Jeremiah and Qoheleth*

Yahweh demands not only his people's admiration and trust but also their fear of him. Is his mode of parenting designed to stymy any attempt by his human children to attain the mature autonomy displayed by characters such as Homer's Odysseus, if not Jonah as well? To what extent does Yahweh's complex personality

---

19. Freud (and his editors) apparently takes for granted that Freud's readers will recognize this phrase from Schiller's poem, "The Song of the Bell." The male of a married couple "must go out into hostile life (*feindliche Leben*), must have an effect and strive and plant and create, be cunning, snatch up, must wager and risk, in order to chase happiness" (Echtermeyer and von Wiese 1966, 295).

create a situation in which humans may be *more* vulnerable than if no god existed at all? In this section, I will address this issue by examining two challenging texts. The books of Jeremiah and Qoheleth both include a tableau which recalls aspects of Constant's bleak portrait of the human world without divine protection. God is indeed present in their sketches, but not in his capacity as a protector or safe haven. In Jer. 4:23-26, the world is experiencing the result of Yahweh's wrath, and the scene is even more unsettling than Constant's depiction of "the universe . . . without life, [in which] generations fleeting, fortuitous, isolated appear, . . . suffer and die." Qoheleth 12:1-7, on the other hand, seems to describe ordinary human activities in a village, although decline, death, and extinction permeate the atmosphere—all without divine anger playing a role.

Jeremiah reports his vision with a fourfold repetition of "I saw . . . and behold":

I looked at the earth, and behold, it was without form and void (תהו ובהו); and to the heavens, and they had no light. I looked at the mountains, and behold, they were quaking and all the hills shook themselves. I looked, and behold, there was no human, and all the birds of the air had fled. I looked, and behold, the fruitful land was a desert, and all its cities were pulled down[20] before the Lord, before his fierce anger. (Jer. 4:23-26)

In this nightmare landscape even the "isolated generations" of humans envisioned by Constant are missing, for there is "no human (אדם)" at all.

Commentators agree that this passage alludes to the creation story in Genesis 1, although the extent of the similarity is debated.[21] The prophet warns his people that God can return the cities of Judah to the state of empty formlessness (or desert waste)[22] which existed prior to creation (Gen. 1:2) by destroying the heavenly light, human cities, arable land, and making even the mountains unstable. In this world, without sustenance, shelter, or stability, birds and humans both disappear. And while Jeremiah claims that there is no human in this world, he himself is an אדם. He describes the imagined devastation as an eyewitness, as though he were observing the scene from outside this arid landscape. Yet this does not imply that Jeremiah or those who see the future through his eyes are safely detached from the danger. Each reader of the vision is invited to conclude that they too, in Constant's words, may find themselves "alone on an earth that may engulf them" if their divine parent is provoked to anger.

O'Connor contends that "Jeremiah himself is a helpless witness of disaster, a horrified onlooker"; he "'looked' and looked and looked, stunned and powerless" (2011, 52). Yet vv. 23-26 offer no evidence that the prophet feels either helpless

---

20. נתץ; cf. Jer. 1:10.
21. See, for example, Vancil (1986, 182–86), Hayes (2002, 83–87), and Kim (2007b, 55–56).
22. See, for example, Hamilton (1990, 108–09) on the various ways in which the phrase תהו ובהו has been understood.

or horrified, although those who see the scene through his description may react with both emotions. Admittedly, the preceding vision in 4:19-21 includes a strong emotional response to the (envisioned?) military attack on Jerusalem, but this cannot be assumed to govern the mood of the following vision as well. Allen (2008, 69) goes far beyond the text in taking the gut-wrenching anguish expressed in vv. 19-21 as the speaker Jeremiah's account of the "psychosomatic effects" his "mind-blowing experience" has had upon him. Yet, as Carroll (1986, 167) rightly points out, Jeremiah may not even be the speaker in vv. 19-21. These verses may represent a community lament, although there is no reason to follow O'Connor (2011, 51) in taking only "the wife" of Jerusalem as the speaker.

The various ways in which one might respond emotionally to a catastrophe—both in anticipation of its occurrence and witnessing its aftermath—can be illustrated by ANE flood narratives. When Atraḫasis realizes that the deluge is about to begin, "his heart was broken and he was vomiting gall" (III, ii, 47; Lambert and Millard 1999, 92-93). When Utnapishtim sees that all humanity had "turned to clay" after the deluge he squatted, sat, and wept (XI 134-37; Parpola 1997, 110). However, when Noah is told by God that the flood will occur, there is no report of any emotional response on his part. In fact, Genesis 6–8 lacks any quoted speech by Noah. Nor do any of the eight people saved in the ark say anything about the state of the world when they disembark, let alone have an emotional reaction to what they must have seen. In addition, the narrator of Genesis 8 says nothing about a ravaged landscape filled with the rotted bodies of dead humans and animals.[23] In contrast, the speaker Jeremiah powerfully depicts the devastated earth in 4:23-26.

Commentators sometimes seek to lessen the impact of this depiction. Lundbom (2013b, 23) makes the consoling observation that this is "only a vision" and that things in Judah never became that "bad." Yet what is described in these verses is presented as something which might really happen and which has already been envisioned—if not experienced—by the prophet. When read in that fashion, the vision resonates with primal human feelings of aloneness and vulnerability in the cosmos.[24] It is one thing to be the sole survivor in a world which has suffered a "natural" cataclysm and quite another to know that the reason for the devastation is the Creator's wrath at his human creatures. The viewer of this scene is placed in the situation of a sole survivor who has been left to witness the abysmal loss and to testify to its justification. Readers, who also witness the scene through Jeremiah's words, know that the same deity who has so often promised to be a safe haven for his human children is also capable of annihilating *all* safe havens when his

---

23. In contrast, artists who depict this scene often make the devastation the focus of their painting (e.g., Kaspar Memberger the Elder, "Leaving the Ark" [1588]).

24. Admittedly, Jer. 4:7, 20 seem to limit the coming destruction to Judah rather than to the entire world. But this does not limit the enormity of the devastation for the people for whom Judah *is* their whole world or for readers who connect the scene in 4:23-26 with a fundamental fear of being alone in an empty hostile world.

anger rises.²⁵ In this sense, those who experienced the fall of Jerusalem, such as the speakers in Lamentations, have had to learn this lesson the hard way. Their human condition is colored by guilt and remorse as well as feelings of loss and divine abandonment.

In contrast, Qoheleth's tableau narrows its focus to a single village after announcing cosmic darkening. The majority of the scene depicts ordinary human activities in a rural setting, not the aftermath of a cataclysmic event. Nevertheless, for some commentators, this portrayal conveys a message about life and death in God's world which is almost as gloomy as Jer. 4:23-26, while others have entirely different understandings of this evocative and elusive poem:

> And remember your Creator in the days of your youth, before the evil days come and the years draw near of which you will say, "I have no delight in them," before the sun darkens and the light and the moon and the stars and the clouds return after the rain; in the day when the men who watch over the house tremble and the worthy men are bent and the grinders cease because they are few and those who look through the windows are dimmed and the double-doors in the market street are shut, when the sound of the grinding is low and one rises at the voice of a bird and all the daughters of song are subdued. Also they are afraid of what is high and terrors are in the way; the almond tree blossoms, the grasshopper is laden and the caper buds,²⁶ because a human (or "humankind"; האדם)²⁷ is going to his eternal house and the mourners go around in the street; before the silver cord is snapped and the golden bowl is broken into pieces and the pitcher is shattered at the fountain and the wheel broken at the cistern (הבור)²⁸ and the dust returns to the earth as it was and the life-spirit returns to God who gave it. (Qoh. 12:1-7)

The passage is often read as an allegory of old age, although the elements of the description are decoded differently by different interpreters. The passage begins

---

25. Or, indeed, without any anger being mentioned, as in the case of the flood; see Lasine (2010, 39–42, 48–49).

26. Reading וְתִפְרַח; MT has וְתָפֵר, "is annulled."

27. For האדם as "humankind" rather than "a human" here, see Lo (2009, 87).

28. The word בור has associations with both life and death. In its meaning of "pit," it can stand for the realm of the dead. As a "spring," it can express renewal of life. Both meanings are illustrated in the Joseph story. Jacob blesses his son with the blessings of heaven above and of the primal depths (תהום) beneath. Jacob acknowledges that others had hated Joseph, even though his father considers Joseph to be a fruitful vine by a fountain (Gen. 49:22-25). Joseph's brothers place him into a בור (cistern) to die, and Potiphar later puts Joseph into a בור (prison). Nevertheless, Joseph rises higher after each of these death-like experiences. From the pit, he becomes the trustworthy slave of his owner Potiphar, and from the prison he becomes the trusted adviser to the king of Egypt, who gives Joseph control over the country's economy.

with a clear evocation of old age which echoes the octogenarian Barzillai in 2 Sam. 19:35-36: the aged cannot experience pleasure. Or, in Constant's more modern version quoted earlier, "old age advances toward us, a gloomy and solemn time when objects grow dark and seem to withdraw, and something cold and dull spreads on everything that surrounds us" (2011, 267).

In Qoh. 12:5, mourners are on the village streets because a human (or humankind) is going to his/its "eternal house." The word בית is often rendered "home" by translators, but this implies that the eternal house of the grave might retain something of the warm, comforting connotations of the home which the deceased might have associated with familial warmth, or at least protective shelter. The בית of v. 5 mirrors the darkened, closed house of v. 3, whose inhabitants are dimmed and whose guards tremble. The house of v. 3 may be shut for a funeral (see Fox 1989, 303). Is this merely a specific person's funeral or symbolic of everyone's mortality and eventual end? The poem allows both readings. Some elements seem to point to the evanescence of any and all human life and activity, if not the eventual return of everything to the kind of pre-Creation condition sketched in Jeremiah 4. The astral bodies grow dark. The rain is followed by more clouds, not by the return of sunshine. There is no covenant war bow in the clouds to give hope for the future.

Are we to learn that when we each die, our world dies with us, as Wittgenstein suggests when he writes that "in death, the world does not change, but ends" (*Tractatus* 6.431; 1961, 146-47)? Wittgenstein's sentence is itself elusive and capable of many interpretations.[29] Fox (2010, 342) makes what seems to be a similar point when discussing "light" and "dark" in Qoh. 11:7-8 and 12:2: "Every individual is a microcosm and every death the end of a world. For the person who dies, the stars blink out, the sun goes dark . . . rigor mortis sets in." However, the person who is dying knows that the stars and sun are still as bright as ever; she knows that it is just for herself that the world is darkening. Nor does a dead person experience the "rigor mortis" which transforms her corpse any more than she can experience the subsequent putrefaction of her flesh. Fox invites us to put ourselves in the position of the dying individual, but when we do so we retain the knowledge that we are still fully alive and have not yet experienced the loss of the light.

Put differently, Fox is imagining a person's death in the way that people dream about witnessing their own funeral. We are still "there" watching (see, for example, Freud 1990, 133), as is the speaker Jeremiah who repeatedly describes what he sees and beholds in Jer. 4:23-26. Are we being invited to watch our own funeral as does the dreaming old professor in Ingmar Bergmann's *Wild Strawberries*?[30]

---

29. It is sometimes assumed that Wittgenstein is espousing solipsism here (and more directly in statements such as "the world is *my* world" [5.62; 1961, 114–15]); see Pihlström (2016, 106) and Glock (1999, 446–49). The present discussion concerns only the sense in which *our own* world dies when we die.

30. Cf. Wolff (1986, 229) who is discussing Emily Dickenson's poem #280 ("I Felt a Funeral, in My Brain"): "Although it is an impossible feat, seeing one's own funeral and reading one's own obituary are among the most common fantasies of our culture."

In Qoheleth's poem, images of decay, enervation, and absence are reported as the cortege makes its way through the streets. Is this how the village looks to the person dying or to mourners who identify with the deceased and see death and decline everywhere? Or is this the report of a house or village in decline (e.g., Krüger 2004, 202–03) or a rendering of how cosmic entropy might be experienced in one rural town? Do those who watch over the house tremble because they recognize that they too will die or because they realize that terrors are on the way?

However, one interprets the scene, in the vignette even the strong among the males are described as bent or bowed, while the women[31] looking out of the windows from inside grow dark (to those looking at the window from outside?) as had the stars in the sky in v. 2. The number of female grinders is diminishing. The villagers experience fear and await terrors. Not everything seems to be vanishing or disintegrating; the almond tree blossoms and the grasshopper may be sated or supplied with food.[32] While the birds have not disappeared as in Jeremiah 4, here the "daughters of song" (often understood to be birds or human singers) are brought low. Everyday tools and precious objects are broken or failing. The pervasiveness of the decay is underscored by the number of specific objects listed. The atmosphere is not only one of entropy but of foreboding as well. Are the inhabitants in the village aware that they too are doomed to extinction, no matter how strong or wealthy they are? Aspects of the scene suggest an affirmative answer; everything human seems to be on its way to the house of eternity, not just the individual being mourned. But, once again, no single interpretation can account for all the elements of this provocative poem.

Qoheleth's poem juxtaposes cosmic and domestic darkening. Weakening and fearful humans and broken utensils are contrasted with blossoming trees (and perhaps budding caper berries). This juxtaposition of the cosmic and the mundane is also found in modern apocalyptic poetry, such as Jakob von Hoddis's prescient poem "*Weltende*" (End of the World), written three years before the outbreak of the First World War (Echtermeyer and von Wiese 1966, 588). In one verse, we are told that a storm rises and the wild seas hop (*hupfen*) ashore in order to crush thick dams, while in the next we learn that most people have the sniffles (*Schnupfen*). The poem begins with the notice that a burgher's hat flies from his pointy head, but in the next lines much more serious events are unfolding: in all the air cries are reverberating, roofers plunge, and break asunder, and on the coasts—one reads— the flood waters are rising. This technique of "cinema style" montage (*Kinostil*; see Hake 2005, 332) shows that even the most trivial annoyance, such as the wind

---

31. The Hebrew participle for those watching (הראות) is feminine, as is the participle (הטחנות) describing the grinders.

32. Alternatively, the חגב may be a species of tree which is either laden with fruit (Fox 2004, 80) or drooping under the weight of its pods after it dies (Seow 1997, 362). Many modern translations (e.g., RSV, NRSV, NIV, ESV, NASB) understand the phrase to mean that the grasshopper drags itself along.

blowing off one's hat, may be only the start of one's quotidian world coming apart at the seams. Once the floodwaters are no longer a distant catastrophe one reads about in the papers but a fact of one's present situation, one might well believe that the whole world was coming to an end.

Even though Qoh. 12:2 evokes imagery associated with the "day of Yahweh" (e.g., Joel 2:2, 10), the gloomy vision of the world in vv. 1-7 is not presented as the result of divine punishment. Does the absence of a punitive context imply that God has arranged human life to inevitably end in this way, even in the haven of one's home town? The very world through which the mourners travel with the deceased has itself dimmed and darkened. If this is the unavoidable end, as Qoheleth has already communicated in other ways,[33] it would seem to imply that God's "protective powers" do not extend to protecting his human children from the extinguishing of life or from the absence of meaning in their deaths. What shelter can be found in a world which itself is in the process of deadening?

5 My death in Yahweh's world

In Chapter 4 §3, I discussed one of Freud's B'nai B'rith addresses to a Jewish audience, presented shortly before the outbreak of hostilities in the First World War. As a Jew, and therefore one of those addressed by Freud's "We and Death," I can say that I have also found it to be "remarkably strange" (*merkwürdig*) that my Bible puts all value on this earthly life and, for the most part, seeks no escape from the inevitability of death through an afterlife promise of celestial milk and honey—or to mix cultural metaphors—ambrosia and nectar. Being in Sheol is nobody's idea of a good time.[34] This is one of many reasons that I feel the biblical world to be my world. The vision of human reality it presents is also the reality in which I live and in which I will die. For me, the genius of the biblical presentation of God is that only a deity with Yahweh's traits and emotions could explain all the paradox, absurdity, beauty, horror, compassion, and injustice that I witness and experience in my life-world.

While Freud clearly views the biblical absence of afterlife dreams as a laudable sign of maturity, he also claims that the modern "cultural-conventional" attitude of denying death and "playing it safe" is exhibited most frequently, and in the

---

33. See Chapter 2 §2.

34. G. Ogden (1984, 33–34) argues that Qoheleth's references to the darkness and lack of pleasure in Qoh. 11:7-8 and 12:1-2 are "a way of speaking of the minimal existence which one enjoys in Sheol," rather than about old age. As Ogden is surely aware, biblical glimpses of underworld existence rarely include reports of enjoyment, except perhaps for a bit of *Schadenfreude* on the part of the shades who witness the king of Babylon's fall into Sheol in Isa. 14:8-9. On Sheol, see Chapter 4 §3.

most extreme fashion, by none other than "we Jews."[35] Freud also finds this to be "*merkwürdig*" (1990, 132). Freud's ambivalence concerning what it means to "take death seriously" (1990, 135; cf. 142) is a function of his peculiar blindness on the subject of death fear.[36] In this speech, and in a number of other essays, he explains heroism as made possible by the fact that deep down we do not accept that we can die; this allows heroes—and soldiers in the Great War raging shortly after he composed his essay—to risk their lives, even though life is like a chess game in which there is no possibility of a rematch if one loses (Freud 1990, 134).

It does not occur to Freud that managing risks to one's life implies that one *has* acknowledged and coped with the fact of irreversible death. One could even argue that taking risks in spite of (or even because of) that awareness is a form of heroism; in support, one could point to Homer's conception of heroic behavior in the *Iliad*[37] or indeed to Jonah's risky behavior in relation to his God. Yet even when Freud is addressing an audience of fellow Jews, he insists that *denying* the possibility of one's death is what makes heroism possible.

In *The Interpretation of Dreams*, Freud relates that he had an early childhood conversation with his mother in which she informed him that she, and therefore he, would inevitably die and be reduced to the dust from which Genesis tells us we were formed (1900, 141).[38] When I was a small child, I had a similar experience when I sought solace from my mother after awaking one night and suddenly realizing in the pit of my stomach that I would surely die, that death meant annihilation and that there was no escape. I woke her up, and she pointed out, quite reasonably, that she too would die someday, as we all will, so I should go back to bed.[39] Now that my death looms much larger on my horizon, I rarely

---

35. He reminds his Jewish audience at the B'nai B'rith of a "characteristically Jewish anecdote" in which a mother runs to her rabbi to report that her son is unconscious from having fallen off a ladder. The rabbi asks, "How does a Jewish child come to be on a ladder?" (1990, 134). In this story—designed to be told by a Jew to fellow Jews—the rabbi expects Jews, even as children, to be too risk-averse (if not cowardly) to climb a ladder.

36. See Razinsky (2007, 356–59, 374–76) and Piven (2004, 21–48, 221).

37. The hero Sarpedon expresses this idea when he encourages his friend Glaucon: "Oh, if escaping this battle we were forever destined to be unaging and undying, neither would I myself fight among the foremost, nor send you into battle bringing men glory; but now, since countless fates of death (κῆρες . . . θανάτοιο) lie in wait for us from which no mortal may escape or flee, let us go on, whether we shall give others something to boast about, or others to us" (*Il.* XII.322-28). As Redfield puts it, the Homeric warrior "becomes a hero because he cannot be a god," that is, immortal (1975, 101; cf. Mueller 1970, 87).

38. The only emotions Freud claims he experienced are "boundless astonishment" at his mother's "*ad oculos*" demonstration of our being made of earth and immediate "submission" to the fact of his own mortality. His pose of detachment is underscored by his use of a technical Latin expression to describe what he witnessed as a small child.

39. To be fair to my mother, this is only my "narrative memory" of that event, as it affected me at the time and later.

experience what I thereafter called the "pit feeling."[40] Can these biblical stories help me understand whether this is a retreat into denial or a sign that I have become resigned to the inevitable?

William James would understand the question. He describes how at one point in his life he awoke "morning after morning with a horrible dread at the pit of my stomach, and with a sense of the insecurity of life that I never knew before, and that I have never felt since" (1920, 160–61).[41] Yet Freud, whose own fear of death is amply documented, does *not* say that he experienced the "pit feeling," either before or after his mother taught him that hard lesson about human mortality.

I do not agree with Freud that accepting death as personal annihilation precludes being heroic any more than denying one's own death is necessary if one is to act heroically. Nor do I share Freud's pride at calling the dream of a blissful afterlife an illusion. I simply cannot convince myself that this dream—and not the pit feeling—is the truth, especially when my Bible seems to accept that truth as well. In fact, biblical speakers such as the character Qoheleth tell me not to waste time trying to convince myself. The only exceptions my Bible offers me are an irascible prophet who is made immortal after declaring that he wants to die (1 Kgs 19:3; 2 Kgs 2:1-11), another irascible prophet who is symbolically reborn from a big fish but then wants to die, and a few silent reanimated corpses padding along in the background of 1–2 Kings with no more personality or consciousness of self than Elisha's bones. These exceptions prove the rule: nothing worthwhile happens after one dies. While we are alive we can indeed listen to Moses and choose life and not death (Deut. 30:11-20); but once life ends, there are no choices left at all, and no consciousness capable of making any. In the meantime, we must content ourselves with eating our bread and drinking our wine with joy and—if you're as lucky as I am—enjoying life with our beloved partner.[42]

---

40. This is hardly unusual; research consistently finds less death anxiety in the elderly than in middle-aged individuals. See, for example, Sinoff (2017).

41. James attributes this account of a state of panic to an anonymous "sufferer" who wrote it in French. However, scholars have demonstrated that James himself is the person who had this experience and authored the account. See R. Richardson (2006, 117–18).

42. I am alluding to Qoh. 9:7-10 and the similar advice of the tavern-keeper in OB *Gilgamesh*, discussed in Chapter 2 §2.

BIBLIOGRAPHY

Abela, Anthony. 2001. When the Agenda of an Artistic Composition Is Hidden: Jonah and Intertextual Dialogue with Isaiah 6, the Confessions of Jeremiah, and Other Texts. Pages 1–30 in *The Elusive Prophet: The Prophet as a Historical Person, Literary Character and Anonymous Artist*. Edited by Johannes C. De Moor. OtSt, 45. Leiden: Brill.

Ackerman, James S. 1987. Jonah. Pages 234–43 in *Literary Guide to the Bible*. Edited by Robert Alter and Frank Kermode. Cambridge, MA: Harvard University Press.

Adam, James, editor. 1897. *The Republic of Plato*. Cambridge: Cambridge University Press.

Affleck, Glenn, Howard Tennen, and Andrea Apter. 2000. Optimism, Pessimism, and Daily Life with Chronic Illness. Pages 147–68 in *Optimism & Pessimism: Implications for Theory, Research, and Practice*. Edited by Edward C. Chang. Washington, DC: American Psychological Association.

Allen, Leslie C. 2008. *Jeremiah: A Commentary*. OTL. Louisville, KY: Westminster John Knox Press.

Allen, Woody. 1982. *Four Films of Woody Allen*. New York: Random House.

Allen, Woody. 1983. *Without Feathers*. New York: Ballantine Books.

Allison, Dale. 1994. *The New Moses: A Matthean Typology*. Minneapolis, MN: Fortress Press.

Ambuel, David. 2013. Pigs in Plato: Delineating the Human Condition in the *Statesman*. Pages 207–26 in *Plato's Statesman: Proceedings of the Eighth Symposium Platonicum Pragense*. Edited by Aleš Havlíček, Jakub Jirsa and Karel Thein. Prague: Oikoymenh.

Annus, Amar and Alan Lenzi. 2010. *Ludlul bēl nēmequi: The Standard Babylonian Poem of the Righteous Sufferer*. State Archives of Assyria Cuneiform Texts, VII. Helsinki: Neo-Assyrian Text Corpus Project.

Arendt, Hannah. 1989. *The Human Condition*. Chicago, IL: The University of Chicago Press.

Auld, A. Graeme. 1983. Prophets through the Looking Glass: Between Writings and Moses. *JSOT* 27: 3–23.

Bachelard, Gaston. 1948. *La Terre et les rêveries du repos*. Paris: Librairie José Corti.

Baines, John. 1990. Interpreting the Story of the Shipwrecked Sailor. *JEA* 76: 55–72.

Barton, John. 2001. *Joel and Obadiah: A Commentary*. OTL. Louisville, KY: Westminster John Knox.

Bayertz, Kurt. 1996. Human Dignity: Philosophical Origin and Scientific Erosion of an Idea. Pages 73–89 in *Sanctity of Life and the Human Condition*. Edited by Kurt Bayertz. Dordrecht, NL: Kluwer Academic Publishers.

Becker, Ernest. 1973. *The Denial of Death*. New York: Free Press.

Becker, Ernest. 1975. *Escape from Evil*. New York: Free Press.

Becking, Bob. 2007. The Prophets as Persons. Pages 53–63 in *Hearing Visions and Seeing Voices: Psychological Aspects of Biblical Concepts and Personalities*. Edited by Gerrit Glas, Moshe Halevi Spero, Peter J. Verhagen, and Herman M. Van Praag. Dordrecht: Springer.

Beiser, Frederick C. 2016. *Weltschmerz: Pessimism in German Philosophy, 1860-1900*. Oxford: Oxford University Press.

Beit-Hallahmi, Benjamin. 2011. Ambivalent Teaching and Painful Learning: Mastering the Facts of Life (?). Pages 41–60 in *Children's Understanding of Death: Biological to Religious Conceptions*. Edited by Victoria Talwar, Paul L. Harris, and Michael Schleifer. Cambridge: Cambridge University Press.

Ben Zvi, Ehud. 2003. *Signs of Jonah: Reading and Rereading in Ancient Yehud*. JSOTSup, 367. London: Sheffield Academic Press.

Ben Zvi, Ehud. 2009. Jonah 4:11 and the Metaprophetic Character of the Book of Jonah. *Journal of Hebrew Scriptures* 9: 1–13. Available online: http://www.jhsonline.org/Articles/article_107.pdf. (Accessed March 17, 2011).

Bergen, Wesley J. 1999. *Elisha and the End of Prophetism*. JSOTSup, 286. Sheffield: Sheffield Academic Press.

Berger, Peter L. 1969. *The Sacred Canopy: Elements of a Sociological Theory of Religion*. Garden City, NY: Doubleday Anchor.

Berger, Peter L. and Thomas Luckmann. 1989. *The Social Construction of Reality: A Treatise in the Sociology of Knowledge*. New York: Anchor Books.

Bernstein, Richard J. 1998. *Freud and the Legacy of Moses*. Cambridge Studies in Religion and Critical Thought, 4. Cambridge: Cambridge University Press.

Bettelheim, Bruno. 1989. *The Uses of Enchantment: The Meaning and Importance of Fairy Tales*. New York: Vintage Books.

Bickerman, Elias. 1967. *Four Strange Books of the Bible*. New York: Schocken Books.

Blackman, Aylward M. 1932. *Middle-Egyptian Stories*. Bibliotheca Aegyptiaca, II. Brussels: Fondation égyptologique reine Élisabeth.

Blank, Sheldon. 1955. "Doest Thou Well to Be Angry?": A Study in Self-Pity. *HUCA* 26: 29–41.

Blumenberg, Hans. 1997. *Shipwreck With Spectator: Paradigm of a Metaphor for Existence* Translated by Steven Rendall; Cambridge, MA: MIT Press.

Boaistuau, Pierre. 1566. *Theatrum Mundi, the Theatre or Rule of the World*. Translated by John Alday. Available online: http://tei.it.ox.ac.uk/tcp/Texts-HTML/free/A16/A16241.html#index.xml- body.1_div.3. (Accessed October 3, 2017).

Boaistuau, Pierre. 1570. *Le théâtre du monde, ou il est faict un ample discours des miseres humaines*. Paris: Christophle Plantin.

Boda, Mark J. 2009. *A Severe Mercy: Sin and Its Remedy in the Old Testament*. Winona Lake, IN: Eisenbrauns.

Bodner, Keith. 2013. *Elisha's Profile in the Book of Kings: The Double Agent*. Oxford: Oxford University Press.

Bonner, Campbell. 1941. Desired Haven. *HTR* 34: 49–67.

Bottéro, Jean. 1992. *Mesopotamia: Writing, Reasoning, and the Gods*. Translated by Zainab Bahrani and Marc Van De Mieroop. Chicago, IL: University of Chicago Press.

Bowlby, John. 1982. *Attachment*. 2nd ed. New York: Basic Books.

Braude, William G., trans. 1959. *The Midrash on Psalms*. Vol. 1. New Haven, CT: Yale University Press.

Brettler, Marc Zvi. 1993. A Bible Commentary for Israel (Review of Zakovitch, *Ruth*). *Prooftexts* 13: 175–81.

Brinton, Daniel G. 1890. Folk-Lore of the Bones. *The Journal of American Folklore* 3: 17–22.

Brown, William P. 2002. *Seeing the Psalms: A Theology of Metaphor*. Louisville, KY: Westminster John Knox Press.

Brueggemann, Walter A. 1997. *Theology of the Old Testament: Testimony, Dispute, Advocacy*. Minneapolis, MN: Fortress Press.
Burckhardt, Jacob. 1998. *The Greeks and Greek Civilization*. Edited by Oswyn Murray. Translated by Sheila Stern. New York: St. Martin's Press.
Burkert, Walter. 1987. *Greek Religion: Archaic and Classical*. Translated by John Raffan. Malden, MA: Blackwell Publishing.
Burkes, Shannon. 1999. *Death in Qoheleth and Egyptian Biographies of the Late Period*. SBLDS, 170. Atlanta, GA: Scholars Press.
Burnett, John, editor. 1911. *Plato's Phaedo*. Oxford: Clarendon Press.
Calvin, Jean. 1960. *Institutes of the Christian Religion, Volume 2*. Edited by John T. McNeill. Translated by Ford L. Battles. Library of Christian Classics. Louisville, KY: Westminster John Knox Press.
Campbell, Joseph. 1968. *The Hero with a Thousand Faces*. 2nd ed. Princeton, NJ: Princeton University Press.
Camus, Albert. 1942. *Le mythe de Sisyphe*. Les Essais, 12. Paris: Gallimard.
Capps, Donald. 1992. *The Depleted Self: Sin in a Narcissistic Age*. Minneapolis, MN: Fortress Press.
Carroll, Robert P. 1986. *The Book of Jeremiah: A Commentary*. OTL. Philadelphia, PA: Westminster Press.
Cassirer, Ernst. 1963. *The Individual and the Cosmos in Renaissance Philosophy*. Translated by Mario Domondi. Chicago, IL: The University of Chicago Press.
Chang, Edward C. 2000. Introduction: Optimism and Pessimism and Moving Beyond the Most Fundamental Question. Pages 3–12 in *Optimism & Pessimism: Implications for Theory, Research, and Practice*. Edited by Edward C. Chang. Washington, DC: American Psychological Association.
Chin, Catherine. 1994. Job and the Injustice of God: Implicit Arguments in Job 13.17-14.12. *JSOT* 64: 91–101.
Chomsky, Noam and Michel Foucault. 2006. *The Chomsky-Foucault Debate: On Human Nature*. New York: New Press.
Christianson, Eric S. 1997. Qoheleth and the Existential Legacy of the Holocaust. *HeyJ* 38: 35–50.
Clement of Alexandra. 1869. *Stromataum I-IV. Opera, Volume 2*. Edited by Wilhelm Dindorf. Oxford: Clarendon.
Clines, David J. A. 1989. *Job 1-20*. WBC 17. Dallas, TX: Word.
Cogan, Mordechai, and Hayim Tadmor. 1988. *II Kings: A New Translation with Introduction and Commentary*. AB, 11. Garden City, NY: Doubleday.
Cogan, Mordecai. 2000. *1 Kings*. AB, 10; New York: Doubleday.
Cohen, A., trans. 1939. Ecclesiastes. Pages i–318 in *The Midrash VIII: Ruth, Ecclesiastes*. London: Soncino.
Cohen, Adam B., Joel I. Siegel, and Paul Rozin. 2003. Faith Versus Practice: Different Bases for Religiosity Judgments by Jews and Protestants. *European Journal of Social Psychology* 33: 287–95.
Cohen, Adam B., John D. Pierce Jr., Jacqueline Chambers, Rachel Meade, Benjamin J. Gorvine, and Harold G. Koenig. 2005. Intrinsic and Extrinsic Religiosity, Belief in the Afterlife, Death Anxiety, and Life Satisfaction in Young Catholics and Protestants. *Journal of Research in Personality* 39: 307–24.
Cohn, Robert L. 2000. *2 Kings*. Berit Olam. Collegeville, MN: Liturgical Press.
Collins, John J. 1978. The Root of Immortality: Death in the Context of Jewish Wisdom. *HTR* 71: 177–92.

Colloti, Carlo. 2010. *Pinocchio*. Translated by Claude Sartirano and Juanita Havill. Edited by Susan Pearson. New York: North-South Books.

Connolly, Cyril. 1940. Comment. *Horizon* 1: 5–6.

Conrad, Joseph. 1989. *Lord Jim*. Edited by Cedric Watts and Robert Hampson. London: Penguin Books.

Constant, Benjamin. 2011. *Principes de Politique applicable à tous les gouvernements représentatifs (texte de 1806). Œuvres Complètes, V*. Edited by Kurt Kloocke. Berlin: Walter de Gruyter.

Constant, Benjamin. 2013. *De la Religion, considérée dans sa source, ses formes, et ses développements, Tome I. Œuvres Complètes, XVII*. Edited by Markus Winkler and Kurt Kloocke. Berlin: Walter de Gruyter.

Cooper, Alan. 1993. In Praise of Divine Caprice: The Significance of the Book of Jonah. Pages 144–63 in *Among the Prophets: Language, Image and Structure in the Prophetic Writings*. JSOTSup 144. Edited by Philip R. Davies and David J. A. Clines. Sheffield: JSOT Press.

Corr, Charles A. 1997. Children and Questions about Death. Pages 217–38 in *Death and the Quest for Meaning: Essays in Honor of Herman Feifel*. Edited by Stephen Strack. Northvale, NJ: Jason Aronson.

Craig, Kenneth M. 1993. *A Poetics of Jonah: Art in the Service of Ideology*. Columbia: University of South Carolina Press.

Crenshaw, James L. 1978. The Shadow of Death in Qohelet. Pages 205–16 in *Israelite Wisdom: Theological and Literary Essays in Honor of Samuel Terrien*. Edited by John G. Gammie, Walter A. Brueggemann, W. L. Humphries, and J. M. Ward. Missoula, MT: Scholars Press.

Crenshaw, James L. 1981. *Old Testament Wisdom: An Introduction*. Atlanta, GA: John Knox Press.

Crenshaw, James L. 1983. Introduction: The Shift from Theodicy to Anthropodicy. Pages 1–16 in *Theodicy in the Old Testament*. Edited by James L. Crenshaw. Issues in Religion and Theology, 4. Philadelphia: Fortress Press.

Crenshaw, James L. 1987. *Ecclesiastes: A Commentary*. OTL. Philadelphia, PA: Westminster Press.

Crenshaw, James L. 1995. *Joel: A New Translation with Introduction and Commentary*. AB, 24C. New York: Doubleday.

Crenshaw, James L. 2013. *Qoheleth: The Ironic Wink*. Columbia: University of South Carolina Press.

Crenshaw, James L. 2014. Qoheleth's Hatred of Life: A Passing Phase or an Enduring Sentiment? Pages 119–31 in *Wisdom for Life: Essay Offered to Honor Prof. Maurice Gilbert, SJ on the Occasion of His Eightieth Birthday*. Edited by Nuria Calduch-Benages. BZAW 445. Berlin: Walter de Gruyter.

Crouch, Walter B. 1994. To Question an End, to End a Question: Opening the Closure of the Book of Jonah. *JSOT* 62: 101–12.

Csapo, Eric. 2005. *Theories of Mythology*. Ancient Cultures. Malden, MA: Blackwell Publishing.

Cyril of Alexandria, St. 2008. *Commentary of the Twelve Prophets, Vol. 2*. Translated by Robert C. Hill. The Fathers of the Church: A New Translation. Washington, DC: Catholic University of America Press.

Dahood, Mitchell, S. J. 1966. *Psalms I: 1-50*. AB, 16. Garden City, NY: Doubleday & Co.

Dalton, Russell. 2007. Perfect Prophets, Helpful Hippos, and Happy Endings: Noah and Jonah in Children's Bible Storybooks in the United States. *RelEd* 102: 298–313.

Daube, David. 1962. Death as a Release in the Bible. *NovT* 5: 82–104.
Daube, David. 1983. Black Hole. *Rechtshistorisches Journal* 2: 177–93.
Davison, Peter, editor. 2013. *George Orwell: A Life in Letters*. New York: Liveright.
Dawson, Terence. 2008. Literary Criticism and Analytical Psychology. Pages 269–98 in *The Cambridge Companion to Jung*. 2nd ed. Edited by Polly Young-Eisendrath and Terence Dawson. Cambridge: Cambridge University Press.
Defoe, Daniel. 1994. *Robinson Crusoe*. Norton Critical Edition. 2nd ed. Edited by Michael Shinagel; New York: Norton.
Dempsey, Carol J. 2000. *The Prophets: A Liberation-critical Reading*. Minneapolis, MN: Augsburg Press.
Dickens, Charles. 1861. *Great Expectations*. Vol. 1. Collection of British Authors, 547. Leipzig: Bernhard Tauchnitz.
Dienstag, Joshua Foa. 2006. *Pessimism: Philosophy, Ethic, Spirit*. Princeton, NJ: Princeton University Press.
Dodds, Eric R. 1968. *The Greeks and the Irrational*. Berkeley: University of California Press.
Dollimore, Jonathan. 2001. *Death, Desire and Loss in Western Culture*. New York: Routledge.
Donne, John. 1839. *The Works of John Donne, Vol. VI*. Edited by Henry Alford. London: John W. Parker.
Donne, John. 1955. *The Sermons of John Donne, Vol II*. Edited by George R. Potter and Evelyn M. Simpson. Berkeley: University of California Press.
Donne, John. 2001. *The Complete Poetry and Selected Prose of John Donne*. Edited by Charles M. Coffin. New York: Modern Library.
Donne, John. 2015. The Annuntiation. Page 149 in *John Donne*. Edited by Janel Mueller. 21st-Century Oxford Authors. Oxford: Oxford University Press.
D'Ooge, Martin L., editor. 1900. *Sophocles Antigone*. Boston, MA: Ginn & Company.
Dostoevsky, Fyodor. 1976. *The Brothers Karamazov*. Norton Critical Edition. Translated by Constance Garnett and Ralph E. Matlaw. Edited by Ralph E. Matlaw. New York: W. W. Norton.
Dougherty, Carol. 2001. *The Raft of Odysseus: The Ethnographic Imagination of Homer's Odyssey*. New York: Oxford University Press.
Dozeman, Thomas B. 1989. Inner-Biblical Interpretation of Yahweh's Gracious and Compassionate Character. *JBL* 108: 207–23.
Dray, Carol A. 2006. *Studies on Translation and Interpretation in the Targum to the Books of Kings*. Leiden: Brill.
Driver, Samuel R. 1920. *Introduction to the Literature of the Old Testament*. New York: Charles Scribner's Sons.
Driver, Samuel R., and George Buchanan Gray. 1921. *A Critical and Exegetical Commentary on the Book of Job, Part I*. ICC. Edinburgh: T&T Clark.
Droge, A. J. 1992. Suicide. Pages 225–31 in *ABD*, vol. 6.
Dundes, Allan, ed. 1989. *Little Red Riding Hood: A Casebook*. Madison, WI: University of Wisconsin Press.
Echtermeyer, Thomas, and Benno von Wiese. 1966. *Deutsche Gedichte von den Anfängen bis zur Gegenwart*. Düsseldorf: August Bagel Verlag.
Edwards, Philip. 1997. *Sea-mark: The Metaphorical Voyage, Spenser to Milton*. Liverpool: Liverpool University Press.
Ehrensaft, Diane. 2008. A Child Is Being Eaten: Failure, Fear, Fantasy, and Repair in the Lives of Foster Children. *Journal of Infant, Child, and Adolescent Psychotherapy* 7: 100–08.

Eliade, Marcel. 1960. *Myths, Dreams, and Mysteries: The Encounter Between Contemporary Faiths and Archaic Realities*. Translated by Philip Mairet. New York: Harper Torchbook.
Eliade, Marcel. 1969. *The Quest: History and Meaning in Religion*. Chicago, IL: University of Chicago Press.
Elias, Norbert. 1997. *Über den Prozeß der Zivilisation: Soziogenetische und psychogenetische Untersuchungen, Band 1*. Frankfurt: Suhrkamp Taschenbuch.
Evelyn-White, Hugh G., trans. 1914. *Hesiod, The Homeric Hymns and Homerica*. LCL. Cambridge, MA: Harvard University Press.
Finch, Casey, trans. 1993. Patience. Pages 184–207 in *The Complete Works of the Pearl Poet*. Edited by Malcolm Andrew, Ronald Waldron and Clifford Peterson. Berkeley: University of California Press.
Fineman, Martha Albertson. 2008. The Vulnerable Subject: Anchoring Equality in the Human Condition. *Yale Journal of Law & Feminism* 20: 1–23.
Fisch, Harold. 1986. The Hermeneutic Quest in *Robinson Crusoe*. Pages 213–35 in *Midrash and Literature*. Edited by Geoffrey H. Hartman and Sanford Budick. New Haven, CT: Yale University Press.
Fishbane, Michael A. 1988. *Biblical Interpretation in Ancient Israel*. Oxford: Clarendon Paperbacks.
Fletcher, John. 1999. The Sins of the Fathers: The Persistence of Gothic. Pages 113–40 in *Romanticism and Postmodernism*. Edited by Edward Larrissey. Cambridge: Cambridge University Press.
Florian, Victor, and Shlomo Kravetz. 1983. Fear of Personal Death: Attribution, Structure, and Relation to Religious Belief. *Journal of Personality and Social Psychology* 44: 600–07.
Forti, Tova. 2011. Of Ships and Seas, and Fish and Beasts: Viewing the Concept of Universal Providence in the Book of Jonah through the Prism of Psalms. *JSOT* 35: 359–74.
Fox, Michael V. 1989. *Qohelet and His Contradictions*. JSOTSup, 71. Sheffield: Almond.
Fox, Michael V. 2004. *Ecclesiastes*. The JPS Bible Commentary. Philadelphia, PA: JPS.
Fox, Michael V. 2010. *A Time to Tear Down and a Time to Build Up: A Rereading of Ecclesiastes*. Eugene, OR: Wipf & Stock.
Fretheim, Terence E. 1999. *First and Second Kings*. WBCom. Louisville, KY: Westminster John Knox.
Fretheim, Terence E. 2007. The Exaggerated God of Jonah. *WW* 27: 125–34.
Fretheim, Terence E. 2010. *Exodus*. IBC. Louisville, KY: Westminster John Knox.
Freud, Sigmund. 1900. *Die Traumdeutung*. Leipzig: Franz Deuticke.
Freud, Sigmund. 1930. *Das Unbehagen in der Kultur*. Vienna: Internationaler Psychoanalytischer Verlag.
Freud, Sigmund. 1940. Jenseits des Lustprinzips. Pages 3–69 in vol. 13 of *GW*.
Freud, Sigmund. 1941. Der Dichter und Das Phantasieren. Pages 213–23 in vol. 7 of *GW*. Edited by Anna Freud. London.
Freud, Sigmund. 1946a. Zeitgemäßes über Krieg und Tod. Pages 324–55 in vol. 10 of *GW*.
Freud, Sigmund. 1946b. Märchenstoff in Träume. Pages 2–9 in vol. 10 of *GW*.
Freud, Sigmund. 1946c. Das Motiv der Kästchenwahl. Pages 24–37 in vol. 10 of *GW*.
Freud, Sigmund. 1947a. Das Unheimliche. Pages 229–68 in vol. 12 of *GW*.
Freud, Sigmund. 1947b. Aus der Geschichte einer infantile Neurose. Pages 29–157 in vol. 12 of *GW*.
Freud, Sigmund. 1948. *Die Zukunft einer Illusion*. Pages 325–80 in vol. 14 *GW*.

Freud, Sigmund. 1950. *Der Mann Moses und die monotheistische Religion*. Pages 103–246 in vol. 16 of *GW*.

Freud, Sigmund. 1990. Wir und der Tod. *Psyche: Zeitschrift für Psychoanalyse und ihre Anwendungen*. 45: 132–42.

Friedlander, Gerald, trans. 1916. *Pirḳê de Rabbi Eliezer: (The Chapters of Rabbi Eliezer the Great) According to the Text of the Manuscript Belonging to Abraham Epstein of Vienna*. London: Kegan Paul, Trench, Trubner.

Frolov, Serge. 1999. Returning the Ticket: God and His Prophet in the Book of Jonah. *JSOT* 86: 85–105.

Fromm, Erich. 1951. *The Forgotten Language: An Introduction to the Understanding of Dreams, Fairy Tales, and Myths*. New York: Rinehart Press.

Gaines, Janet Howe. 2003. *Forgiveness in a Wounded World: Jonah's Dilemma*. Atlanta, GA: SBL Press.

Gay, Peter. 1995. *The Bourgeois Experience, Victoria to Freud, Vol. 4: The Naked Heart*. New York: W. W. Norton.

Geiringer, Erich. 1952. Fear of Death. *The Spectator* 189: 179–80.

Geller, Stephen A. 1996. *Sacred Enigmas: Literary Religion in the Hebrew Bible*. London and New York: Routledge.

George, Andrew, ed. and trans. 2003. *The Babylonian Gilgamesh Epic: Introduction, Critical Edition and Cuneiform Texts, Volume I*. Oxford: Oxford University Press.

Gerber, Douglas E., trans. and ed. 1999. *Greek Elegiac Poetry: From the Seventh to the Fifth Centuries BC*. LCL. Cambridge, MA: Harvard University Press.

Gilbert, Daniel T., and Patrick S. Malone. 1995. The Correspondence Bias. *Psychological Bulletin* 117: 21–38.

Gildersleeve, Basil L., editor. 1885. *Pindar: The Olympian and Pythian Odes*. New York: American Book Company.

Ginzberg, Louis. 1968. *The Legends of the Jews, Volume 4*. Philadelphia, PA: Jewish Publication Society of America.

Glasson, T. Francis. 1969. The Final Question—in Nahum and Jonah. *ExpTim* 81: 54–55.

Glock, Hans-Johann. 1999. Schopenhauer and Wittgenstein: Representation as Language and Will. Pages 422–58 in *The Cambridge Companion to Schopenhauer*. Edited by Christopher Janaway. Cambridge: Cambridge University Press.

Goedde, Lawrence O. 1989. *Tempest and Shipwreck in Dutch and Flemish Art: Convention, Rhetoric and Interpretation*. University Park: The Pennsylvania State University Press.

Goedicke, Hans. 1974. *Die Geschichte des Schiffbrüchigen*. ÄgAbh, 30. Wiesbaden: Otto Harrassowitz.

Goldhill, Simon. 2012. *Sophocles and the Language of Tragedy*. New York: Oxford University Press.

Good, Edwin M. 1962. Booth. Page 455 in *IDB*, vol. 1.

Good, Edwin M. 1981. *Irony in the Old Testament*. 2nd ed. Bible and Literature, 3. Sheffield: Almond Press.

Greenwood, Kyle R. 2012. Debating Wisdom: The Role of Voice in Ecclesiastes. *CBQ* 74: 476–91.

Gregory, Russell. 1990. Irony and the Unmasking of Elijah. Pages 93–169 in *From Carmel to Horeb: Elijah in Crisis*. Edited by Alan J. Hauser and Russell Gregory. Bible and Literature, 19. JSOTSup, 85. Sheffield: Almond Press.

Groenewegen-Frankfort, Henriette A. 1987. *Arrest and Movement: An Essay on Space and Time in the Representational Art of the Ancient Near East*. Cambridge, MA: Harvard University Press.

Guggenheimer, Heinrich W., trans. 1998. *Seder Olam: The Rabbinic View of Biblical Chronology*. Northvale, NJ: Jason Aronson.
Guillaume, Philippe. 2006. The End of Jonah is the Beginning of Wisdom. *Bib* 87: 243–50.
Guillaume, Philippe. 2009. Review of Lowell K. Handy, *Jonah's World: Social Science and the Reading of Prophetic Story. Journal of Hebrew Scripture* 9:1. Available online: http://www.jhsonline.org/reviews/reviews_new/review378.htm. (Accessed July 12, 2012).
Gunn, David M., and Danna Nolan Fewell. 1993. *Narrative in the Hebrew Bible*. Oxford Bible Series. New York: Oxford University Press.
Guthrie, W. K. C. 1965. *In the Beginning: Some Greek Views on the Origins of Life and the Early State of Man*. Ithaca, NY: Cornell Paperbacks.
Guttmacher, Adolph. 1903. *Optimism and Pessimism in the Old and New Testaments*. Baltimore, MD: Friedenwald.
Habel, Norman C. 1981. "Naked I came": Humanness in the Book of Job. Pages 373–90 in *Die Botschaft und die Boten: Festschrift für Hans Walter Wolff zum 70. Geburtstag*. Edited by Jörg Jeremias and Lothar Perlitt. Neukirchen-Vluyn: Neukirchener Verlag.
Habel, Norman C. 1985 *The Book of Job: A Commentary*. OTL. Philadelphia, PA: Westminster Press.
Hahn, Joachim. 1981. *Das "Goldene Kalb": Die Jahwe-Verehrung bei Stierbildern in der Geschichte Israels*. Frankfurt a. M.: Peter Lang.
Hake, Sabine. 2005. Expressionism and Cinema: Reflections on a Phantasmagoria of Film History. Pages 321–41 in *A Companion to the Literature of German Expressionism*. Edited by Neil H. Donahue. Rochester, NY: Camden House.
Hall, Amy Laura. 2012. Ruth's Resolve: What Jesus' Great-Grandmother May Teach about Bioethics and Care. Pages 561–68 in *On Moral Medicine: Theological Perspectives on Medical Ethics*. Edited by M. Therese Lysaught and Joseph J. Kotva, Jr. 3rd ed. Grand Rapids, MI: Eerdmans.
Hall, Bishop Joseph. 1837. *The Works of Joseph Hall, D. D., With Some Account of His Life and Sufferings, Volume 6*. Oxford: D.A. Talboys.
Hamel, Gildas. 1995. Taking the Argo to Nineveh: Jonah and Jason in a Mediterranean Context. *Judaism* 44: 341–59.
Hamilton, Victor P. 1990. *The Book of Genesis, Chapters 1-17*. NICOT. Grand Rapids, MI: Eerdmans Publishing Company.
Hamilton, Victor P. 2001. *Handbook on the Historical Books: Joshua, Judges, Ruth, Samuel, Kings, Chronicles, Ezra-Nehemiah, Esther*. Grand Rapids, MI: Baker Academic.
Hare, D. R. A., trans. 1985. The Lives of the Prophets. Pages 385–99 in *The Old Testament Pseudepigrapha, Vol. 2*. Edited by James H. Charlesworth. Garden City, NY: Doubleday & Company.
Hartmann, Eduard von. 1904. *Philosophie des Unbewussten, zweiter Teil: Metaphysik des Unbewussten*. 11th ed. Ausgewählte Werke, vol. 8. Leipzig: Hermann Hacke.
Hayes, Katherine M. 2002. *"The Earth Mourns": Prophetic Metaphor and Oral Aesthetic*. Academia Biblica, 8. Atlanta, GA: SBL Press.
Hays, J. Daniel. 2010. *The Message of the Prophets: A Survey of the Prophetic and Apocalyptic Books*. Grand Rapids, MI: Zondervan.
Heims, Neil. 1983. Robinson Crusoe and the Fear of Being Eaten. *Colby Quarterly* 19: 190–93.
Herbert, George. 2007. *The English Poems of George Herbert*. Edited by Helen Wilcox. Cambridge: Cambridge University Press.

Hill, Scott D. 1992. The Local Hero in Palestine in Comparative Perspective. Pages 37–73 in *Elijah and Elisha in Socioliterary Perspective*. Edited by Robert B. Coote. Atlanta, GA: Scholars Press.
Holbert, John C. 1996. "Deliverance Belongs to Yahweh": Satire in the Book of Jonah". Pages 334–54 in *The Prophets: A Sheffield Reader*. Edited by Philip R. Davies. Sheffield: Sheffield Academic Press.
Holladay, William L. 1964. The Background of Jeremiah's Self-Understanding: Moses, Samuel, and Psalm 22. *JBL* 83: 153–64.
Holladay, William L. 1986. *Jeremiah 1: A Commentary on the Book of the Prophet Jeremiah, Chapters 1-25*. Hermeneia; Philadelphia, PA: Fortress.
Howard, Donald Roy. 1969. Introduction. Pp. xiii–xliii in Lothario dei Segni, *On the Misery of the Human Condition, De miseria humane conditionis*. Edited by Donald R. Howard. Translated by Margaret M. Dietz. Indianapolis, IN: Bobbs Merrill Company.
Howard, Donald Roy. 1974. Renaissance World-Alienation. Pages 47–76 in *The Darker Vision of the Renaissance: Beyond the Fields of Reason*. Edited by Robert S. Kinsman. Berkeley: University of California Press.
Hume, David. 2007a. *A Treatise of Human Nature, A Critical Edition*. Vol. 1: Texts. Edited by David F. Norton and Mary J. Norton. Oxford: Clarendon Press.
Hume, David. 2007b. The Natural History of Religion. Pages 33–87 in *A Dissertation on the Passions: The Natural History of Religion, A Critical Edition*. Edited by Tom L. Beauchamp. The Clarendon Edition of the Works of David Hume. Oxford: Clarendon Press.
Hunter, A. G. 2001. Jonah From the Whale: Exodus Motifs in Jonah 2. Pages 142–58 in *The Elusive Prophet: The Prophet as a Historical Person, Literary Character and Anonymous Artist*. Edited by Johannes C. De Moor. OtSt, 45. Leiden: Brill.
Huxley, Aldous. 2009. *Island*. New York: Harper Perennial Modern Classics.
Ingram, Virginia. 2012. Satire and Cognitive Dissonance in the Book of Jonah, in Light of Ellens' Laws of Psychological Hermeneutics. Pages 140–55 in *Psychological Hermeneutics for Biblical Themes and Texts: A Festschrift in Honor of Wayne G. Rollins*. Edited by J. Harold Ellens. New York: T&T Clark International.
Jacobsen, Thorkild. 1976. *The Treasures of Darkness: A History of Mesopotamian Religion*. New Haven, CT: Yale University Press.
James, William. 1920. *The Varieties of Religious Experience: A Study in Human Nature*. New York: Longmans, Green and Co.
James, William. 1962. Is Life Worth Living? Pages 1–31 in *Essays on Faith and Morals*. Edited by Ralph Barton Perry. Cleveland, OH: Meridian.
Johns, Elizabeth. 1979. Washington Allston's Dead Man Revived. *The Art Bulletin* 61: 78–99.
Johnstone, Steven. 1994. Virtuous Toil, Vicious Work: Xenophon on Aristocratic Style. *CP* 89: 219–40.
Jones, D. A. N. 1972. Arguments against Orwell. Pages 154–58 in *The World of George Orwell*. Edited by Miriam Gross. New York: Simon and Schuster.
Jong, Jonathan and Jamin Halberstadt. 2016. *Death Anxiety and Religious Belief: An Existential Psychology of Religion*. London: Bloomsbury Academic.
Judson, J. Richard. 1964. Marine Symbols of Salvation in the Sixteenth Century. Pages 136–52 in *Essays in Memory of Karl Lehmann*. Edited by Lucy Freeman Sandler. New York: Institute of Fine Arts, New York University.

Jung, Carl G. 1967. *Symbols of Transformation: An Analysis of the Prelude to a Case of Schizophrenia*. 2nd ed. Translated by R. F. C. Hull. Princeton, NJ: Princeton University Press.

Kafka, Franz. 1953. Brief an dem Vater. Pages 162–223 in *Hochzeitsvorbereitungen auf dem Lande und andere Prosa aus dem Nachlass*. Edited by Max Brod. Frankfurt: Fischer Verlag.

Kafka, Franz. 1970. Beschreibung eines Kampfes. Pages 197–232 in *Sämtliche Erzählungen*. Edited by Paul Raabe. Frankfurt a. M.: Fischer Taschenbuch Verlag.

Kafka, Franz. 1994. *Der Proceß: Originalfassung*. Frankfurt a. M.: Fischer Taschenbuch Verlag.

Kartje, John. 2014. *Wisdom Epistemology in the Psalter: A Study of Psalms 1, 73, 90, and 107*. BZAW 472. Berlin: De Gruyter.

Kassel, Maria. 2012. Jonah: The Jonah Experience—for Women Too? Pages 411–20 in *Feminist Biblical Interpretation: A Compendium of Critical Commentary on the Books of the Bible and Related Literature*. Edited by Luise Schottroff and Marie-Theres Wacker. Translated by Nancy Lukens. Grand Rapids, MI: Eerdmans.

Kaufman, Gordon D. 1981. *The Theological Imagination: Constructing the Concept of God*. Philadelphia, PA: John Knox Press.

Kaufmann, M. 1904. Was "the Weeping Prophet" a Pessimist? *The Expositor*. 6th series. 9.3: 186–200.

Keen, Suzanne. 2007. *Empathy and the Novel*. New York: Oxford University Press.

Keltner, Dacher, Phoebe C. Ellsworth, and Kari Edwards. 1993. Beyond Simple Pessimism: Effects of Sadness and Anger on Social Judgement. *Journal of Personality and Social Psychology* 64: 740–52.

Kim, Hyun Chul Paul. 2007a. Jonah Read Intertextually. *JBL* 126: 497–528.

Kim, Hyun Chul Paul. 2007b. Tsunami, Hurricane, and Jeremiah 4:23-28. *BTB* 37: 54–61.

Kissling, Paul J. 1996. *Reliable Characters in the Primary History: Profiles of Moses, Joshua, Elijah and Elisha*. JSOTSup 224. Sheffield: Sheffield Academic.

Klug, Leo and A. Sinha. 1987–88. Death Acceptance: A Two-Component Formulation and Scale. *Omega* 18: 229–35.

Knox, Bernard M. W. 1971. *Oedipus at Thebes: Sophocles' Tragic Hero and His Time*. New York: Norton.

Knox, Bernard M. W. 1989. Theognis. Pages 95–105 in *The Cambridge History of Classical Literature, Vol. I, Part 1: Early Greek Poetry*. Edited by P. E. Easterling and B. M. W. Knox. Cambridge: Cambridge University Press.

Koestler, Arthur. 1979. *Janus: A Summing Up*. New York: Vintage Books.

Kohut, Heinz. 1972. Thoughts on Narcissism and Narcissistic Rage. *The Psychoanalytic Study of the Child* 27: 360–400.

Krašovec, Jože. 1992. The Source of Hope in the Book of Lamentations. *VT* 42: 223–33.

Kreuzberg, Claus. 1960. Zur Seesturm-Allegorie Breugels. Pages 33–49 in *Zwischen Kunstgeschichte und Volkskunde: Festschrift für Wilhelm Fraenger*. Edited by Reinhard Peesch. Akademic Verlag: Berlin.

Krüger, Thomas. 2004. *Qoheleth: A Commentary*. Translated by O. C. Dean, Jr. Hermeneia. Minneapolis, MN: Fortress Press.

Kübler-Ross, Elizabeth. 1970. *On Death and Dying: What the Dying Have to Teach Doctors, Nurses, Clergy and Their Own Families*. New York: Macmillan Paperbacks Edition.

LaCocque, André and Pierre-Emmanuel Lacocque. 1990. *Jonah: A Psycho-Religious Approach to the Prophet*. Columbia: University of South Carolina Press.

LaCocque, André. 2004. A Psychological Approach to the Book of Jonah. Pages 83–92 in *Psychology and the Bible: From Genesis to Apocalyptic Vision, Vol. 2*. Edited by J. Harold Ellens and Wayne G. Rollins. Westport, CT: Praeger Publishers.

LaCocque, André. 2007. The Story of Jonah. Pages 166–70 in *Psychological Insight into the Bible*. Edited by Wayne G. Rollins and D. Andrew Kille. Grand Rapids, MI: Eerdmans.

Lacocque, Pierre-Emmanuel. 1984. Fear of Engulfment and the Problem of Identity. *Journal of Religion and Health* 23: 218–28.

Lambert, Wilfred G. and Alan R. Millard. 1999. *Atra-ḫasīs: The Babylonian Story of the Flood*. Winona Lake, IN: Eisenbrauns.

Lambert, Wilfred G. 2016. Morals in Mesopotamia. Pages 11–27 in *Ancient Mesopotamian Religion and Mythology: Selected Essays*. Edited by A. R George and T. M. Oshima. Orientalische Religionen in der Antike, 15. Tübingen: Mohr Siebeck.

Landes, G. M. 1999. Textual "Information Gaps" and "Dissonances" in the Interpretation of the Book of Jonah. Pages 273–93 in *Ki Baruch Hu: Ancient Near Eastern, Biblical, and Judaic Studies in Honor of Baruch A. Levine*. Edited by R. Chazan, W.W. Hallo and L. H. Schiffman. Winona Lake, IN: Eisenbrauns.

Landow, George P. 1982. *Images of Crisis: Literary Iconology, 1750 to the Present*. Boston, MA: Routledge & Kegan Paul.

Lanzmann, Claude. 1985. *Shoah: An Oral History of the Holocaust*. New York: Pantheon Books.

Lasine, Stuart. 1984a. Fiction, Falsehood, and Reality in Hebrew Scripture. *HS* 25: 24–40.

Lasine, Stuart. 1984b. Guest and Host in Judges 19: Lot's Hospitality in an Inverted World. *JSOT* 29: 37–59.

Lasine, Stuart. 1986. Indeterminacy and the Bible: A Review of Literary and Anthropological Theories and Their Application to Biblical Texts. *HS* 27: 48–80.

Lasine, Stuart. 1988. Bird's-Eye and Worm's-Eye Views of Justice in the Book of Job. *JSOT* 42: 29–53.

Lasine, Stuart. 1991. Jehoram and the Cannibal Mothers (2 Kings 6.24-33): Solomon's Judgment in an Inverted World. *JSOT* 50: 27–53.

Lasine, Stuart. 2001. *Knowing Kings: Knowledge, Power and Narcissism in the Hebrew Bible*. SemeiaSt, 40. Atlanta, GA: SBL Press.

Lasine, Stuart. 2002. Divine Narcissism and Yahweh's Parenting Style. *BibInt* 10: 36–56.

Lasine, Stuart. 2004 Matters of Life and Death: The Story of Elijah and the Widow's Son in Comparative Perspective. *BibInt* 12: 117–44.

Lasine, Stuart. 2010. Everything Belongs To Me: Holiness, Danger, and Divine Kingship in the Post-Genesis World. *JSOT* 35: 31–62.

Lasine, Stuart. 2011. "Go in peace" or "Go to Hell"? Elisha, Naaman and the Meaning of Monotheism in 2 Kings 5. *SJOT* 25: 3–28.

Lasine, Stuart. 2012. *Weighing Hearts: Character, Judgment and the Ethics of Reading the Bible*. LHBOTS. New York: T&T Clark International.

Lasine, Stuart. 2013. Observations on the Rollins *Festschrift*. Available online: http://psybibs.revdak.com/2013/Lasine-Rollins_Festschrift.pdf (Accessed November 3, 2013).

Lasine, Stuart. 2016a. Characterizing God in His/Our Own Image. Pages 465–77 in *The Oxford Handbook to Biblical Narrative*. Edited by Danna Fewell. New York: Oxford University Press.

Lasine, Stuart. 2016b. Holy Men In Space. Pages 3–22 in *Constructions of Space III: Biblical Spatiality and the Sacred*. Edited by Jorunn Økland, Cor de Vos, and Karen Wennell. LHBOTS. New York: Bloomsbury.

Lefkowitz, Mary R. 1977. Pindar's Pythian 8. *CJ* 72: 209–21.

Levenson, Michael. 2007. The Fictional Realist: Novels of the 1930s. Pages 59–75 in *The Cambridge Companion to George Orwell*. Edited by John Rodden. Cambridge: Cambridge University Press.

Lifton, Robert Jay. 1961. *Thought Reform and the Psychology of Totalism: A Study of "Brainwashing" in China*. New York: W. W. Norton & Co.

Limburg, James. 1993. *Jonah: A Commentary*. Louisville, KY: Westminster/John Knox Press.

Lo, Alison. 2009. Death in Qohelet. *JANES* 31: 85–98.

Lockwood, Peter F. 2004. The Elijah Syndrome: What is Elijah up to at Mt. Horeb? *Lutheran Theological Journal* 38: 51–62.

Long, Burke O. 1984. *1 Kings, with an Introduction to Historical Literature*. FOTL 9. Grand Rapids, MI: Eerdmans.

Loraux, Nicole. 1982. Ponos: Sur quelques difficultés de la peine comme nom du travail. *Annali del Seminario di Studi del Mundo Classico, Archeologia e Storia Antica* 4: 171–92.

Lundbom, Jack R. 2013a. *Deuteronomy: A Commentary*. Grand Rapids, MI: Eerdmans.

Lundbom, Jack R. 2013b. *Jeremiah among the Prophets*. Cambridge: James Clark & Co.

Macdonald, William. 1937. "The Beatitude of 'Them that trust.'" *ExpTim* 48: 325–27.

Mackie, C. J. 2001. The Earliest Jason. What's in a Name? *GR* 48: 1–17.

Magonet, Jonathan. 1992. Review of *Jonah: A Psycho-Religious Approach to the Prophet*, by André LaCocque and Pierre Emmanuel LaCocque. *HS* 33: 141–44.

Mahler, Margaret S. 1952. On Child Psychosis and Schizophrenia: Autistic and Symbiotic Infantile Psychoses. *Psychoanalytic Study of the Child* 7: 286–305.

Mahler, Margaret S. 1979. *Separation-Individuation*. Selected Papers, Vol. 2. New York: Jason Aronson.

Malraux, André. 1946. *La Condition Humaine*. Le Livre de Poche. Paris: Gallimard.

Malraux, André. 1997. *Les Noyers de l'Altenburg*. Collection Folio. Paris: Gallimard.

Mann, Thomas. 1964. *Joseph und seine Brüder*. Frankfurt: Fischer.

Marcus, David. 1995. *From Balaam to Jonah: Anti-prophetic Satire in the Hebrew Bible* Brown Judaic Studies 301. Atlanta, GA: Scholars Press.

Marcus, Paul. 2003. *Ancient Religious Wisdom, Spirituality, and Psychoanalysis*. Westport, CT: Praeger.

Marcus, Ralph, trans. 1937. *Josephus: Jewish Antiquities, Books IX-XI*. LCL. Cambridge, MA: Harvard University Press.

Marks, Peter. 2011. *George Orwell the Essayist: Literature, Politics and the Periodical Culture*. London: Continuum.

Marlow, Hilary. 2016. The Human Condition. Pages 293–312 in *The Hebrew Bible: A Critical Companion*. Edited by John Barton. Princeton, NJ: Princeton University Press.

Maslow, Abraham H. 1971. *The Farther Reaches of Human Nature*. New York: Viking Press.

Masson, Michel. 2001. Rois et prophètes dans la cycle d'Élie. Pages 119–31 in *Prophètes et Rois: Bible et Proche-Orient*. Edited by André Lemaire. Lectio Divina Hors Série. Paris: Cerf.

McCarthy, James. 1980. *Death Anxiety: Loss of the Self*. New York: Gardener Press.

McConville, J. Gordon. 2016. *Being Human in God's World: An Old Testament Theology of Humanity.* Grand Rapids, MI: Baker Academic.

McKane, William. 1980. אשׁמ in Jeremiah 23,33-40. Pages 35–54 in *Prophecy: Essays Presented to Georg Fohrer on his sixty-fifth birthday 6 September 1980.* Edited by J. A. Emerton. BZAW, 150. Berlin: Walter de Gruyter.

McKane, William. 1986. *A Critical and Exegetical Commentary on Jeremiah.* Vol. 1. ICC. Edinburgh: T&T Clark.

McKane, William. 1996. *A Critical and Exegetical Commentary on Jeremiah.* Vol. 2. ICC. Edinburgh: T&T Clark.

Mejía, Jorge. 1975. Some Observations on Psalm 107. *BTB* 5: 56–66.

Melville, Herman. 2002. *Moby-Dick.* 2nd ed. Edited by Hershel Parker and Harrison Hayford. Norton Critical Edition. New York: Norton & Company.

Mentz, Steve. 2013. Donne at Sea: The Islands Voyage and Poetic Form. *Forum for Modern Language Studies* 49: 355–68.

Meyer, Wulf-Uwe, Reisenzein, Rainer, and Schützwohl, Achim. 1997. Toward a Process Analysis of Emotions: The Case of Surprise. *Motivation and Emotion* 21: 251–74.

Meyer, Wulf-Uwe. 1988. Die Rolle von Überraschung im Attributionsprozeß. *Psychologische Rundschau* 39: 136–47.

Michaels, Leonard. 1987. Jonah. Pages 232–37 in *Congregation: Contemporary Writers Read the Jewish Bible.* Edited by David Rosenberg. San Diego, CA: Harcourt Brace Jovanovich, Publishers.

Milgrom, Jacob. 1990. *Numbers: The Traditional Hebrew Text With the New JPS Translation.* JPS Torah Commentary. Philadelphia, PA: Jewish Publication Society.

Milgrom, Jacob. 1992. Numbers, Book of. Pages 1146–55 in *ABD*, vol. 4.

Miller, Henry. 1959. Un Etre Etoilique. Pages 287–306 in *The Henry Miller Reader.* Edited by Lawrence Durrell. New York: New Directions.

Moberly, R. Walter L. 2011. Miracles in the Hebrew Bible. Pages 57–74 in *The Cambridge Companion to Miracles.* Edited by Graham H. Twelftree. Cambridge: Cambridge University Press.

Modell, Arnold H. 1976. "The Holding Environment" and the Therapeutic Action of Psychoanalysis. *Journal of the American Psychoanalytical Association* 24: 285–307.

Montaigne, Michel de. 2003. *The Complete Essays.* Edited and translated by M. A. Screech. London: Penguin Books.

Morton, Jamie. 2001. *The Role of the Physical Environment in Ancient Greek Seafaring.* Leiden: Brill.

Mueller, Martin. 1970. Knowledge and Delusion in the *Iliad. Mosaic: An Interdisciplinary Critical Journal* 3: 86–103.

Murphy, Roland. 2000. Death and Afterlife in the Wisdom Literature. Pages 101–16 in *Judaism in Late Antiquity, Part IV: Death, Life-After-Death, Resurrection and the World-to- Come in the Judaisms of Antiquity.* Edited by Alan J. Avery-Peck and Jacob Neusner. Leiden: Brill.

Murray, Oswyn. 1998. Introduction. Pages xi–xliv in Jakob Burckhardt, *The Greeks and Greek Civilization.* Edited by Oswyn Murray. Translated by Sheila Stern. New York: St. Martin's Press.

Neil, W. 1962. Book of Jonah. Pages 964–67 in *IDB*, vol. 2.

Nell, Victor. 2002. Mythic Structures in Narrative: The Domestication of Immortality. Pages 17–37 in *Narrative Impact: Social and Cognitive Foundations.* Edited by Melanie C. Green, Jeffrey Strange and Timothy Brock. Mahwah, NJ: Erlbaum.

Nesse, Randolph M., MD. 2000. Is Depression an Adaptation? *Archives of General Psychiatry* 57: 14–20.
Nietzsche, Friedrich. 1964a. *Die Geburt der Tragödie.* Pages 45–191 in *Die Geburt der Tragödie. Der griechische Staat.* Kröners Taschenausgabe, 70. Stuttgart: Alfred Kröner Verlag.
Nietzsche, Friedrich. 1964b. Vom Nutzen und Nachteil der Historie für das Leben. Pages 97–195 in *Unzeitgemässe Betrachtungen. Sämtliche Werke in zwölf Bänden*, Vol. 2. Stuttgart: Kröner Verlag.
Norem, Julie K. and Edward C. Chang. 2000. Full Glass: Adding Complexity to our Thinking about the Implications and Applications of Optimism and Pessimism Research. Pages 347–67 in *Optimism & Pessimism: Implications for Theory, Research, and Practice.* Edited by Edward C. Chang. Washington, DC: American Psychological Association.
Norem, Julie K. 2000. Defensive Pessimism, Optimism, and Pessimism. Pages 77–100 in *Optimism & Pessimism: Implications for Theory, Research, and Practice.* Edited by Edward C. Chang. Washington, DC: American Psychological Association.
Nugel, Bernfried. 2009. Aldous Huxley's Revisions of the Old Raja's *Notes on What's What* in His Final Typescript of *The Island*. *Aldous Huxley Annual* 9: 69–90.
Oatley, Keith. 2011. *Such Stuff as Dreams: The Psychology of Fiction.* West Sussex: Wiley-Blackwell.
O'Connor, Kathleen M. 2011. *Jeremiah: Pain and Promise.* Minneapolis, MN: Fortress Press.
Oesterley, W. O. E. and Robinson, Theodore H. 1934. *An Introduction to the books of the Old Testament.* London: S. P. C. K.
Ogden, Daniel. 2013. *Dragons, Serpents & Slayers in the Classical and Early Christian Worlds: A Sourcebook.* New York: Oxford University Press.
Ogden, Graham S. 1984. Qoheleth XI 7-XII 8: Qoheleth's Summons to Enjoyment and Reflection. *VT* 34: 27–38.
Ortega y Gasset, José. 1963. *Man and People.* Translated by Willard R. Trask. New York: Norton Library.
Ortega y Gasset, José. 1968. *The Dehumanization of Art and Other Essays on Art, Culture, and Literature.* Translated by Willard R. Trask. Princeton, NJ: Princeton University Press.
Orwell, George. 1950. *Coming Up for Air.* San Diego, CA: Harcourt.
Orwell, George. 1968. The Frontiers of Art and Propaganda. Pages 123–27 in *The Collected Essays, Journalism and Letters of George Orwell, II.* Edited by Sonia Orwell and Ian Angus. New York: Harcourt, Brace & World.
Orwell, George. 1981. Inside the Whale. Pages 210–52 in *A Collection of Essays.* Orlando: Harcourt.
Ostriker, Alicia Suskin. 2007. *For the Love of God: The Bible as an Open Book.* New Brunswick, NJ: Rutgers University Press.
Ostry, Elaine. 2002. *Social Dreaming: Dickens and the Fairy Tale.* New York: Routledge.
Otzen, Benedikt. 2001. עָמָל *ʿāmāl*. Pages 196–202 in *TDOT*, vol. 11.
Overholt, Thomas. 1996. *Cultural Anthropology and the Old Testament.* Minneapolis, MN: Fortress Press.
Park, Jongsoo. 2004. The Spiritual Journey of Jonah: From the Perspective of C. G. Jung's Analytical Psychology. Pages 276–85 in *Inspired Speech: Prophecy in the Ancient Near East, Essays in Honor of Herbert B. Huffmon.* JSOTSup, 378. Edited by John Kaltner and Louis Stulman. London: T&T Clark International.

Parkinson, R. B. 1998. *The Tale of Sinuhe and Other Ancient Egyptian Poems, 1940-1640 BC*. Oxford World's Classics. New York: Oxford University Press.
Parpola, Simo, editor. 1997. *The Standard Babylonian Epic of Gilgamesh*. State Archives of Assyria Cuneiform Texts, I. Helsinki: Neo-Assyrian Text Corpus Project.
Pascal, Blaise. 1966. *Œuvres complètes*. Edited by Louis Lafuma. Paris: Aux Éditions du Seuil.
Patrides, C. A. 1989. John Donne: The Aesthetics of Morality. Pages 89–116 in *Figures in a Renaissance Context*. Edited by Claude J. Summers and Ted-Larry Pebworth. Ann Arbor: University of Michigan Press.
Paul, Robert A. 1991. Freud's Anthropology: A Reading of the "Cultural Books." Pages 267–86 in *The Cambridge Companion to Freud*. Edited by Jerome Neu. Cambridge: Cambridge University Press.
Pell, Olive. 1952. *Olive Pell Bible*. New York: Exposition Press.
Perry. T. A. 2006. *The Honeymoon is Over: Jonah's Argument with God*. Peabody, MA: Hendrickson Publishers.
Petersen, David L. 2006. The Ambiguous Role of Moses as Prophet. Pages 311–24 in *Israel's Prophets and Israel's Past: Essays on the Relationship of Prophetic Texts and Israelite History in Honor of John H. Hayes*. Edited by Brad E. Kelle and Megan Bishop Moore. LHBOTS, 446. New York and London: T&T Clark.
Pico della Mirandola. 2010. *Oration on the Dignity of Man: A New Translation and Commentary*. Edited and translated by Francesco Borghesi, Michael Papio, and Massimo Riva. Cambridge: Cambridge University Press.
Pihlström, Sami. 2016. *Death and Finitude: Toward a Pragmatic Transcendental Anthropology of Human Limits and Mortality*. Lanham, MD: Lexington Books.
Pinker, Aron. 2007. Job's Perspectives on Death. *JBQ* 35: 73–85.
Piven, Jerry S. 2004. *Death and Delusion: A Freudian Analysis of Mortal Terror*. Greenwich, CT: Information Age Publishing.
Priest, John F. 1968. Humanism, Skepticism, and Pessimism in Israel. *JAAR* 36: 311–26.
Provan, Iain W. 1995. *1 and 2 Kings*. NIBCOT. Peabody, MA: Hendrickson.
Rank, Otto. 2004. *The Myth of the Birth of the Hero: A Psychological Exploration of Myth*. Revised ed. Translated by Gregory C. Richter and E. James Lieberman. Baltimore, MD: Johns Hopkins University Press.
Razinsky, Liran. 2007. A Psychoanalytic Struggle with the Concept of Death: A New Reading of Freud's "Thoughts for the Times on War and Death." *Psychoanalytic Review* 94: 355–85.
Redditt, Paul L. 2008. *Introduction to the Prophets*. Grand Rapids, MI: Eerdmans.
Redfield, James M. 1975. *Nature and Culture in the* Iliad: *The Tragedy of Hector*. Chicago, IL: University of Chicago Press.
Richardson, N. J. 1985. Early Greek views about life after death. Pages 50–66 in *Greek Religion and Society*. Edited by P. E. Easterling and I. V. Muir. Cambridge: Cambridge University Press.
Richardson, Robert D. 2006. *William James in the Maelstrom of American Modernism: A Biography*. Boston, MA: Houghton Mifflin Co.
Ricoeur, Paul. 1983. Action, Story and History: On Re-Reading *The Human Condition*. *Salmagundi* 60: 60–72.
Rindge, Matthew S. 2011. Mortality and Enjoyment: The Interplay of Death and Possessions in Qoheleth. *CBQ* 73: 265–80.
Robinson, Bernard P. 1991. Elijah at Horeb, 1 Kings 19:1-18: A Coherent Narrative? *RB* 98: 513–36.

Rose, Peter W. 1976. Sophocles' Philoctetes and the Teachings of the Sophists. *Harvard Studies in Classical Philology* 80: 49–105.

Rosen, Norma. 1987. Jonah: Justice for Jonah, or a Bible Bartleby. Pages 222–31 in *Congregation: Contemporary Jewish Writers Read the Jewish Bible*. Edited by David Rosenberg. San Diego, CA: Harcourt Brace Jovanovich.

Rosenberg, A. J., trans. and ed. 1989. *Kings II*. Mikraoth Gedoloth. New York: Judaica Press.

Rossi, John. 2007. "My Country Right or Left": Orwell's Patriotism. Pages 87–99 in *The Cambridge Companion to George Orwell*. Edited by John Rodden. Cambridge: Cambridge University Press.

Roth, Leon. 1969. Job and Jonah. Pages 71–74 in *The Dimensions of Job: A Study and Selected Readings*. Edited by Nahum N. Glatzer. New York: Schocken Books.

Rowley, Harold H. 1980. *Job*. NCBC. Grand Rapids, MI: W. B. Eerdmans Publishing Co.

Russell, M. 1983. *Visions of the Sea: Hendrick C. Vroom and the Origins of Dutch Marine Painting*. Leiden: Brill.

Rutherford, R. B. 1986. The Philosophy of the Odyssey. *JHS* 106: 145–62.

Salberg, Jill. 2008. Jonah's Crisis: Commentary on Paper by Avivah Gottlieb Zornberg. *Psychoanalytic Dialogues* 18: 317–28.

Sandars, Nancy K. 1972. Introduction. Pages 7–58 in *The Epic of Gilgamesh*. London: Penguin Classics.

Sanders, Paul. 1996. *The Provenance of Deuteronomy Thirty-two*. Leiden: Brill.

Sartre, Jean-Paul. 1943. *L'être et le néant: Essai d'ontologie phénoménologique*. Paris: Éditions Gallimard.

Sartre, Jean-Paul. 1946. *L'Existentialisme est un Humanisme*. Paris: Éditions Nagel.

Sartre, Jean-Paul. 1947. *Une idée fondamentale de la phénoménologie de Husserl: l'intentionnalité*. Pages 29–32 in *Situations, I: Essais critiques*. Paris: Gallimard.

Sasson, Jack M. 1990. *Jonah: A New Translation with Introduction, Commentary, and Interpretation*. AB, 24B. New York: Doubleday.

Schachtel, Ernest G. 1959. *Metamorphosis: On the Development of Affect, Perception, Attention, and Memory*. New York: Basic Books.

Schein, Seth L., editor. 2013. *Sophocles: Philoctetes*. Cambridge Greek and Latin Classics. New York: Cambridge University Press.

Schiller, Friedrich. 1953. *Schiller's Werke, Nationalausgabe, Band 3: Die Räuber*. Edited by Herbert Stubenrauch; Weimar: Verlage Hermann Böhlaus Nachfolger.

Schmidt, Werner. 2001. Jeremias Konfessionen. *JBTh* 16: 3–23.

Schökel, Luis Alonso. 2000. Jeremiah as an Anti-Moses. Pages 27–38 in *The Literary Language of the Bible: The Collected Essays of Luis Alonso Schökel*. Translated by Harry Spencer. Edited by Tawny Holm. BIBAL Collected Essays, 3. North Richland Hills, TX: BIBAL Press.

Schopenhauer, Arthur. 1819. *Die Welt als Wille und Vorstellung, vier Bücher nebst einem Anhange, der die Kritik der Kantischen Philosophie enthält*. Leipzig: Brockhaus.

Schopenhauer, Arthur. 1960. *Sämtliche Werke, Band II: Die Welt als Wille und Vorstellung, II*. Edited by Wolfgang Frhr. von Löhneysen. Stuttgart: Cotta-Insel Verlag.

Schopenhauer, Arthur. 1963. Aphorismen zur Lebensweisheit. Pages 373–592 in *Sämtliche Werke, Band IV: Parerga und Paralipomena, I*. Edited by Wolfgang Frhr. von Löhneysen. Stuttgart: Cotta-Insel Verlag.

Schopenhauer, Arthur. 1965. Über Religion. Pages 382–466 in *Sämtliche Werke, Band V: Parerga und Paralipomena, II*. Edited by Wolfgang Frhr. von Löhneysen. Stuttgart: Cotta-Insel Verlag.

Segal, Charles. 2001. *Oedipus Tyrannus: Tragic Heroism and the Limits of Knowledge*. 2nd ed. New York: Oxford University Press.

Segal, Robert A. 2004. Introductory Essay. Pages vii–xxxviii in Otto Rank, *The Myth of the Birth of the Hero: A Psychological Exploration of Myth*. Baltimore, MD: Johns Hopkins University Press.

Segni, Lothario dei (Pope Innocent III). 1969. *On the Misery of the Human Condition, De miseria humane conditionis*. Edited by Donald R. Howard. Translated by Margaret M. Dietz. Indianapolis, IN: Bobbs Merrill Company.

Seitz, Christopher R. 1989. The Prophet Moses and the Canonical Shape of Jeremiah. *ZAW* 101: 3–27.

Seow, Choon-Leong. 1997. *Ecclesiastes*. AB, 18C. New York: Doubleday.

Seow, Choon-Leong. 1999. Qohelet's Eschatological Poem. *JBL* 118: 209–34.

Shemesh, Yael. 2008. The Elisha Stories as Saints' Legends. *Journal of Hebrew Scriptures* 8/5: 2–41.

Shemesh, Yael. 2009. Suicide in the Bible. *JBQ* 37: 157–68.

Sherwood, Yvonne. 2000. *A Biblical Text and its Afterlives: The Survival of Jonah in Western Culture*. Cambridge: Cambridge University Press.

Sim, Stuart. 2015. *A Philosophy of Pessimism*. London: Reaktion Books.

Simmel, Georg. 1903. Die Großstädte und das Geistesleben. Pages 186–206 in *Die Großstaat. Vorträge und Aufsätze zur Städteausstellung*. Jahrbuch der Gehe-Stiftung zu Dresden, 9. Edited by Theodor Petermann. Dresden: Zahn & Jaensch.

Simon, Erika. 1981. *Die griechischen Vasen*. Munich: Hirmer Verlag.

Simon, Uriel. 1999. *Jonah*. JPS Bible Commentary. Philadelphia, PA: Jewish Publication Society.

Sinoff, Gary. 2017. Thanatophobia (Death Anxiety) in the Elderly: The Problem of the Child's Inability to Assess Their Own Parent's Death Anxiety State. *Frontiers in Medicine* (Lausanne) 4:11. Available online: https://www.ncbi.nlm.nih.gov/pmc/articles/PMC5326787/. (Accessed February 23, 2017).

Skehan, Patrick W., and Alexander A. Di Lella. 1987. *The Wisdom of Ben Sira*. The Anchor Yale Bible, 39. New Haven, CT: Yale University Press.

Smith, E. L. 1997. *The Hero Journey in Literature: Parables of Poesis*. Lanham, MD: University Press of America.

Sneed, Mark R. 2012. *The Politics of Pessimism in Ecclesiastes: A Social-Science Perspective*. Ancient Israel and Its Literature, 12. Atlanta, GA: Society of Biblical Literature.

Sobecki, Sebastian I. 2008. *The Sea and Medieval English Literature*. Cambridge: D. S. Brewer.

Sokel, Walter H. 2002. *The Myth of Power and the Self: Essays on Franz Kafka*. Detroit, MI: Wayne State University Press.

Solmes, Mark. 1993. Death and Us, by Sigmund Freud. Pages 11–39 in *Freud and Judaism*. Edited by David Meghnagi. London: Karnac Books.

Solomon, Sheldon, Jeff Greenberg, and Tom Pyszczynski. 2004. The Cultural Animal: Twenty Years of Terror Management Theory and Research. Pages 13–34 in *Handbook of Experimental Existential Psychology*. Edited by Jeff Greenberg, Sander Koole, and Tom Pyszczynski. New York: Guilford Press.

Solomon, Sheldon, Jeff Greenberg, and Tom Pyszczynski. 2015. *The Worm at the Core: On the Role of Death in Life*. New York: Random House.

Sommer, Benjamin D. 1999. Reflecting on Moses: The Redaction of Numbers 11. *JBL* 118: 601–24.

Sourvinou-Inwood, Christiane. 1996. *"Reading" Greek Death: To the End of the Classical Period*. Oxford: Clarendon Press.

Spronk, Klaas. 1997. *Nahum*. Historical Commentary on the Old Testament, Book. Kampen: Kok Pharos.

Stanford, W. B., editor. 1967. *The Odyssey of Homer, Vol I (Books I-XII)*. Vol. I. London: Macmillan.

Stark, Caroline. 2012. Renaissance Anthropologies and the Conception of Man. Pages 173-94 in *New Worlds and the Italian Renaissance: Contributions to the History of European Intellectual Culture*. Edited by Andrea Moudarris and Christiana Purdy Moudarris. Brill's Studies in Intellectual History, 216. Leiden: Brill.

Steffen, Uwe. 1982. *Jona und der Fisch: Der Mythos von Tod und Wiedergeburt*. Stuttgart: Kreuz Verlag.

Stephen, James Fitzjames. 1862. The Minister's Wooing. Pages 307-19 in *Essays by a Barrister*, London: Smith, Elder & Co.

Stobaeus, Joannes. 1856. *Ioannis Stobaei Florilegium, Vol. 3*. Edited by August Meineke. Leipzig: B. G. Teubner.

Stubbs, John. 2008. *John Donne: The Reformed Soul*. New York: W. W. Norton & Company.

Stulman, Louis. 2005. *Jeremiah*. Abingdon Old Testament Commentaries. Nashville: Abingdon Press.

Talwar, Victoria. 2011. Talking to Children about Death in Educational Settings. Pages 98-115 in *Children's Understanding of Death; Biological to Religious Conceptions*. Edited by Victoria Talwar, Paul L. Harris, and Michael Schleifer. Cambridge: Cambridge University Press.

Targoff, Ramie. 2006. Facing Death. Pages 217-31 in *The Cambridge Companion to John Donne*. Edited by Achsah Guibbory. Cambridge: Cambridge University Press.

Tatar, Maria. 2003. *The Hard Facts of the Grimms' Fairy Tales*. 2nd ed. Princeton, NJ: Princeton University Press.

Taylor, Charles H., Jr. 1963. The Obstacles to Odysseus' Return. Pages 87-99 in *Essays on the Odyssey: Selected Modern Criticism*. Edited by Charles H. Taylor, Jr. Bloomington: Indiana University Press.

Thelle, Rannfrid I. 2002. *Ask God: Divine Consultation in the Literature of the Hebrew Bible*. BBET, 30. Frankfurt a. M.: Peter Lang.

Thompson, E. P. 1978. Outside the Whale. Pages 211-43 in *The Poverty of Theory & Other Essays*. New York: Monthly Review Press.

Thompson, John A. 1980. *The Book of Jeremiah*. NICOT. Grand Rapids, MI: Eerdmans.

Thompson, Thomas L. 1999. *The Mythic Past: Biblical Archaeology and the Myth of Israel*. New York: Basic Books.

Tigay, Jeffrey H. 1996. *The JPS Torah Commentary: Deuteronomy*. Philadelphia, PA: Jewish Publication Society.

Todorov, Tzvetan. 1970. *Introduction à la littérature fantastique*. Paris: Éditions du Seuil.

Trible, Phyllis. 1994. *Rhetorical Criticism: Context, Method, and the Book of Jonah*. Minneapolis, MN: Fortress Press.

Trible, Phyllis. 1996. The Book of Jonah: Introduction, Commentary, and Reflections. Pages 463-529 in *NIB*. Vol. 7. Nashville: Abingdon Press.

Tucker, W. Dennis, Jr. 2006. *Jonah: A Handbook on the Hebrew Text*. Waco, TX: Baylor University Press.

Vail, Kenneth E., III, Zachary Rothschild, Dave R. Weise, Sheldon Solomon, Tom Pyszczynski, and Jeff Greenberg. 2010. A Terror Management Analysis of the Psychological Functions of Religion. *Personality and Social Psychology Review* 14: 84-94.

Vancil, Jack W. 1986. From Creation to Chaos: An Exegesis of Jeremiah 4:23-26." Pages 181–92 in *Biblical Interpretation: Principles and Practices*. Edited by F. Furman Kearley, Edward P. Myers, and Timothy D. Hadley. Grand Rapids, MI: Baker Book House.

Van Heerden, Willie. 2003. Psychological Interpretations of the Book of Jonah. OTE 16: 717–29.

Van Peer, Willie, Anna Chesnokova, and Matthias Springer. 2017. Distressful Empathy in Reading Literature: The Case for Terror Management Theory? *Science and Education* 26: 33–41.

Versnel, H. S. 2011. *Coping With the Gods: Wayward Readings in Greek Theology*. Leiden: Brill.

Vidal-Naquet, Pierre. 1978. Plato's Myth of the Statesman, the Ambiguities of the Golden Age and of History. *JHS* 98: 132–41.

Volkan, Vamik D. 1979. The "Glass Bubble" of the Narcissistic Patient. Pages 405–31 in *Advances in Psychotherapy of the Borderline Patient*. Edited by J. Le Boit and A. Capponi. New York: Jason Aronson.

Von Rad, Gerhard. 1965. *Old Testament Theology, Volume II: The Theology of Israel's Prophetic Traditions*. Translated by D. M. G. Stalker. New York: Harper & Row.

Von Rad, Gerhard. 1973. *Genesis: A Commentary*. Rev. ed. OTL. Translated by John H. Marks. Philadelphia, PA: Westminster Press.

Wachtel, Paul L. 1973. Psychodynamics, Behavior Therapy, and the Implacable Experimenter: An Inquiry into the Consistency of Personality. *Journal of Abnormal Psychology* 82: 324–34.

Walsh, Jerome T. 1982. Despair as a Theological Virtue in the Spirituality of Ecclesiastes. *BTB* 12: 46–49.

Walsh, Jerome T. 1996. *1 Kings*. Berit Olam. Collegeville, MN: Liturgical Press.

Watson, Francis. 1994. *Text, Church and World: Biblical Interpretation in Theological Perspective*. Edinburgh: T&T Clark.

Watson, Robert N. 1994. *The Rest is Silence: Death as Annihilation in the English Renaissance*. Berkeley: University of California Press.

Weitzman, Steven. 1997. *Song and Story in Biblical Narratives: The History of a Literary Convention in Ancient Israel*. Bloomington: Indiana University Press.

Westermann, Claus. 1994. *Genesis 1-11: A Continental Commentary*. Trans. John J. Scullion, S. J. Minneapolis, MN: Fortress Press.

White, David A. 2007. *Myth, Metaphysics, and Dialectic in Plato's Statesman*. Burlington, VT: Ashgate.

White, Hayden V. 1973. *Metahistory: The Historical Imagination in Nineteenth-Century Europe*. Baltimore, MD: Johns Hopkins University Press.

Whybray, Norman. 1998. *Job*. Readings: A New Biblical Commentary. Sheffield: Sheffield Academic Press.

Widmer, Michael. 2004. *Moses, God, and the Dynamics of Intercessory Prayer: A Study of Exodus 32-34 and Numbers 13-14*. FAT, 2d series, 8. Tübingen: Mohr Siebeck.

Wilkin, Peter. 1999. Chomsky and Foucault on Human Nature and Politics: An Essential Difference? *Social Theory and Practice* 25: 177–210.

Williamson, Robert Jr. 2014. "In the Way of Righteousness Is Life": Symbolic Death Transcendence in Proverbs 10–29. *JSOT* 38: 363–82.

Wineman, Aryeh. 1990. The Zohar on Jonah: Radical Retelling or Tradition? *HS* 31: 57–69.

Wink, Paul and Julia Scott. 2005. Does Religiousness Buffer against the Fear of Death and Dying in Late Adulthood? Findings From a Longitudinal Study. *Journal of Gerontology: Psychological Sciences* 60B/4: 207–14.

Winnicott, Donald W. 1992. *Psycho-analytic Explorations.* Edited by Clare Winnicott, Ray Shepherd, and Madeleine Davis. Cambridge, MA: Harvard University Press.

Wittgenstein, Ludwig. 1961. *Tractatus Logico-Philosophicus.* Translated by D. F. Pears and B. F. McGuinness. London: Routledge & Kegan Paul.

Wohlgelernter, Devora. 1981. Death Wish in the Bible. *Tradition* 19: 131–40.

Wolff, Cynthia Griffin. 1986. *Emily Dickenson.* New York: Alfred A. Knopf.

Wolff, Hans W. 1986. *Obadiah and Jonah: A Commentary.* Translated by Margaret Kohl. Minneapolis, MN: Augsburg Press.

Wordsworth, William. 1947. *The Poetical Works of William Wordsworth.* Vol. 4. Edited by Ernest de Selincourt and Helen Darbishire. Oxford: Clarendon.

Wordsworth, William. 1979. *The Prelude, 1799, 1805, 1850.* Edited by Jonathan Wordsworth, M. H. Abrams, and Stephen Gill. New York: W. W. Norton & Co.

Würthwein, Ernst. 1984. *Die Bücher der Könige, 1. Kön. 17–2. Kön. 25.* ATD 11/2. Göttingen: Vandenhoeck & Ruprecht.

Young, F. W. 1962. Suicide. Pages 453–54 in *IDB*, vol. 4.

Zijderveld, Anton C. 1987. On the Nature and Function of Clichés. Pages 26–40 in *Erstarrtes Denken: Studien zu Klischee, Stereotyp und Vorurteil in englischsprachiger Literatur.* Edited by Günther Blaicher. Tübingen: Gunter Narr Verlag.

Ziolkowski, Jan M. 2007. *Fairy Tales from Before Fairy Tales: The Medieval Latin Past of Wonderful Lies.* Ann Arbor: University of Michigan Press.

Zornberg, Avivah Gottlieb. 2008. Jonah: A Fantasy of Flight. *Psychoanalytic Dialogues* 18: 271–99.

Zuckermann, Ghil'ad. 2010. Do Israelis Understand the Hebrew Bible? *The Bible and Critical Theory* 6: 6.1–6.7.

INDEX OF ANCIENT SOURCES

Hebrew Bible/Old Testament

Genesis
1–2	14
1	15, 127
1:2	127
1:26-27	4
1:28	4
1:31	22, 23
2:7	4
2:15	7, 8
3	8
3:14	13
3:16-17	12
3:16	13, 17
3:17-19	8, 13
3:17	7, 13
3:19	7, 123
3:22	13
3:23-24	47
4:14	82
4:16	82
5:23-24	67
6–8	128
6:5	33
6:6-7	82
6:7	82
8	128
8:21	16, 33
32:32-33	120
37:21-22	86
42:22	86
43:33	67
49:22-25	129

Exodus
1:22–2:10	38
2:11-15	34
2:15	38
3	67
4:14	82
4:19-24	38
4:19	38
4:23	38
4:24	38
6:1	47
11:1	47
12:1-7	132
13:21-22	58
14	86
14:12	85, 86
15:10-12	49
15:15	50
15:16	50
15:24	39
16:2	39
17:4	38, 39
20:4	111
32	111
32:10	111
32:19	111
32:32	36, 39
33:3	112
33:5	112
34:6-7	50, 85, 111, 112
34:6	42, 85, 111, 112
34:7	112
34:10	111
34:14	111

Numbers
11	37
11:10-15	38
11:14-15	39
11:15	39
11:29	39
12	39
13–14	38
14:2	39
14:10	38
16	39
17:6	39
25:11-13	39
27:16-17	34

Deuteronomy
4	33
4:26-31	33
4:29-31	34
5:6 Heb.	33
9:7	34
9:24	34
10:16	34
10:20-21	34
10:29	34
20:5-7	35
28	32
28:29	119
28:30	35
29	32
29:1-3	33
29:11-19	33
29:17-20	33
29:21-27	33
30	32
30:1-10	34
30:11-20	134
31–32	23
31	17, 21, 32–34
31:15-21	33
31:19	33
31:20-21	33
31:27	32
32	34, 48

32:4	45	2:1-11	134	11:8	35
32:10-11	48	4	63	11:18-21	38
32:10	114	4:9	69	11:18-20	40
32:15	45	5	63	11:19-20	40
32:18	45	5:1-14	63	11:20	40
		5:25-27	63	11:21	38
Joshua		6:13-23	62	11:21 MT	38
24:1-27	32	8	62	14:9	67
24:21	32	8:4	70	15	40, 41
24:24	32	8:7-13	62	15:5	40
		8:28-29	65	15:10	41
Judges		9	63	15:15-18	40
5:4-5	109	9:14-28	65	15:15	37, 40–42
19	69	13	63–65, 71	15:17-18	40
		13:14	65	15:17	40
2 Samuel		13:20-21	65, 68–71	15:20	41
8:11	4	14:25	62	15:21	41
19:35-36	130	20	62	16:2	35
		21:13	84	17:9	16
1 Kings		22:19	35	17:17-18	41
5:1	4	23	71	17:23	35
5:4	4	23:17-18	71	20	40–43
9:26	52			20:2	38
10:22	52	*Isaiah*		20:7-12	40
13	71	1:8	86	20:7-8	40
13:31	71	11:6	45	20:8	40
14	62	14:8-9	132	20:11-12	40
17–18	63	14:9-20	74	20:11	41
17	88	14:11	7	20:12	40
18–19	37	21:4	50	20:14-18	40, 60, 101
18:10	38	59:16	67	20:14	35
18:39-40	40	63:1-3	109	20:16	84
18:40	63	63:5	67	20:17	35, 38, 42
19	39, 42			23:33-40	35
19:1-3	38	*Jeremiah*		23:33	35
19:3	134	1:5	41	25:4	35
19:4	38–40	1:10	127	26:11	38
19:10	38, 40	1:17	41	29:5-6	35
19:11-12	109	1:18	41	31:32-33	34
19:14	38, 40	4	20, 130, 131	34:14	35
19:18	39	4:7	128	35:15	35
21:28-29	40	4:9	67	37:15	38
22:11-24	70	4:19-21	128	38:6	38
22:49	47, 52	4:20	128	44:5	35
		4:23-26	127–30	51:34	101
2 Kings		7:24	35	51:44	101
1	62, 63	7:26	35		
1:9-15	63	9:20	42	*Ezekiel*	
2–6	69	11	40	7:18	50

27:25-34	52	4:5	86	32:7	49	
27:25-29	47	4:6	82, 87	32:10	49	
27:26	51	4:7-8	87	33	35	
		4:7	7	39	6	
Hosea		4:8	35, 39, 42, 87	39:6-7	6	
5:14	45	4:9	82	39:6	4	
		4:10-11	87	39:12	6	
Joel		4:11	87	44	54, 60, 110	
2:2	132	4:12	82	44:12	45	
2:10	132	10:1-11	88	44:23	45, 119	
2:12-14	85	48:7	47	44:24-25	54	
				48:5	67	
Jonah		*Nahum*		48:8	47	
1–2	17, 52	1:1-3	82	49:16	72	
1	80, 83, 85, 90	1:2-10	112	54:4 LXX	50	
1:2	81	1:2-6	112	55	50	
1:4	46, 47	1:2-3	81	55:5 MT	50	
1:5	83	1:2	112	55:5-9	50	
1:9	84	1:3	85	55:6	50	
1:10	83, 110	3:19	112	55:11	9	
1:11-12	52			55:16	49	
1:12	85, 110	*Habakkuk*		69	50	
2	47, 83, 84	1:5	67	69:14-17	50	
2:3-5	47	3:3-15	109	69:16	50	
2:3	90			71	50	
2:4	47, 83	*Malachi*		71:6	51	
2:6	47	1:23	118	72:8	4	
2:7	83			88	47, 50, 51	
2:11	90, 103	*Psalms*		88:4-6	51	
3	84	1	35	88:7-8	51	
3:1	90	8	15	88:9	51	
3:2	81	8:5-7	4	88:18	49	
3:3	98	8:5	4	90:5-6	7	
3:4	81, 84, 85	8:6 Vg.	15	90:10	9	
3:5	83	8:7	4	10:17	53	
3:6-9	83	10:7	9	107	46, 47, 51–53, 56	
3:8	81	16:10	72			
3:9	82	17:8	114	107:11	53	
3:10	84, 85	17:9	49	107:23-32	15	
4	83, 85, 87, 88, 98, 100, 110, 111, 120	17:11	49	107:23-30	110	
		18	50	107:23-28	47, 52	
		18:5-6	50	107:23	52	
4:1	82, 85	22	50	107:27	119	
4:2	41, 82, 83, 85, 86, 95, 111	22:2-3	50	107:30	52	
		22:10-12	50	107:39-40	53	
		22:10	51	107:40	53	
4:3	35, 39	22:13	49, 50	111:1-16	57	
4:4	84, 87	22:17	50	112	35	
4:5-7	48	24:7-8	54	116:3	47	

125:2	49	7:17-18	4	4:1	30, 31
140:10	49	7:17	4	4:2-3	25
144	5, 6	10:4	5	5:7	67
144:2	5	10:16	45	5:8	30, 31
144:3-4	5, 7	12	53	6:1-2	45
144:3	4	12:21	53	6:12	6
144:5-7	6	12:24-25	53	6:22	30
144:11	6	12:25	119	7:2	30
		13–14	23	7:13	31
Proverbs		13:24	109	7:15	30
1:12	49	14:1-2	9	8:8	30
10–29	26	14:1	6	8:11	30
31:6-7	14	14:13-15	43	8:14	31
		14:13	101	9:2-3	30
Job		15:14-16	5, 9	9:3	30
1–2	44	15:14	4, 5	9:4	30
1:10	50	16:12-13	99	9:5	30
1:21	51	16:12	99	9:7-10	134
2:3	50	16:14	41	9:9	31
2:7	48	19:13-19	51	11:7-8	130, 132
2:9-10	51	21:6	50	12	20, 30
2:10	87	24:1-2	31	12:1-7	6, 127, 129
2:11	87	24:8	45	12:1-2	122, 132
3–31	44	25:4-6	5	12:2	130–32
3	51	25:4	5	12:3	130
3:3-19	60	27:18	86	12:5	130
3:12	51	28	15	12:7	122
3:20-23	48	31:30	39		
3:23	50, 51	40:4	5	*Daniel*	
4:6-7	8	42	44	3:24	67
4:7-8	9	42:5-6	5	12:2	71
4:7	8	42:6	91		
4:8	9			*2 Chronicles*	
4:17-21	9	*Lamentations*		20:37	47, 52
4:17-20	5	3:10	45	30:8	34
4:17	5	3:18	23		
4:19	6	3:24	23	Apocrypha/	
5:6-7	6, 9			Deuterocanonical	
5:6	9	*Qoheleth/Ecclesiastes*		Books	
5:7	7, 9	1	30		
5:14	119	1:1	31	*Wisdom of Solomon*	
6–7	51	1:12	31	2:23	73
7:1-10	9	2:3	30	3:1-4	73
7:1-3	9	2:14	30	5:15-16	73
7:1-2	9	2:16	30		
7:3-5	9	2:23	26, 30	*Sirach/Ecclesiasticus*	
7:12	5	2:24	31	40:1-17	24
7:13	6	3:19	30	40:1	26
7:17-19	5	4:1-3	28, 29, 31, 35	40:2	26

40:5-7	26	I, 99-100	39	Hesiod	
40:5	26			*Catalogue of Women*	
40:9	26	*Midrash Tehillim*		98	28
41:1	26	I, 26, 7	70, 88		
48:13	69			Homer	
		Pirqe de Rabbi Eliezer		*Iliad*	
New Testament		33	70	X.70-71	13
				XII.322-38	133
Matthew		*Qoheleth Rabbah*		XV.140-41	111
8:27	68	8.10	70	XXIV. 527-33	45
9:33	68				
12:40	108	*Seder ʿOlam*		*Odyssey*	
15:31	68	18–19	63	1.62	109
				4.563	22
Mark		Josephus		5.162-79	108
5:42	68	*Antiquities*		5.234-62	108
		9.8.6	69	5.340	109
Luke		9.10.2	83, 87	5.366-70	119
5:9	68			5.406-23	119
7:16	68	Greek, Roman and		5.415-22	108
8:56	68	Classical Works		5.423	109
				6.127-7.347	56
Acts		Aeschylus		9–12	105
3:10	68	*Prometheus Bound*		9.489-91	73
13:13-14	57	467	11	11.29-635	74
				12.73-110	106
		Aristotle		12.235-59	106
Pseudepigrapha		*Ethica nicomachae*		12.260	11
		1115b23-28	109	12.423-25	108
3 Maccabees				12.430-46	106
6:8	87	Baccylides		23.183-204	109
		Odes			
Babylonian Talmud		5	28	*Homeric Hymn to*	
		5.115-64	28	*Poseidon*	
Baba Meṣiʿa		5.160	28	22	109
87a	65				
		Euripides		Horace	
Sanhedrin		*Bacchae*		*Epistulae*	
47a	70, 71	280-83	14	1.2.22	106
107b	65				
		Heracles		Lucian	
Midrash and Other		1192	13, 103	*A True History*	
Jewish Works		356-57	13	1, §§30-31	108
Mekilta		Hippolytus		Lucretius	
Baḥodesh		189-90	13	*De rerum natura*	
6	111			2.1-12	64
		Herodotus			
Pisḥa		*Histories*			
I, 88-99	82	2.24	107	5.222-34	54

Lycophron
Alexandra
35   103
475-78   103

Ovid
Metamorpheses
9.99-272   28

Pindar
Nem.
1:33   13

Olympian Odes
2.62-72   14

Pythian Ode
5.54   13
8.95   10
8.96-97   10
10.41-43   14

Plato
Leges
664e   11
732a   11
803b   46
803c   11
804d   11

Phaedrus
85c-d   107
85d   108

Politicus
272e   12
274b   12

Respublica
379de   45

604b-c   10
614b   105

Plutarch
Consolation to Apollonius
27   28

The Contest between Homer and Hesiod
315   28

Seneca
Epistulae morales
53, §4   109

Solon
Fragment 14   22

Sophocles
Antigone
334   10
335-37   10
337-40   11
369   11

Oedipus at Colonus
1225-31   28

Philoctetes
5   55
501-3   55
504-6   55
703   55
979-98   55
1419-22   13

Theognis
181-82   29
271-78   29
425-27   26
1013-16   29

Valerius
Flaccus Argonautica
2.451-578 103

Xenophon
Memorabilia
2.1.28   14

Qur'an
37.142-45 43

ANCIENT NEAR EASTERN SOURCES

Egyptian Tale of the Shipwrecked Sailor
16   104
28–39   52
31–39   105
38–42   104
77–80   104
132   104
183   105
185–86   105

Atraḥasis
III, ii, 47   128
XI, 134-37   128

Gilgamesh Epic
III, 45   107
VII, 184-93   74
VII, 185   74
XII, 20   74

Ludlul bēl nēmequi
I. 5   57
I. 7-8   57
I. 10   57

INDEX OF AUTHORS

Abela, Anthony 83
Ackerman, James S.   81, 90
Adam, James   10
Aeschylus   11
Affleck, Glenn   26
Allen, Leslie C.   128
Allen, Woody   23, 45
Allison, Dale   36
Ambuel, David   11
Annus, Amar   57
Arendt, Hannah   13
Aristotle   109
Auld, A. Graeme   36

Baccylides   28
Bachelard, Gaston   89
Baines, John   105
Barton, John   111
Bayertz, Kurt   15
Becker, Ernest   70, 106
Becking, Bob   37
Beiser, Frederick C.   24, 25, 35
Beit-Hallahmi, Benjamin   99, 101
Ben Zvi, Ehud   37, 81, 82, 87
Bergen, Wesley J.   69, 70
Berger, Peter L.   95, 123
Bergmann, Ingmar   130
Bernstein, Richard J.   73
Bettelheim, Bruno   18, 91
Bickerman, Elias   26, 80
Blackman, Aylward M.   104
Blank, Sheldon   80
Blumenberg, Hans   46
Boaistuau, Pierre   3, 47
Boda, Mark J.   32
Bodner, Keith   69
Bonner, Campbell   46
Bottéro, Jean   74
Bowlby, John   52
Braude, William G.   70, 88
Brettler, Marc Zvi   24

Brinton, Daniel G.   70
Brown, William P.   47, 53
Brueggemann, Walter A.   56
Burckhardt, Jacob   13, 22, 28, 74
Burkert, Walter   109, 111
Burkes, Shannon   26
Burnett, John   107

Calvin, Jean   43, 58
Campbell, Joseph   94
Camus, Albert   66
Capps, Donald   80
Carroll, Robert P.   34, 128
Cassirer, Ernst   15
Chang, Edward C.   24, 26
Chin, Catherine   23
Chomsky, Noam   3
Christianson, Eric S.   6
Clement of Alexandria   26
Clines, David J. A.   4, 6–9
Cogan, Mordechai   39, 66
Cohen, A.   70
Cohen, Adam B.   72
Cohn, Robert L.   65
Collins, John J.   26
Colloti, Carlo   101
Connolly, Cyril   116
Conrad, Joseph   118
Constant, Benjamin   121–4, 127, 130
Cooper, Alan   87
Corr, Charles A.   99
Craig, Kenneth M.   80
Crenshaw, James L.   7, 8, 21, 23–5, 27, 47, 72, 111
Crouch, Walter B.   119
Csapo, Eric   13
Cyril of Alexandria   103

Dahood, Mitchell   72
Dalton, Russell   98
Dante Alighieri   109

Daube, David 42, 43
Davison, Peter 116
Dawson, Terence 91
Defoe, Daniel 48, 120
Dempsey, Carol J. 110
Dickens, Charles 99
Dienstag, Joshua Foa 25, 37, 43
Di Lella, Alexander A. 24
Dodds, Eric R. 11
Dollimore, Jonathan 25
Donne, John 17, 57–60
D'Ooge, M. L. 10
Dostoevsky, Fyodor 107
Dougherty, Carol 106
Dozeman, Thomas B. 82
Dray, Carol A. 70
Driver, Samuel R. 8, 9, 37
Droge, A. J. 43, 44
Dundes, Alan 89

Echtermeyer, Thomas 126, 131
Edwards, Philip 46
Ehrensaft, Diane 99
Eliade, Marcel 22, 90
Elias, Norbert 95
Euripides 13, 14, 42, 103, 111
Evelyn-White, Hugh G. 28

Fewell, Danna Nolan 41, 86, 90
Finch, Casey 100
Fineman, Martha Albertson 124
Fisch, Harold 48, 89
Fishbane, Michael A. 112
Fletcher, John 68
Florian, Victor 72
Forti, Tova 56
Foucault, Michel 3
Fox, Michael V. 7, 8, 26, 130, 131
Fretheim, Terence E. 110, 111
Freud, Sigmund 63, 64, 66, 68, 69, 72–4, 91, 102, 118, 120–2, 125, 126, 130, 133
Friedlander, G. 70
Frolov, Serge 40, 81, 107
Fromm, Erich 89, 90

Gaines, Janet Howe 79–82
Gay, Peter 123
Geiringer, Erich 72
Geller, Stephen A. 36

George, Andrew 31
Gerber, Douglas E. 28
Gilbert, Daniel T. 96
Gildersleeve, B. L. 10
Ginzberg, Louis 65, 94
Glasson, T. Francis 63, 112
Glock, Hans-Johann 43, 130
Goedde, Lawrence O. 46, 55, 57
Goedicke, Hans 104
Goldhill, Simon 28, 29
Good, Edwin M. 37, 86
Greenwood, Kyle R. 30
Gregory, Russell 36, 43
Groenewegen-Frankfort, Henriette A. 74
Guggenheimer, Heinrich W. 63
Guillaume, Philippe 83, 87
Gunn, David M. 41, 86, 90
Guthrie, W. K. C. 12
Guttmacher, Adolph 22–3

Habel, Norman C. 6, 8, 44, 99
Hahn, Joachim 43
Hake, Sabine 131
Halberstadt, Jamin 72
Hall, Amy Laura 24
Hall, Bishop Joseph 37
Hamel, Gildas 103
Hamilton, Victor P. 70, 127
Hare, D. R. A. 88
Hartmann, Eduard von 43
Hayes, Katherine M. 127
Hays, J. Daniel 80
Heims, Neil 48, 89
Heine, Heinrich 28, 73
Herbert, George 51
Herodotus 107
Hesiod 28
Hill, Scott D. 70
Holbert, John C. 80
Holladay, William L. 40, 41
Homer 10, 19, 22, 45, 47, 56, 73–4, 98, 104–9, 126, 133
Horace 106
Howard, Donald R. 3, 15
Hume, David 108, 125, 126
Hunter, A. G. 83
Huxley, Aldous 16, 115, 121–2

Ingram, Virginia 84, 91, 92

Jacobsen, Thorkild   111
James, William   20, 24–5, 72, 118–19, 134
Johns, Elizabeth   67
Johnstone, Steven   13
Jones, D. A. N.   116
Jong, Jonathan   72
Josephus   69, 83, 87–8
Judson, J. Richard   46, 54, 57
Jung, Carl G.   18, 90–2

Kafka, Franz   66–7, 99, 101–2, 119
Kartje, John   52, 53, 56
Kassel, Maria   80
Kaufman, Gordon D.   52
Kaufmann, M.   35
Keen, Suzanne   64
Keltner, Dacher   24
Kim, Hyun Chul Paul   80, 127
Kissling, Paul J.   32
Klug, Leo   29
Knox, Bernard M. W.   11, 28
Koestler, Arthur   56, 92
Kohut, Heinz   44
Krašovec, Jože   23
Kravetz, Shlomo   72
Kreuzberg, Claus   57
Krüger, Thomas   28, 131
Kübler-Ross, Elizabeth   29

LaCocque, André   37, 42, 80, 83, 95
Lacocque, Pierre-Emmanuel   37, 42, 79, 81
Lambert, Wilfred G.   128
Landes, G. M.   81, 84
Landow, George P.   55
Lanzmann, Claude   60, 61
Lasine, Stuart   5, 11, 30, 36–9, 44, 45, 48, 55, 57, 63, 65–9, 71, 72, 75, 80, 82, 89, 91, 94–6, 100, 102, 110, 111, 118, 120, 126, 129
Lefkowitz, Mary R.   10
Lenzi, Alan   57
Levenson, Michael   116
Lifton, Robert Jay   29
Limburg, James   81, 82, 87
Lo, Alison   129
Lockwood, Peter F.   37
Long, Burke O.   40

Loraux, Nicole   13
Lucian   108
Luckmann, Thomas   118
Lucretius   47, 54–6, 64, 117
Lundbom, Jack R.   32, 128
Lycophron   103

Macdonald, William   35
Mackie, C. J.   103
Magonet, Jonathan   82, 83
Mahler, Margaret S.   99
Malone, Patrick S.   96
Malraux, André   16
Mann, Thomas   16
Marcus, David   37, 80
Marcus, Paul   6
Marcus, Ralph   88
Marks, Peter   116
Marlow, Hilary   5
Maslow, Abraham H.   18, 79, 89–91
Masson, Michel   36
McCarthy, James   80, 90
McConville, J. Gordon   5, 36
McKane, William   34, 35, 37, 38, 42
Mejía, Jorge   52, 53
Melville, Herman   49, 83, 103
Mentz, Steve   59
Meyer, Wulf-Uwe   65
Michaels, Leonard   80, 85
Milgrom, Jacob   37, 38
Millard, Alan R.   128
Miller, Henry   115, 117
Moberly, R. Walter L.   66
Modell, Arnold H.   87, 95
Montaigne, Michel de   3, 27
Morton, Jamie   108
Mueller, Martin   133
Murphy, Roland   27
Murray, Oswyn   22

Neil, W.   80
Nell, Victor   64
Nesse, Randolph M.   24
Nietzsche, Friedrich   28, 89
Norem, Julie K.   24
Nugel, Bernfried   122

Oatley, Keith   64
O'Connor, Kathleen M.   127, 128

Oesterley, W. O. E. 92
Ogden, Daniel 103
Ogden, Graham S. 132
Ortega y Gasset, José 16, 46, 54
Orwell, George 19–20, 59, 98, 114–18
Ostriker, Alicia Suskin 31, 45, 79–81
Ostry, Elaine 102
Otzen, Benedikt 7
Overholt, Thomas 70
Ovid 28

Park, Jongsoo 92, 93
Parkinson, R. B. 22, 105
Parpola, Simo 74, 107, 128
Pascal, Blaise 124
Patrides, C. A. 58
Paul, Robert A. 79
Pearl Poet 100
Pell, Olive 91
Perry, T. A. 85
Petersen, David L. 36
Pico della Mirandola, Giovanni 15
Pihlström, Sami 130
Pindar 10, 13, 14
Pinker, Aron 67
Piven, Jerry S. 69, 100, 110, 133
Plato 10, 11–12, 14, 45, 46, 105, 107, 108
Plutarch 28
Priest, John F. 27
Provan, Iain W. 40

Rank, Otto 102
Razinsky, Liran 133
Redditt, Paul L. 82
Redfield, James M. 133
Richardson, N. J. 22
Richardson, Robert D. 134
Ricoeur, Paul 16
Rindge, Matthew S. 31
Robinson, Bernard P. 36, 80
Robinson, Theodore H. 92
Rose, Peter W. 55
Rosen, Norma 85
Rosenberg, A. J. 71
Rossi, John 117
Roth, Leon 82
Rowley, Harold H. 9
Russell, M. 57
Rutherford, R. B. 106

Salberg, Jill 80, 93, 94
Sandars, Nancy K. 22
Sanders, Paul 32
Sartre, Jean-Paul 3, 89
Sasson, Jack M. 7, 37, 42, 80, 81, 84–6
Schachtel, Ernest G. 90
Schein, Seth L. 13, 55
Schiller, Friedrich 54, 126
Schmidt, Werner 40
Schökel, Luis A. 37
Schopenhauer, Arthur 22–3, 25, 35, 36, 42, 43, 54, 55, 61, 105–6, 114–15
Schützwohl, A. 66
Scott, Julia 72
Segal, Charles 79
Segal, Robert A. 102
Segni, Lothario dei (Pope Innocent III) 3, 15
Seitz, Christopher R. 36
Seneca 27, 109
Seow, Choon-Leong 7, 131
Shakespeare, William 42
Shemesh, Yael 44, 65, 66, 69
Sherwood, Yvonne 37, 80, 82, 92, 116
Sim, Stuart 24, 25
Simmel, Georg 125
Simon, Erika 37, 40, 103
Simon, Uriel 80, 81, 84, 86
Sinha, A. 29
Sinoff, Gary 134
Skehan, Patrick W. 24
Smith, E. L. 94
Sneed, Mark R. 23, 24, 26, 29, 31, 45
Sobecki, Sebastian I. 100
Sokel, Walter H. 101, 102
Solmes, Mark 73
Solomon, Sheldon 63
Solon 22
Sommer, Benjamin D. 37
Sophocles 10, 11, 13, 28, 35, 47, 55, 79, 120, 123
Sourvinou-Inwood, Christiane 22, 74
Spronk, Klaas 112
Stanford, W. B. 106, 108
Stark, Caroline 15
Steffen, Uwe 90, 94

Stephen, James Fitzjames 60, 61
Stobaeus, Joannes 22
Stubbs, John 58, 59
Stulman, Louis 44

Tadmor, Hayim 66
Talwar, Victoria 99
Targoff, Ramie 58
Tatar, Maria 66, 101, 102
Taylor, Charles H., Jr. 106
Thelle, Rannfrid I. 39
Theognis 26, 28–9
Thompson, E. P. 116, 117
Thompson, John A. 44
Thompson, Thomas L. 37
Tigay, Jeffrey H. 32, 34
Todorov, Tzvetan 66–8
Trible, Phyllis 80, 85, 119
Tucker, W. Dennis, Jr. 46, 86

Vail, Kenneth E. 72
Valerius 103
Vancil, Jack W. 127
Van Heerden, Willie 92
Van Peer, Willie 63, 64
Versnel, H. S. 22
Vidal-Naquet, Pierre 12
Volkan, V. D. 117
Von Rad, Gerhard 13, 85
Von Wiese, Benno 126, 131

Wachtel, Paul L. 96
Walsh, Jerome T. 26, 37
Watson, Francis 30, 31
Watson, Robert N. 51, 58
Weitzman, Steven 23, 32
Westermann, Claus 8
White, David A. 11
White, Hayden V. 123
Whybray, Norman 8, 9
Widmer, Michael 38
Wilkin, Peter 3
Williamson, Robert Jr. 26, 27, 29
Wineman, Aryeh 46
Wink, Paul 72
Winnicott, Donald W. 100
Wittgenstein, Ludwig 130
Wohlgelernter, Devora 42, 43
Wolff, Cynthia Griffin 130
Wolff, Hans W. 37, 80, 82, 86
Wordsworth, William 68, 101
Würthwein, Ernst 66

Xenophon 13–14

Young, F. W. 43, 44

Zijderveld, Anton C. 29
Ziolkowski, Jan M. 104
Zornberg, Avivah Gottlieb 80, 93
Zuckermann, Ghilʻad 8

www.ingramcontent.com/pod-product-compliance
Lightning Source LLC
Chambersburg PA
CBHW052048300426
44117CB00012B/2021